Palgrave Studies in Democracy, Innovation, and Entrepreneurship for Growth

Series Editor

Elias G. Carayannis, PhD
School of Business
George Washington University
Washington, DC, USA

The central theme of this series is to explore why some areas grow and others stagnate, and to measure the effects and implications in a trans-disciplinary context that takes both historical evolution and geographical location into account. In other words, when, how and why does the nature and dynamics of a political regime inform and shape the drivers of growth and especially innovation and entrepreneurship? In this socio-economic and socio-technical context, how could we best achieve growth, financially and environmentally. This series aims to address such issues as:

- How does technological advance occur, and what are the strategic processes and institutions involved?
- How are new businesses created? To what extent is intellectual property protected?
- Which cultural characteristics serve to promote or impede innovation?
- In what ways is wealth distributed or concentrated?

These are among the key questions framing policy and strategic decision-making at firm, industry, national, and regional levels.

A primary feature of the series is to consider the dynamics of innovation and entrepreneurship in the context of globalization, with particular respect to emerging markets, such as China, India, Russia, and Latin America. (For example, what are the implications of China's rapid transition from providing low-cost manufacturing and services to becoming an innovation powerhouse? How do the perspectives of history and geography explain this phenomenon?)

Contributions from researchers in a wide variety of fields will connect and relate the relationships and inter-dependencies among

- Innovation,
- Political Regime, and
- Economic and Social Development.

We will consider whether innovation is demonstrated differently across sectors (e.g., health, education, technology) and disciplines (e.g., social sciences, physical sciences), with an emphasis on discovering emerging patterns, factors, triggers, catalysts, and accelerators to innovation, and their impact on future research, practice, and policy. This series will delve into what are the sustainable and sufficient growth mechanisms for the foreseeable future for developed, knowledge-based economies and societies (such as the EU and the US) in the context of multiple, concurrent and inter-connected "tipping-point" effects with short (MENA) as well as long (China, India) term effects from a geo-strategic, geo-economic, geo-political and geo-technological set of perspectives. This conceptualization lies at the heart of the series, and offers to explore the correlation between democracy, innovation and growth.

More information about this series at
http://www.springer.com/series/14635

Manlio Del Giudice

Understanding Family-Owned Business Groups

Towards a Pluralistic Approach

Manlio Del Giudice
Link Campus University
Rome, Italy

Palgrave Studies in Democracy, Innovation, and Entrepreneurship for Growth
ISBN 978-3-319-82535-9   ISBN 978-3-319-42243-5 (eBook)
DOI 10.1007/978-3-319-42243-5

© The Editor(s) (if applicable) and The Author(s) 2017
Softcover reprint of the hardcover 1st edition 2017
This work is subject to copyright. All rights are solely and exclusively licensed by the Publisher, whether the whole or part of the material is concerned, specifically the rights of translation, reprinting, reuse of illustrations, recitation, broadcasting, reproduction on microfilms or in any other physical way, and transmission or information storage and retrieval, electronic adaptation, computer software, or by similar or dissimilar methodology now known or hereafter developed. The use of general descriptive names, registered names, trademarks, service marks, etc. in this publication does not imply, even in the absence of a specific statement, that such names are exempt from the relevant protective laws and regulations and therefore free for general use.
The publisher, the authors and the editors are safe to assume that the advice and information in this book are believed to be true and accurate at the date of publication. Neither the publisher nor the authors or the editors give a warranty, express or implied, with respect to the material contained herein or for any errors or omissions that may have been made. The publisher remains neutral with regard to jurisdictional claims in published maps and institutional affiliations.

Cover illustration: Reinhard Krull / EyeEm

Printed on acid-free paper

This Palgrave Macmillan imprint is published by Springer Nature
The registered company is Springer International Publishing AG
The registered company address is: Gewerbestrasse 11, 6330 Cham, Switzerland

CONTENTS

1 Untangling the Origins of Family Business   1
   1.1   Definition of Family Business   1
   1.2   The Institutional Overlap Between Business and Family   3
   1.3   The Diffusion of Family Businesses in the National and Global
      Context   4
   1.4   Advantages and Criticalities of Family Businesses   6
      1.4.1   Advantages   6
      1.4.2   Criticalities   10
   References   15

**2 Family Business Between Family and Business: Theoretical
and Practical Perspectives**   19
   2.1   The Entrepreneurial and Managerial Model   19
      2.1.1   The Entrepreneurial Formula of Family Businesses   20
      2.1.2   The Governance System of a Family Business   21
      2.1.3   The Models of Corporate Governance in a Family
         Business Led by a Non-family CEO   24
   2.2   Family Business Governance: Constraints and Opportunities
      Related to Family Governance   25
   2.3   The Pink Aspect of the Corporate Governance of Family
      Businesses   31

viii CONTENTS

2.4	The Process of Succession	33
	2.4.1 Generational Change	33
	2.4.2 The Transfer Models	35
	2.4.3 The Conclusion of the Succession Process	37
2.5	Growth Dynamics and Continuity of Success	38
2.6	Funding Management and Financial Structure of Family Businesses: A Look on Italy	41
	2.6.1 A New Model of Finance for Knowledge Growth in Family Businesses: The Serial Family Entrepreneur	47
2.7	The Value of Family Business	54
References		56

3 From Family Businesses to Business Groups — 61

3.1	The Problem of Enterprise Size	61
3.2	The Nature of Company Aggregations	63
3.3	Toward a Definition of Business Groups	66
	3.3.1 Motivations for the Formation of Groups	69
	3.3.2 Modalities for the Formation of Business Groups	70
	3.3.3 Classification of Business Groups	74
3.4	The Family Enterprise Structured as a Group: Peculiarities of Family Groups	78
3.5	Understanding the Family Holdings	80
	3.5.1 Types of Holdings	81
	3.5.2 Juridical Forms of the Family Holding	83
	3.5.3 Advantages and Disadvantages of the Family Holding	86
3.6	Designation of the Company Assets to the Holding Company	87
3.7	The Family Holding: Tutelage Instruments of the Assets During the Generational Change	89
3.8	The Phenomenon of Generational Drift	90
	3.8.1 The Effects of the Generational Drift on Share Leverage	91
	3.8.2 Reinforcing Control Through the Family Holding	92
3.9	The Value of the Business Group	94
	3.9.1 Asymmetries in the Spread of Value	95
	3.9.2 Measurement of Value: Return of Capital and Evaluation of Group Performance	96
	3.9.3 The Group Economic Value Added	97
References		100

4 Emerging Markets: Institutional Problems and Entrepreneurial Models

		105
4.1	Emerging Markets: A Variety of Definitions	105
4.2	The Rise of Emerging Markets	111
4.3	A New Growth Model	113
4.4	The Importance of the Emerging Economies for Investors	115
4.5	The Relevance of Informal Institutions	116
4.6	Institutional Vacuums	117
4.7	The Product Market	118
	4.7.1 Capital Markets	119
	4.7.2 The Labor Market	120
4.8	Methods for Overcoming Institutional Vacuums	121
	4.8.1 By-Passing the Formal Institutions	123
	4.8.2 Organization into Business Groups: Relying on Informal Institutions	125
References		126

5 Business Groups in the Emerging Markets

		133
5.1	Business Groups in the World	133
5.2	Family Group Versus Non-family Group	136
5.3	The Role of Family Conglomerates in Emerging Markets	139
	5.3.1 The Formation of Family Conglomerates	142
	5.3.2 Drivers of Growth, Development and Expansion	144
	5.3.3 Evolution of the Family Conglomerate	152
5.4	Conclusions	153
References		156

References 163

Index 187

LIST OF FIGURES

Fig. 3.1	Distribution of share participations before acquisition	71
Fig. 3.2	Distribution of share participations after the acquisition	71
Fig. 3.3	Distribution of the quotas before conferring "backward development"	73
Fig. 3.4	Distribution of the shares after what is conferred	73
Fig. 4.1	Global growth (advanced economies vs emerging market and developing economies)	112
Fig. 4.2	Demographics in Asian EMDEs	113

LIST OF TABLE

Table 5.1   Heterogeneity of groups in the world   135

CHAPTER 1

Untangling the Origins of Family Business

1.1 Definition of Family Business

Family business plays a major role in developed economies, but the management literature has still not found an agreement on a single definition of this entity (Del Giudice et al. 2011, 2013a, b; Campanella et al. 2013a, b; Ward 2011; Zellweger et al. 2010; Zahra et al. 2000; Westhead and Cowling 1997; Zachary 2011; Zahra and Sharma 2004).

At first, some authors used a single-variable approach to describe a firm as a family business, based on a single dimension: the degree of control. In this regard, a definition may be quoted of family business as "a firm controlled by members of a single family"; totally restrictive and lacking in specification, this definition creates complications in the case of single-owned businesses, or when people outside the family are involved in the ownership and management of the firm. The same applies by defining a family business as "a firm in which venture capitalists and workforce belong to a single family or to a few families linked by ties of kinship or affinity". In fact, referring specifically to the family as the only source of capital and labor, family members and firm fully overlap.

Thus, it is useful to highlight another definition that describes a family business as the place where "relationships of mutual conditioning are established between the production firm and the consumer firm of one or a few families linked by kinship or affinity, which own the capital provided with the bond of full risk". This definition would broaden the horizon by also including among family businesses those in which the economic actors,

© The Author(s) 2017
M. Del Giudice, *Understanding Family-Owned Business Groups,*
DOI 10.1007/978-3-319-42243-5_1

1

personal institutions and assets of the firms involved are different and distinct.

Other perspectives have considered family businesses as firms set up by "one or a few families linked by ties of kinship, affinity or strong alliances, which hold a share of risk capital sufficient to ensure the control of the firm".

However, the studies and empirical research of business economy all converge toward a definitional proposal that identifies as a family business a firm that, regardless of its size or its national or international importance, falls under the ownership or control of one or more families; a firm in which the entire management is run by an owner-entrepreneur and, potentially, by the co-workers from his family.

The aforesaid definitions highlight features and elements that, differently combined, can generate various types of family businesses present in reality. Precisely for this reason, in the literature, both for a systematization of the present case, and for purely empirical purposes, there was an urge to proceed with classifications that take into account a combination of factors, such as the stage of development and the size of the firm, the generational phase and the ownership structure (Vilaseca 2002; Chua et al. 1999; Martínez et al. 2007; Habbershon et al. 2003; Sciascia and Mazzola 2008; Harvey and Evans 1994; James 1999).

A contribution in this direction is provided by Corbetta (1995), who, by taking as reference three variables (capital ownership model, presence of family members in the Board of Directors (BoD) and in the firm's management bodies, size of staff) and identifying for each of them, three or more measures, recognizes:

- *Household family businesses*, with complete ownership (single owner) or limited (more owners, but not many), small, with total presence of family members in the government and management of the business;
- *Traditional family businesses*, different from the previous ones in size (larger) and for the presence of external members besides the family in the management bodies;
- *Extended family businesses*, with capital owned by a larger number of people (always within the family) and the presence of non-family members, both in the BoD and in the management bodies;
- *Open family businesses*, medium or large, with people not descended from the founder as owners of shares, with a multifaceted composition of both the BoD and the management bodies, and the presence of both family and non-family members.

1.2 The Institutional Overlap Between Business and Family

A family business, to be regarded as such, must be represented at the same time by the presence of the family, the firm and the equity component. The simultaneous presence of these three factors may lead to the development of the so-called phenomenon of "institutional overlap" (Chua et al. 2003; Lansberg 1983; Astrachan and Kolenko 1994).

In fact, in family businesses, since the conduct is influenced by the behavior and values of the entrepreneur and his family, pressure from the latter is so significant that it leads to a substantial overlap between entrepreneurial, family and management roles. In organizational terms, this means that decision-making processes and management policies are conceived within the family institution, and mainly to meet the needs of the family and its members (Barnes and Hershon 1976; Donnelley 1964; Dyer 1986; Kepner 1983; Beckhard and Dyer 1983; Levinson 1971; De Mik et al. 1985; Ward 2011; Davis 1983).

This phenomenon is not always a disturbing element for the firm. In fact, the maintenance of a broad area of institutional overlap is a resource the firm cannot ignore in the start-up phases. The family, in this case, becomes a vital resource, resulting in a greater involvement and higher motivation. It also allows to govern conflicts and encourage communication, by identifying the interests and objectives shared by the firm and the family; it transforms the compliance of the objectives, the cohesion, trust, willingness to sacrifice and to reinvest the proceeds in instruments to obtain consent.

These factors of success, however, become obstacles when the firm is facing problems of development, business restructuring and leadership succession. The sacrifices the family was willing to endure in order to achieve social extraction shared by all, if success is reached, tend to fade to the advantage of fulfillment and a progressive aversion to risk.

According to Lansberg (1983), the main difficulties caused by the institutional overlap between family and business emerge in the phases of:

- selection, in which family members claim to occupy a position within the firm, despite not having the appropriate expertise, only to enjoy their right to business ownership. The solution to the problem could be the establishment of a regulation with guiding principles in the selection of new members (e.g. a qualification threshold, work experience in other firms, etc.);

4   M. DEL GIUDICE

- training, in which the distinction between the individual and the firm's needs can be solved through a planned management of the training and selection processes;
- assessment, which discloses the difficulties arising from assessing objectively the family members without, therefore, being conditioned by the emotional component. For this reason, evaluation committees made up of both family and non-family members are usually established;
- reward, which differs according to the needs of the family compared to those of the firm. In fact, for the former, reward is determined by the needs of the individual in order to ensure his long-term wealth, while for the latter it is based on a more meritocratic path.

It is clear that, at the time of convergence of the different objectives, family managers will act in order to provide the firm with an enduring competitive advantage (Carney 2005; Arregle et al. 2007; Zahra 2005).

1.3   The Diffusion of Family Businesses in the National and Global Context

The extensive and in-depth analysis, the economic doctrine has long been conducting on family businesses, documents the complex issue of their government in relation to the changing conditions of the context where they operate. This would justify, following the changes in the processes of industrialization, the economic development of different countries and of different forms of family-based capitalism.

Family business is the ownership and governance model numerically more common in the world; in all the countries considered, the percentage of family businesses exceeds, often widely, 50%. According to a research conducted by Aidaf,[1] in the ranking of the top 100 companies by revenue, 42 appear to have been "passed down" from father to son. Furthermore, according to Aidaf (Report 2010), Italian family businesses always appear to be distributed 60% in the northwest, 13% in the northeast, 17% in central Italy and the remaining 10% in the south.

As confirmed by the International Family Enterprise Research Academy (IFERA) survey,[2] family businesses in Italy are the prevalent business reality, both as SMEs and as large companies or industrial groups. A more accurate estimate, based on the ownership and control structure is provided by the Bank of Italy, which shows that the ownership is highly concentrated with an average size of the share held by the largest shareholder of 52% of capital. This analysis indicates that 48% of firms is legally controlled by a single shareholder or a group formed by a few family members; a minority of firms is controlled by few people who do not have family ties.

The results obtained confirm the absence of widespread ownership and that direct ownership is held in most cases by individuals, as evidence of the low degree of separation between ownership and control. Then, the instruments used to exercise control were identified, which integrate or replace ownership, and are both formal and informal. The former include the restrictive terms of freedom of movement of shareholdings or the social pacts, while the latter include the family ties, which decrease as the business size increases.

The dominant control model among SMEs is the family model (46%), followed by the absolute (22%), the group (17%) and the coalition (13%). Then, the links between the actors at the top of the group structure were identified, showing how control is exercised two-thirds by family, while the rest consists of absolute and coalition control. The family nature of the SMEs' control structure is clear; it increases with size, and families manage it differently by switching to forms mediated by group structures.

Astrachan et al. (2009) have reported the high presence of family businesses also in the rest of the world, and the IFERA data confirm that in France these firms appear to be approximately 83% of listed companies; in Germany, the percentage appears to be 79%, in Spain 83% and in Sweden 79%. In the East, however, data suggest that 70% of listed companies appear to be concentrated in the area of Malaysia, Hong Kong and Thailand.

Similar results, although with lower percentages, are found in Asian countries (Hong Kong, South Korea and Singapore), with the exception of Japan, due, above all, to the different way of exercising control. Furthermore, after experiencing an explosive business growth in a few decades, Japan appears to have the lowest degree of concentration of family businesses, with a percentage that almost reaches 10% (Chu 2009). Hence, with regard to the Asian countries, there is still little data available, despite the presence of the oldest family businesses in the world.

This is a phenomenon diametrically opposed to the Indian evidence, where family capitalism appears to be responsible for the overall profitability of the 250 largest private companies; while the 15 most influential families control over 60% of corporate assets listed in Indonesia.

Data indicating the percentage of family businesses in the USA and, in part, the UK is surprising: unlike the common belief about the insignificance of the phenomenon in Anglo-Saxon countries (where managerial capitalism and public companies are prevalent), the survey shows that in both the USA and the UK, family businesses represent a significant share in the economy of the country.

In fact, according to the international organization Family Firm Institute (FFI), between 80% and 90% of businesses in North America pertain to family capitalism (Poutziouris et al. 2008), and 65% of those in the UK (Hartley and Griffith 2009). In particular, in the USA (Zahra 2003), family businesses (Astrachan and Shanker 2003) are more than 20 million today, equivalent to 92% of all firms operating in the economic and production context.

1.4 Advantages and Criticalities of Family Businesses

The evolution of business economics studies and the constant success of family business management have prompted a revision of the original theoretical perspectives on the family business topic. The studies on family businesses, in fact, were characterized by a rather negative connotation; the authors used to focus attention on the limits of family businesses, arguing that the link between business and family could jeopardize their survival (Graves 2006).

The international management literature has recorded, over the years, a number of strengths and weaknesses related to family businesses for which an explanation will be later attempted (Dumas and Blodgett 1999).

1.4.1 Advantages

Long-Term Orientation
One element that is often recognized as one of the major strengths of family businesses is represented by long-term orientation, by focusing on the potential for growth and investment projects due to the inseparability between the objectives of the family and those of the firm.

The goal is to maximize the well-being of current and future generations in a trans-generational perspective, while managerial enterprises are linked to the maximization of shareholder value with a short-term horizon in order to increase the managers' personal benefits.

This orientation is the result of several factors (Koiranen 2002): the willingness of family members to pass down to their heirs a healthy and competitive firm; the strong economic and emotional involvement of family members in the enterprise, which implies that the firm itself is an asset to be safeguarded and, at the same time, to be developed; the financial and reputational consequences that would arise from a possible situation of business disruption.

With regard to ownership, the presence of a long-term vision favors: the existence of "patient" capital to support growth; the stability of the firm's basic strategy; the guarantee for stakeholders of a partner with whom long-term relationships may be initiated.

With regard to management, the main advantage is the ability to evaluate investments in accordance with cost effectiveness criteria, which necessarily require prolonged assessments, because investments in real assets are characterized by a medium- to long-term return period, in monetary form.

The long-term view, in essence, should be consistent with the classic shareholder economic objective: the creation of value.

The Creation of Inimitable Resources

The competitive advantage that family businesses are able to generate is due to the presence of inimitable resources, that is, rare resources, difficult to replicate by competitors (García-Álvarez and López-Sintas 2001; Aronoff 2004).

The process of creating unique resources goes through different elements:

- Human capital: it expresses the set of knowledge, skills and abilities of a person and/or an organization. In family businesses, human capital has a sort of "added value" resulting from the fact that every family member, participating both in the business and the family life, contributes with original and inimitable elements;
- Capital stock: it expresses the set of current and potential resources arising from the system of relationships that are established among a variety of individuals and/or organizations. In family businesses, the network of relationships created between family members and stakeholders promotes the creation of stable and productive ties over time;
- Financial capital: it identifies all financial resources available to the firm. Investment and growth activities are encouraged by the ability of family businesses to keep resources within the firm over a long

period of time, thus excluding the fact that the funds are threatened by the risk of repayment;

- "Informal" capital: it expresses the overall resources that family members decide to "personally" contribute with (working for the firm without any remuneration, granting personal loans, etc.). The exploitation of these resources is normally concentrated in the start-up phase of the business and in moments of difficulty for the enterprise;
- Costs related to the governance structure: family businesses, through family and fiduciary ties, have less need to adopt expensive tools to limit agency costs (management monitoring, performance-related rewards, etc.). These costs, in fact, do not exist or are minimized, when the principal and the agent are the same person, which results in cost advantage and greater efficiency.

Altruism
This term intends to describe the special nature of actors with kin relationships (especially if close) to adopt an attitude aimed at mutual prosperity and support. Applying a similar concept to the management of a firm implies that the family should opt for a cooperative behavior, which is able to prefer the interests of the enterprise to those strictly personal of a single family member. Such an attitude assumes the existence of a strong link between the fate of the enterprise and that, not only economic, of the family (Hall et al. 2001).

In short, *altruism* considers:

- the willingness of family members to prefer the firm's interests to their own;
- the behavior of "older" family members (founder, parents, etc.) aimed at passing down to their heirs, values such as loyalty, honesty, commitment, respect, mutual trust, etc.;
- their willingness to be particularly generous with the descendants within the firm (by ensuring them a job, allowing them to take advantage of business resources, etc.).

According to a positive vision of the concept, altruism appears to be a unique element in family businesses that could reduce agency costs through positive effects arising from fiduciary ties, mutual support, engagement in the enterprise, etc.

In particular, the effective functioning of altruism, as a governance element aimed at limiting agency costs, must be based on the culture, understood as the set of personal and business values, which are long-lasting and shared among family members, and shape the behavior of the family itself toward the company and, more generally, the environment. Thus, the culture within a firm involves the overlap between personal and business values, as well as the commitment and involvement of the family in the business.

Increased Flexibility

In general, flexibility is defined as the ability to adapt one's resources to the external conditions preferable for business development (Tàpies and Fernández Moya 2012).

Thus, from a strategic viewpoint, a firm's flexibility increases together with the potential rapidity of the adaptations of the objectives and strategy to the evolution of the external environment, and with the cost reduction of resource changes. The pursuit of flexibility is an important lever, which together with other variables, such as time, quality and variety, helps to improve business performance.

In family businesses, the decisions taken informally make the entire organization flexible, facilitating its development, with a slim and rapid structure.

Thanks to the more simple decision path, family businesses can react rapidly, thus seizing purchase opportunities when they reach the market. Most of the time, their acquisitions are set in a long-term strategy. They do not aim so much for the acquisitions that make headlines and flatter the managers' ego, but for really advantageous transactions.

Healthier Balance Sheets

One of the interesting characteristics of family businesses is also the greater financial health of their balance sheets. This advantage arises from the different perspective of a family compared to that of an external shareholder. In fact, the latter is especially attentive to the maximization of profits, even if they are "inflated" artificially, provided that the share is appealing to the eyes of the market and the stock prices rise (Thomas 2002).

In most cases, the approach of family shareholders is quite different; they rather aim at reducing the tax burden, and this leads them to adopt a more conservative accounting management, with significant reserves and a policy of rapid amortization. This translates into healthier balance sheets and

10   M. DEL GIUDICE

better cash-flow conversion, with a substantial equity capital and significant hidden reserves. As a result, the family business is less dependent on stock exchange movements and may embark on more substantial infrastructure and R&D expenditures.

1.4.2   Criticalities

Risk Aversion

There is a widespread belief, also supported by various empirical evidence that family businesses have a very cautious approach, oriented to preservation rather than growth, with a strategic approach not keen on risk-taking (Fernández and Nieto 2005).

The increased risk aversion that characterizes family businesses may:

- constitute a barrier to the development of innovative processes;
- lead to the undercapitalization of the firm, limiting the collection of resources in the form of equity and debt to support growth;
- encourage the "closure" of capital and/or management positions toward external parties in order to avert risks of loss of control and inability to manage more complex relationships with the increase of shareholding;
- limit the firm's expansion strategy in international markets.

Moreover, risk aversion may induce the family, especially those in which the heirs have reached leading positions in the firm's ownership and hold large assets acquired through inheritance, to seek for positions of political privilege, in order to preserve the status quo that could be threatened by new and innovative companies entering the market (Morck and Yeung 2003).

A direct outcome of such an attitude could be a problem of delay in the economic growth resulting from positions of economic and political privilege related to the maintenance of the firm's control and the reluctance of family businesses to invest in innovation and R&D.

Recent studies (Zahra 2005), on the contrary, have focused on the potential for innovation transfer of family businesses (Ward 2011), noting that the involvement of family members in the ownership and/or management causes a positive effect on innovation.

Succession Issues

The phenomenon of generational transfer is one of critical importance as it comes from a kind of categorical imperative related to any business experience, which is the firm's survival.

Looking at the entrepreneurial reality, it can be stated that the phenomenon of generational change is especially significant when referring to family businesses, where it is particularly complex. Moreover, the overlap between the family and the enterprise system may cause several issues in the transition from one generation to another, going as far as undermining business continuity. For this reason, some authors argue that "the great secret to deal virtuously with family succession in a firm is to convince yourself that you are not faced with a fact, but a process." Entrepreneurial succession, therefore, is a real process in which, on the one hand, there is a founder or a second generation entrepreneur ready to transfer to their successor their knowledge and experience in business management; on the other, a successor increasing his level of preparation, training and presence in the firm, so as to acquire the skills needed to manage the company.

A number of surveys (IFC 2010) show that, worldwide, about 7% of family businesses are sold within the first generation and 10% retain the same size; in the transition from second to third generation about 80% of US companies and 86% of Asian ones cease activities.

The theme of generational change is a mandatory stage for all firms; however, it would be important to plan transfer time so that the firm appears prepared for the event, also to prevent it from occurring in extreme or emergency situations, the consequences of which could be disastrous for the company.

The topic of succession will be dealt with in depth later in the discussion.

The (Managerial) Labor Market

Some studies claim that, at the time of succession and, in particular, when the future managers of the enterprise are to be selected, family businesses are in a penalizing condition. Specifically, some criticalities are detected (Habbershon and Pistrui 2002):

- Nepotism, which is the tendency to promote and systematically assign key roles to members of the family. This preference places kinship ties above professional expertise, not recognizing the skills of capable and deserving collaborators. It is a choice that sets the stage for future conflicts among people inside and outside the family, and is decisive in the phase of generational transfer. Corporate nepotism, which is demotivating for non-family staff, is associated with the authoritarian paternalism toward family members employed by the firm, that is, the tendency to manage relationships with relatives and in-laws in the same way as those within the family. Consequently, this propensity confuses the roles and lines of authority resulting in a situation that is advantageous neither for managerial rationality nor for family harmony;

- Adverse selection, that is, limitations in the selection process of human resources that force the firm to face the risk of hiring qualitatively poor individuals. Adapting the argument to family businesses, the competitiveness of the labor market is reduced, because the group of potential suitors to managerial positions is limited, often to the sole heirs. This involves a greater risk of having in command individuals with insufficient expertise, and results, in turn, in higher managerial monitoring costs. The most talented managers, in fact, in the absence of career opportunities in family businesses, will turn to large listed companies with an organizational structure without the burden of the family. The problem of adverse selection is reduced in the presence of a competitive transparent labor market, where the firm has the opportunity to choose from a wide circle of individuals attracted by remuneration, good career prospects within the company and, generally, by the structure of the employment contracts, which are all more flexible elements in listed companies (consider, e.g. the impossibility for a private firm to offer options to managers due to the absence of a stock market and the reluctance of the main shareholder to reduce its stake);

- demotivation of workers, which is caused by the possibility that the family pursues exclusively its own utility function (maximization of personal wealth), and results in a lack of commitment and productivity.

Integration Between Family and Business

The merger between family unit and business on the one hand can be a source of unique and inimitable resources for the enterprise, but on the other hand can lead to problems in the management of the family business, since the conflicts among family members, which also emerge outside the

UNTANGLING THE ORIGINS OF FAMILY BUSINESS   13

business sphere, negatively influence the formation and pursuit of the firm's economic goals (Vallejo 2008).

This risk is normally higher where sharing of strategies is only limited to some family members, or in the case of a family that sees the presence on the BoD of shareholders not involved in the management of the business, or of individuals representing a branch of the family. For example, a family-manager aims at the firm's growth, so reinvestment of profits is considered an important source of funding, while a family-shareholder expects to be able to receive adequate remuneration in the form of dividends, considering also possible difficulties in liquidating the securities.

Another consequence resulting from the integration between family and business could be the expropriation of wealth (the use of business resources for personal satisfaction, group transactions to transfer wealth from one business to another, sub-optimal investments to pursue relatively costly objectives, etc.) to the detriment of any other shareholder.

Some studies claim that the family, having control of the firm, is more prone to extract private benefits, when the financial involvement in the business of the family itself is lower, through equity leveraged instruments (pyramidal groups, limited-voting shares, shareholders' agreements, etc.).

The Distortion of Altruism
The distortion of altruism generally results both from a possible radicalization of the phenomenon by "elderly" family members that causes negative effects, and from a number of opportunistic behaviors potentially enforced by family members, in particular by the heirs (Schulze et al. 2003).

Some family members (usually the descendants) are encouraged by the generosity of other family members (usually parents) to adopt a behavior guided by free riding and shirking.

In the first case, the reference is to the behavior of those family members who, in order to avoid the most tedious or difficult tasks they have been assigned to, leave the job to others, aware that those assignments will be fulfilled.

Shirking, instead, is the behavior, for example, of those who squander their parents' money in unprofitable expenses and play no active role in the enterprise.

With regard to the criticalities related to altruism, the concept of self-control is particularly significant. In general, the issues concerning self-control arise from the situation in which the parties to a contract are driven and able to violate the terms of the agreement by implementing actions that can harm both themselves and the individuals close to them. The problems associated with self-control can arise both from its practice and from its lack.

With regard to the former, in the specific case of family businesses, the ruling party can make decisions by taking into account both the objectives and the economic preferences of the majority shareholder (which can be reasonably considered common to all shareholders), but also the non-economic ones which, on the contrary, may diverge from subject to subject and, for this reason, are not measurable with reasonable certainty, that is, using the monetary criteria. It follows that the owner could assign greater importance to "personal preferences", by engaging in a conduct aimed at maximizing his own welfare and this, accordingly, may not be efficient both for the owner and for all the other shareholders. Therefore, self-control expresses the risk of acting, in an attempt to improve one's own utility function, in a way that threatens the common welfare and, hence, also one's own.

The loss of self-control, however, is due to the failure by elderly family members to adopt a preventive behavior toward their heirs (e.g., the decision to subject the transfer of a part of the inheritance to the implementation of certain behaviors by the descendants).

In family businesses, self-control may be particularly emphasized to the extent that some family members, by controlling the firm's resources, decide to grant unconditionally economic and non-economic privileges to their heirs at the risk of causing the aforementioned phenomena of free riding and shirking.

The Diversification of the Portfolio

Family businesses are the most common ownership-concentrated structure in the world. The family has basically poorly diversified assets, being, for the most part, conveyed in the enterprise, and this results in the default of one of the terms to apply risk pricing models: the existence of a diversified portfolio (Astrachan and Jaskiewicz 2008).

Some authors argue that shareholders with poorly diversified portfolios may make investment decisions based on different criteria than those used by "diversified" shareholders. Specifically, there may be a violation of the rule of "value enhancing" toward other criteria (survival, dimensional growth, etc.). In particular, the family could have an approach toward risk characterized by high aversion, which could lead them to reject affordable investment projects, because they are deemed too risky.

Overall, the previously highlighted positive and negative aspects confirm the complexity of a phenomenon that, in itself, has so many facets interconnected with one another that it is extremely difficult to isolate in what way and extent a single element may have some effect in characterizing the family business compared to other organizational forms.

NOTES

1. Italian Association of Family Businesses, born in Italy in 1997 to protect and disseminate the values of family capitalism.
2. International Family Enterprise Research Academy, founded in 2001 by a group of professors and researchers with the goal of developing studies on family businesses on a global scale.

REFERENCES

Aronoff, C. (2004). Self-perpetuation family organization built on values: Necessary condition for long-term family business survival. *Family Business Review, 17*(1), 55–59.

Arregle, J. L., Hitt, M. A., Sirmon, D. G., & Very, P. (2007). The development of organizational social capital: Attributes of family firms*. *Journal of Management Studies, 44*(1), 73–95.

Astrachan, J. H., & Jaskiewicz, P. (2008). Emotional returns and emotional costs in privately held family businesses: Advancing traditional business valuation. *Family Business Review, 21*(2), 139–149.

Astrachan, J. H., & Kolenko, T. A. (1994). A neglected factor explaining family business success: Human resource practices. *Family Business Review, 7*(3), 251–262.

Astrachan, J. H., & Shanker, M. C. (2003). Family businesses' contribution to the U.S. economy: A closer look. *Family Business Review, 16*(3), 211–219.

Astrachan, J. H., Torsten, M. P., & Jaskiewicz, P. (2009). *Family business.* London: Edward Elgar Publishing Limited.

Barnes, L. B., & Hershon, S. A. (1976). Transferring power in family business. *Harvard Business Review, 54*(4), 105–114.

Beckhard, R., & Dyer, W. G. (1983). Managing continuity in the family-owned business. *Organizational Dynamics, 12*(1), 5–12.

Campanella, F., Del Giudice, M., & Della Peruta, M. R. (2013a). The role of information in the credit relationship. *Journal of Innovation and Entrepreneurship, 2*, 17. doi:10.1186/2192-5372-2-17.

Campanella, F., Della Peruta, M. R., & Del Giudice, M. (2013b). Informational approach of family spin-offs in the funding process of innovative projects: An

16   M. DEL GIUDICE

empirical verification. *Journal of Innovation and Entrepreneurship, 2,* 18. doi:10. 1186/2192-5372-2-18.

Carney, M. (2005). Corporate governance and competitive advantage in family-controlled firms. *Entrepreneurship Theory and Practice, 29*(3), 249–265.

Chu, W. (2009). The influence of family ownership on SME performance: Evidence from public firms in Taiwan. *Small Business Economics, 33*(3), 353–373.

Chua, J. H., Chrisman, J. J., & Sharma, P. (1999). Defining the family business by behavior. *Entrepreneurship: Theory and Practice, 23*(4), 19–40.

Chua, J. H., Chrisman, J. J., & Steier, L. P. (2003). Extending the theoretical horizons of family business research. *Entrepreneurship Theory and Practice, 27*(4), 331–338.

Corbetta, G. (1995). Patterns of development of family businesses in Italy. *Family Business Review, 8*(4), 255–265.

Davis, P. (1983). Realizing the potential of the family business. *Organizational Dynamics, 12*(1), 47–56.

De Mik, L., Anderson, R. M., & Johnson, P. A. (1985). *The family in business.* San Francisco: Jossey-Bass Publishers.

Del Giudice, M., Della Peruta, M. R., & Carayannis, E. G. (2011). *Knowledge and family business. The governance and management of family firms in the new knowledge economy* (Innovation, technology and knowledge management series editor). New York: Springer. ISBN: 978-1-4419-7352-8.

Del Giudice, M., Della Peruta, M. R., & Maggioni, V. (2013a). Spontaneous processes of reproduction of family-based entrepreneurship: An empirical research on the cognitive nature of the spin-offs. *Journal of Innovation and Entrepreneurship, 2,* 12. doi:10.1186/2192-5372-2-12.

Del Giudice, M., Della Peruta, M. R., & Maggioni, V. (2013b). One man company or managed succession: The transfer of the family dream in Southern-Italian firms. *Journal of Organizational Change Management, 26*(4), 703–719.

Donnelley, R. G. (1964). The family business. *Harvard Business Review, 42*(4), 93–105.

Dumas, C., & Blodgett, M. (1999). Articulating values to inform decision making: Lessons from family firms around the world. *International Journal of Value-Based Management, 12*(3), 209–221.

Dyer, W. G. (1986). *Cultural change in family firms.* San Francisco: Jossey-Bass.

Fernández, Z., & Nieto, M. J. (2005). Internationalization strategy of small and medium-sized family businesses: Some influential factors. *Family Business Review, 18*(1), 77–89.

García-Álvarez, E., & López-Sintas, J. (2001). A taxonomy of founders based on values: The root of family business heterogeneity. *Family Business Review, 14*(3), 209–230.

Graves, C. (2006). Internationalization of Australian family businesses: A managerial capabilities perspective. *Family Business Review, 19*(3), 207–224.

Habbershon, T. G., & Pistrui, J. (2002). Enterprising families domain: Family-influenced ownership groups in pursuit of transgenerational wealth. *Family Business Review, 15*(3), 223–237.

Habbershon, T. G., Williams, M., & MacMillan, I. C. (2003). A unified systems perspective of family firm performance. *Journal of Business Venturing, 18*(4), 451–465.

Hall, A., Melin, L., & Nordqvist, M. (2001). Entrepreneurship as radical change in the family business: Exploring the role of cultural patterns. *Family Business Review, 14*(3), 193–208.

Hartley, B. B., & Griffith, G. (2009). *Family wealth transition planning: Advising families with small businesses, Bloomberg Press, New York, USA.*

Harvey, M., & Evans, R. E. (1994). Family business and multiple levels of conflict. *Family Business Review, 7*(4), 331–348.

International Finance Corporation–World Bank Group, *Family Business Governance Handbook.* Edition 2010.

James, H. S. (1999). Owner as manager, extended horizons and the family firm. *International Journal of the Economics of Business, 6*(1), 41–55.

Kepner, E. (1983). The family and the firm: A coevolutionary perspective. *Organizational Dynamics, 12*(1), 57–70.

Koiranen, M. (2002). Over 100 years of age but still entrepreneurially active in business: Exploring the values and family characteristics of old Finnish family firms. *Family Business Review, 15*(3), 175–187.

Lansberg, I. S. (1983). Managing human resources in family firms: The problem of institutional overlap. *Organizational Dynamics, 12*(1), 39–46.

Levinson, H. (1971). Conflicts that plague family businesses. *Harvard Business Review, 49*(2), 90–98.

Martínez, J. I., Stöhr, B. S., & Quiroga, B. F. (2007). Family ownership and firm performance: Evidence from public companies in Chile. *Family Business Review, 20*(2), 83–94.

Morck, R., & Yeung, B. (2003). Agency problems in large family business groups. *Entrepreneurship Theory and Practice, 27*(4), 367–382.

Poutziouris, P., Smyrnios, K., & Klein, S. (Eds.). (2008). *Handbook of research on family business.* Cheltenham: Edward Elgar Publishing.

Schulze, W. S., Lubatkin, M. H., & Dino, R. N. (2003). Toward a theory of agency and altruism in family firms. *Journal of Business Venturing, 18*(4), 473–490.

Sciascia, S., & Mazzola, P. (2008). Family involvement in ownership and management: Exploring nonlinear effects on performance. *Family Business Review, 21*(4), 331–345.

Tàpies, J., & Fernández Moya, M. (2012). Values and longevity in family business: Evidence from a cross-cultural analysis. *Journal of Family Business Management, 2*(2), 130–146.

Thomas, J. (2002). Freeing the shackles of family business ownership. *Family Business Review*, *15*(4), 321–336.

Vallejo, M. C. (2008). Is the culture of family firms really different? A value-based model for its survival through generations. *Journal of Business Ethics*, *81*(2), 261–279.

Vilaseca, A. (2002). The shareholder role in the family business: Conflict of interests and objectives between nonemployed shareholders and top management team. *Family Business Review*, *15*(4), 299–320.

Ward, J. L. (2011). *Keeping the family business healthy: How to plan for continuing growth, profitability, and family leadership*. New York: Palgrave Macmillan.

Westhead, P., & Cowling, M. (1997). Performance contrasts between family and non-family unquoted companies in the UK. *International Journal of Entrepreneurial Behavior & Research*, *3*(1), 30–52.

Zachary, R. K. (2011). The importance of the family system in family business. *Journal of Family Business Management*, *1*(1), 26–36.

Zahra, S. A. (2003). International expansion of US manufacturing family businesses: The effect of ownership and involvement. *Journal of Business Venturing*, *18*(4), 495–512.

Zahra, S. A. (2005). Entrepreneurial risk taking in family firms. *Family Business Review*, *18*(1), 23–40.

Zahra, S. A., & Sharma, P. (2004). Family business research: A strategic reflection. *Family Business Review*, *17*(4), 331–346.

Zahra, S. A., Neubaum, D. O., & Huse, M. (2000). Entrepreneurship in medium-size companies: Exploring the effects of ownership and governance systems. *Journal of Management*, *26*(5), 947–976.

Zellweger, T. M., Eddleston, K. A., & Kellermanns, F. W. (2010). Exploring the concept of familiness: Introducing family firm identity. *Journal of Family Business Strategy*, *1*(1), 54–63.

CHAPTER 2

Family Business Between Family and Business: Theoretical and Practical Perspectives

2.1 The Entrepreneurial and Managerial Model

The management literature, besides the extraordinary development of the "BRIC" countries, the success of the European Single Market introduced by the advent of the euro and the 2008 financial crisis, has long focused its analysis on corporate governance, bringing back to the top the economic and political debate on corporate governance, its purposes, the functioning of the firms' management bodies and the strategic decisions made by these (Ward 2011).

The topic of the governing structures in family businesses has gained importance in the broad discipline of corporate governance only in the last 20 years, in spite of very little interest shown by scholars, until half way through the 1980s.

Although family businesses have always been an "invariant" in the different forms of capitalism (Anglo-Saxon, Rhine-Japanese and continental European), rarely in the past have the scientific community showed an interest in the analysis of the ownership structure and governance mechanisms in firms of this type.

Accurate analysis of the evolving trends of business management from a strategic and organizational point of view is the basis of the future economic performance the company can generate. The reflection on the strengths and weaknesses of family businesses with regard to the management strategy of the enterprise and of the organization adopted allows us to concretely

© The Author(s) 2017
M. Del Giudice, *Understanding Family-Owned Business Groups*,
DOI 10.1007/978-3-319-42243-5_2

20   M. DEL GIUDICE

observe its consistency with the evolution of the surrounding environment and the firm's life cycle (Jaffe and Lane 2004).

2.1.1   The Entrepreneurial Formula of Family Businesses

According to the general systems theory (Von Bertalanffy 1972), a firm is seen as a complex system, where system means a structured and coordinated entirety of all its parts, participants and relationships between those elements, addressed to achieve a specific goal in its reference context. In particular, a family business is considered a semi-open system: the partiality of its degree of openness stems from the strong sense of belonging and from the influence of family members in the enterprise.

Systematic requirements should be added to the construction of the entrepreneurial formula that provides each company with a firm-specific added value.

The entrepreneurial formula is essentially the past history of the firm, its cultural background and the competitive advantages it carries, which are functional to meet specific needs or critical success factors on the market from which it receives output, resources and partnerships. Thus, the entrepreneurial formula of a family business is constituted by various elements (Zahra and Shama 2004; Salvato 2004):

- the organizational structure, the operational mechanisms and the set of competitive resources, through which the company itself develops its offer in the competitive environment;
- the competitive micro-environment, where it finds its own place and to whom the offer itself is addressed;
- the system of stakeholders (funders, workers, public administrators, etc.);
- the product system, which refers to all the elements that characterize the firm's offer;
- the project proposal addressed by the firm to the economic and social forces, in order to obtain their consent.

These elements are linked by relationships through which it is possible to highlight two sub-systems that show the competitive arena, that is, the setting through which the firm operates in an industry, and the social dynamics typical of the company, that is, its way of being and surviving in the system of economic forces. The two sub-systems are articulate, in turn, within the structure.

For the success of the entrepreneurial formula, all the aforementioned elements must exhibit a high degree of consonance and express internal and external consistency. Consistency ensures the family business both competitive success, by generating an enduring advantage based on critical success factors, and a higher profitability, consequential to the competitive advantage developed.

Ultimately, more careful consideration is given to the entrepreneurial formula, integrated within the environment and based on the logic of competitiveness, aimed at finding a common value among all the stakeholders (Carney et al. 2015).

2.1.2 *The Governance System of a Family Business*

In the early stages of development of a family business, the ownership participates in the production activity with an economic interest, the control body exercises the power of guidance and the management coordinates all the actions in the company's best interest.

The growth path will inevitably lead to a change in the governing body, with possible alterations of the family balance and with the arrival of external non-owner managers. With the increase in shareholding, the complexity of the relationships between family and business, and of the governance system, will increase.

Corporate governance is to be understood as the set of business activities from the formulation of the objectives to their achievement, through planning of suitable strategies and the organization of the management structure. The concept recalls various elements, such as the system of relations between ownership, board of directors and management, as well as the set of rules that should protect the interests of these parties, including the other enterprise stakeholders. It is simply the explicit representation of the way the family decides to set up its relationship with the company, the distribution of roles within it, the composition and functioning of the government bodies, and therefore the way decision-making processes should be carried out.

Generally, the governing bodies of a family business are (Tricker 2015; Corbetta and Salvato 2004):

- Board of Directors (BoD), which contributes to the process of creating value for the company that will result in the economic and financial performance, in stability and remuneration, in a collective growth. The role that a BoD can take on in a family business is distinguished by the importance assigned to its tasks;

In particular, the roles undertaken by the directors can be summarized in four points: to serve as a source of advice to the family that controls the company; to act as arbitrators and conciliators in the event of conflicts and differences of opinion among family members; to act as "governing" elements for the management; to appoint a substitute for the general president-manager if, for any reason, he were no longer present;

Danco and Jonovic (1981), after a complete analysis of the role of the BoD in family businesses, agree that the members of this body can be assigned different tasks, namely as planners, which help the owner-manager define the business goals; regulators, which limit the excesses of the owner-manager's absolute power; supporters, which help to offset the risks associated with excessive risk-taking, any lack of information on the markets, a lack of professionalism in the management; elder brothers, who act as guides;

- Family Council (FC), the body responsible for the prevention and/or the management of family disputes by promoting assistance. It is generally composed of all family members, or in the case of a high number, by their representatives, in order to facilitate the process of communication;

  Mostly, the FC interfaces with the BoD to exchange information about the operating performance and to formulate guidelines on corporate strategic choices. Therefore, it may be assumed that the purpose and functions of this Council are intended to provide the family members with "*a place where they can express and discuss their needs, views, concerns, opinions, values, and develop policies and procedures to serve the family, its long-term interests and hopes for the future*";

- Management Committee, which is mainly involved in coordinating the strategic choices regarding the different strategic business units. Establishing this Committee means acting on the corporate structure by inserting a body whose main task is to fulfill a function of decision-making coordination on extensive management problems, usually of a strategic nature, involving the interests of or the effects of which fall within several functional areas of the company.

The increasing complexity of the market in which firms operate requires the development of these bodies in order to govern the family business, by complying with certain guidelines specified in the family pact.

The family pact guarantees, at the time of succession, a stable generational transfer, the result of shared agreements between entrepreneurs and successors, pondered upon for some time (Bennedsen and Foss 2015).

The opportunity to use a regulation of institutional relations between family and business permits to formalize the operating rules of the governing bodies by regulating their participation in the capital of the company, the recruitment criteria of family members, their career paths and the calculation of their remuneration. However, this excess of formalization is likely to harm the instinctive predisposition that characterizes family businesses rather than educating family members to respect the need for autonomy and the principle of sustainable economic efficiency of the firm. It should be noted that the family pact has no legal value, and therefore, it does not help to ensure compliance with the provisions contained in it, but it leads the family to become aware of the relationship with the company and to think systematically in a context of transparency of everyone's actual motives. The result is a full acknowledgment of the firm's autonomy and the belief that family relationships should follow and be consistent with market criteria.

A related theme is represented by the differences between formal systems and substantial systems, where the distinction is based on the effective functioning of the legally existing bodies. Not infrequently, in fact, there is a mismatch between the formal articulation of the governing bodies and the way they actually perform their duties. With the evolution of the firm and the gradual separation between ownership and government, the board of directors becomes more important and turns into the only link between the family, the ownership and the company. In fact, in a closed ownership model, in this case a domestic family business, the governance is totally centralized; in a traditional family business, it is unlikely to see a board of directors made up of non-family members, while in an extended family business it is possible to find managers who are responsible for managing the whole company or a functional area. Only in an open family business, given the complexity of the governance structure, there are external parties in positions of directors or managers of the enterprise.

Many family businesses do not survive due to conflicts within the family that then affect the business management itself, and are often due to the lack of separation between corporate and family assets, or to the lack of a suitable strategic planning. Additional potential conflicts arise from the choice of the family members that should hold governance roles within the business, and that may affect business continuity by endangering it.[1]

2.1.3 The Models of Corporate Governance in a Family Business Led by a Non-family CEO

In case of absence of successors or the presence of individuals not suitable for business management, it is necessary to include external managers in a firm, thus ensuring the survival of the family business. The appointment of a person outside the owner family to Chief Executive Officer (CEO), that is the role of leader representative of the company's management, is the most delicate decision within the process of managerialization of family businesses, as it covers a role that is traditionally held by a member of the owning family. Generally, as long as the company does not exceed a certain size, the owner family shows a reluctance to open up the bodies of government and management to external members (Brumana et al. 2015).

An analysis to be carried out is linked to corporate governance reports that are generated within the family business led by a non-family CEO.

From an "external" perspective, corporate governance can be defined as *"the set of rules, institutions and procedures designed to protect investors from opportunistic behavior of entrepreneurs and managers, ensuring adequate return on invested capital and influencing the activities of the latter through a series of mechanisms and incentives".*

When the leader representative of the company's management is an individual outside the owner family, there is a clear separation between ownership and management of the family business; the aim of the owner family is the maximization of business value, while that of the management tends to be to maximize its own utility function. This affects the value of the company itself. To re-align the management's interests with those of the ownership, it is necessary that the BoD plays a key role in family businesses. This body, in fact, has the task of assessing the CEO's work and of firing him in the event of poor performance.

The analysis of the relations between a non-family CEO and the BoD permits us to observe the possible conflicts and the related costs arising between the two parties and it can be conducted through references to two important business theories, namely the theories of agency and stewardship.

The agency theory is used by researchers of corporate governance to explain the behavior resulting from the separation between ownership and management of an enterprise. Agency costs arise from an attempt to match the objectives of principal and agent by monitoring their behavior. If the non-family CEO is tempted by pursuing individualistic goals, and the BoD, expecting this behavior, monitors his work attentively, a situation occurs whereby both parties adopt a behavior in line with the agency theory. The costs generated by this type of relationship are mainly associated with the review by the BoD of the CEO's work and to the opportunistic behavior undertaken by the latter.

The stewardship theory, which is mostly opposed to the agency theory, interprets the relationship between principal and agent not necessarily as conflicting, but believes that the management acts as a steward for the investor, and pursues the creation of shareholder value as a basic objective in the management of corporate resources. If the non-family CEO is driven by collectivistic and pro-organizational interests aimed at managing at best the family business, and at the same time, the BoD provides excellent support in its aim of improving business results, there will be no conflicts (and, therefore, costs) between managers and shareholders. This way, a partnership between the above parties is established, which guarantees the company the maximization of corporate value.

Intermediate situations may occur, when the non-family CEO acts accordingly with the assumptions of the stewardship theory and the BoD accordingly with those of the agency theory, or vice versa; and this could lead to an interruption of the working relationship between the two parties at the expense of firm value (Gnan et al. 2015).

2.2 FAMILY BUSINESS GOVERNANCE: CONSTRAINTS AND OPPORTUNITIES RELATED TO FAMILY GOVERNANCE

Recent international literature on family business and corporate governance has attached considerable importance to the topic of business ownership, regarded as one of the elements that most affect the types of corporate governance (Breton-Miller and Miller 2006; Young et al. 2008).

Corporate governance is a key element for the purpose of corporate disclosure and for the proper distinction between ownership and control; in more detail, not only does the model of corporate governance adopted by a firm affect its ability to establish correct relations with the different company stakeholders, and, in particular, with the financial capital providers, but it also influences the prevailing relationship model adopted by senior management toward business interlocutors. However, this occurs because academia has neglected or at least underestimated the existence of the direct influence of governance on corporate performance. Moreover, it has been empirically proven that this relationship becomes certain in family businesses. Such an attitude is partly attributable to a traditional approach in corporate governance studies, which chose as units of analysis, large companies with a pulverized and variable ownership resulting from being traded in numerous stock exchanges, and characterized above all by a separation between ownership and government, that is between those who finance the company and those who run it. The fundamental premise of these studies established the primary need to regulate the relations between two types of stakeholders—owners/shareholders and management—who pursue different interests and goals, which above all are still conflicting, to the extent that the two clusters of economic actors sought economic benefits, some at the expense of others. As shown in the Agency Theory (Jensen and Meckling 1976), the arm's length relationships between principal and agent were based on bargaining power and on these actors' ability to exercise a dominant influence on corporate governance.

It has been noted that such an approach has no *raison d'etre* for family businesses, in which the institutional overlap between ownership and governance is an essential and defining element of the agency relationship that, albeit with varying degrees of intensity, establishes a kind of *pax romana* between those who control and those who govern the company, in order to maximize the economic value in the medium to long term. Faced with these considerations, some scholars have provocatively asked themselves what was the point of studying the governance in family businesses and in most small and medium-sized firms, if there was no separation between ownership and governance; in fact, the solidity of the matter has stigmatized this provocation, highlighting the need to establish effective governance mechanisms also for family businesses, in which the overlap between shareholders and managers is not free from problems, and generates many risks arising from the expropriation of personal revenues from control. When outlining the features of family business governance, the immediate finding is that it is not possible to identify one single model that may be adapted and used for family business, but a particularly complex and articulated scenario appears; family business governance, in fact, introduces elements of complexity that would lead many scholars to argue that the governance structure of family businesses is even more complex compared to other types of firms. If, from a formal point of view, the government bodies are the same in all companies

(Shareholders' Meeting, Board of Directors, Board of Statutory Auditors), regardless of the degree of ownership concentration and of the type of actors in the role of shareholders, it is in substance, however, that governance mechanisms take on different functions and importance; in family businesses, in particular, other government bodies, such as the family council, committees or other instruments, such as family pacts, have emerged (Gnan et al. 2015).

In this writer's opinion, the governance structure of a family business formally consists of a dual overlap:

(a) in the ownership structure, characterized by a considerable overlap between business, family and assets;
(b) in the control structure, characterized by an atypical overlap between those who govern the firm and those who own it.

The intensity of the overlap is related to the number of family parties involved in the business, to their contribution and expected rewards; the way in which these elements interact and relate, determines the dynamic balance between contributions and rewards that hold the structure together. The overlap between firm and family mainly reveals itself in two ways: first, through the transfer of family wealth within the firm (and vice versa), or even through the daily work of family members within the organization.

Compared to non-family firms, the typical governance mechanisms of a family business tend to govern also the relationship between business and family, and sometimes even the difficult field of relations among family members, often influenced by the choices made within the firm (Tricker 2015; Corbetta and Salvato 2004). In the face of these demands, informal governance mechanisms have emerged, ranging from "family pacts" and family offices, which have found wide consensus also in practice, to the "kitchen tables", which are family meetings "around the table" during which important decisions for the firm are made. The governing structure of family businesses is described as basically stable or "inertial", because once balance shared by the different actors is reached, it is often necessary to wait for important events, such as the generational succession or a shift in the ownership (to be limited to the two major ones), to see a substantial change in governance mechanisms.

When it comes to governance, in the sense of family management, it is impossible to limit oneself to exclusive reference to the relationship established between the different categories of stakeholders (administrators, managers and shareholders), but there is interaction with a variety of actors revolving around the firm, to an end that is dynamically changing in order to meet the needs of the entrepreneurial family. The owners of a firm, especially one of small size and with family features, are, in fact, the economic actors of the company, those who have the "supreme volitional power" (Del Giudice et al. 2011, 2013a, b; Campanella et al. 2013a, b; Ward 2011; Zellweger et al. 2010; Zahra et al. 2000; Westhead and Cowling 1997; Zachary 2011; Zahra and Sharma 2004).

In this view, it is possible to define corporate governance as the set of rules of the game through which the most significant corporate decisions are originated and developed, and which articulate and determine the prosperity or failure of the business itself; it can also be theoretically framed as "the set of rules and institutions designed to reconcile the interests of entrepreneurs and investors, in order to ensure that the control of businesses is allocated efficiently".

In family businesses, the governance structure receives its imprinting by the family, and is a synthesis, or, in some cases, a "fair compromise" between family values and business rules; the search for an effective structure is influenced by organizational, personal and family aspects, and may lead to the redefinition of the content brought by the actors to the firm, whether they are the entrepreneur and his family rather than external collaborators, in order to ensure a dynamic balance between contributions and rewards, external resources and expertise at critical moments. Government stability may be a factor of development, in case of a well-established correct understanding of the relationship between business and family, together with a responsible exercise of ownership and control; thus, keeping the family sphere separate from the business sphere is not sufficient, however, there is the need to be aware that an incorrect design of the governance rules may lead to imbalances and inefficiencies in the management. In other words, the achievement of the corporate goal, which in most cases is to realize the common good of the firm and of the family, may be discouraged by inadequate governance rules that relate to insufficient knowledge of sub-systems and mechanisms on which family business is based.

That is why family businesses must necessarily adopt a proper governance framework and shared cognitive scripts, in order to provide an effective and efficient management, which does not neglect the interests of each interpreter of the family business (Ward 2011; Zellweger et al. 2010; Zahra et al.

2000; Westhead and Cowling 1997; Zachary 2011; Zahra and Sharma 2004).

This framework must be able to hold together, in a firm way, the family and the business; it must establish a symbiosis between the two institutions by creating the conditions for a two-way relationship of mutual exchange.

Some guiding principles that may be expressed in relation to the governance of family business concerns, in brief:

- planning of the relations between firm and family;
- formulation of plans in writing;
- integration between the different types of plans;
- control by the bodies responsible for governance choices and processes.

In general, the role of economic governance can be analyzed along three dimensions, which are content, structure and process (Vilaseca 2002; Chua et al. 1999; Martínez et al. 2007; Habbershon et al. 2003; Sciascia and Mazzola 2008; Harvey and Evans 1994; James 1999).

The "content" dimension regards the maps and cognitive scripts of government choices, both in its "invisible" profile, about the values and basic guidelines, and in its "visible" profile, that of the decisions made based on those values and guidelines.

The governance choices of family businesses are of two types: on the one hand, there are the corporate governance decisions in the strict sense, that is, the set of fundamental business decisions and choices about the establishment and extinction of the enterprise, and the management and guide of the operational firm; choices and decisions that, for their structural systemic long-term impact, generally have a strategic nature; decisions that may be attributable to the ownership, the BoD and, possibly, the supreme management bodies.

On the other hand, instead, there are the government decisions on ownership—regarding its internal configuration, the operating rules and the definition of the relationships with the firm. Clearly, these government decisions on ownership have a major impact on corporate governance choices, because they determine the context in which these choices are reached and accomplished.

The second dimension concerns the "structure" of economic government, represented by the so-called decision tables, or the system of governance bodies.

This system includes, in family businesses, the presence, alongside the so-called "official" bodies (shareholders' meeting, the company's president, BoD, executive committee, etc.), of typical family governing bodies, such as the family council, which is a body supporting the government of this category of businesses; it can be variously articulated and formalized, or structured in the form of regular informal meetings.

The third dimension regards the "process", that is, the ways of formulation and implementation of the decisions made by managing the bodies mentioned above or by using traditional mechanisms of family businesses, such as the stipulation of family pacts or other similar agreements.

Another staple concerning the governance of family businesses is the fact that the key player that is directly or indirectly responsible for government decisions is deemed to be the ownership. The cases of potential conflict between family and business are different, and experience shows that they multiply with increasing management criticalities: size growth, expansion of ownership structure, recruitment policy of young family members and imminence of a succession process.

Despite being a highly flexible document, free of regulatory constraints and adaptable to the changing needs of the ownership structure, the family pact introduces a certain uniformity of content among different firms; and it tends to regulate all or part of the following aspects heralding the generation of criticalities in the relationship between business and family (Barnes and Hershon 1976; Donnelley 1964; Dyer 1986; Kepner 1983; Beckhard and Dyer 1983; Levinson 1971; De Mik et al. 1985; Ward 2011; Davis 1983):

- Recruitment of family members;
- Education and career of the young aspiring to enter the firm;
- Transfer of succession shares;
- Liquidation of shares to resigning members;
- Investment policy and sources of funding;
- Conditions of access by external parties to the positions of partner, administrator or manager.

The use of the family pact generates many advantages in terms of sharing of rules and principles among all the members, preliminary to the achievement of a single goal and the establishment of a strong cohesion among them; it facilitates a perfect information symmetry and constitutes the preservation of the historical memory of a family business, able to pass on to future generations, the reasons for the success or failure of the enterprise itself.

2.3 The Pink Aspect of the Corporate Governance of Family Businesses

Closely related to the principles and values stored and transferred within this particular type of business is the role of women in family firms; this is why more and more often you hear about the so-called Pink Entrepreneurship and the "culture" of difference (Danes et al. 2007).

Especially in family businesses, the "female" lever is particularly strong, to the extent that women are often those who actually run the company (in the dual role of wives and mothers) and act, both in terms of processes and structure, by mediating with informal and direct tools, and scripts the divergent and different positions at stake.

Although the investigations on this subject are few and the phenomenon generally appears to be scarcely explored, available data confirms that in recent years, the number of women involved in the ownership, management and governance of family businesses is increasing, although in some cases, as in Italy, growth has been slower and rather limited.

Some recent studies also indicate that the presence of women in family firms is more noticeable than in non-family businesses. Today women, who in the past were assigned very marginal roles, of back-office and minor importance compared to core activities, settle down with ever more momentum and force in the positions that "count" within the process of family business management.

Thus, there is a positive trend of change that converts into a state of law what already, in economic substance, women produce and bring to business management. Among the determinants that have allowed this escalation of female power in family firms, there certainly are factors such as the gradual overcoming of the customary gender differentiation (gender equality), the longevity and size of the company, the corporate philosophy and set of value and social status aspects, the growing demographic development, and the overcoming of political, cultural and institutional barriers.

Women's contribution in family businesses is definitely crucial, since they are able to provide help, support and extend unconditional loyalty; they are custodians of the values, traditions and business climate bringing added value for the welfare of the family business. The influence of women—mothers, wives, daughters or sisters—in the dual cognitive and affective dimension that distinguishes their own role, facilitates the transfer to the next generation of values that will be crucial for the continuity and success of the business.

Some recent research shows, moreover, that family businesses constitute a more favorable environment for women's professional success; female leaders are more numerous than in non-family firms, the presence of women on the boards of directors is more accentuated, women have more chances to become part of the leadership team. The studies on gender diversity emphasize also the importance of strengthening the presence of women in top management, on the basis both of the peculiarities of the women's leadership style, recognized as particularly effective in the current environment, and especially in the context of family businesses, and by virtue of the positive empirical evidence about the relationships between female leaders, and economic performance (Danes et al. 2005).

It must be also stressed that family firms provide women with greater career opportunities, allow them to reach higher positions, to make more money and have the flexibility required to combine work and family (Dumas 1989, 1992).

The integration of women in a family business context creates the basis for building a fertile ground on which to lay a foundation for the activation and implementation of numerous entrepreneurial skills.

Among the various determinants, sharing of cultural values is no doubt a very profitable channel for the personal and professional development of women within family firms, overcoming a sort of "sexual apartheid", which was widespread in certain businesses until a few decades ago.

Women nowadays display a leadership role in many contexts and in vital functions of the enterprise system, which is well associated with their propensity to have a higher rate of productivity within the family business compared to their male colleagues; when women are managers, the load of values is amplified, and there is an efficient implementation of the networks of relations and the consolidation of the share capital, as well as a better approach to the always delicate moment of generational transition (Cadieux et al. 2002; Cole 1997; Curimbaba 2002; Danes and Olson 2003).

Over time, women have managed to gain intelligent voice and thoughts independent from those of men; these are women suspended between the coveted goal of empowerment and new management styles. In the name of the cohesion of the family/enterprise system, they find themselves entrusted with the task of weaving a common identity and ensuring a personal ethic of responsibility, offering moral reasons to capture consensus, searching for the connections between business goals and people's motives with the aim of increasing the participation of family members to the general purposes.

2.4   THE PROCESS OF SUCCESSION

The generational change has to redefine the roles and relationships between the family, the business and the management, according to the orientation toward the entrepreneur's future and his willingness to delegate. In the start-up phase of this process, timing is defined and the ways of managing the relationships between family and external members are designed. These activities can be supported by the creation of an organizational unit by drawing up a succession plan with subsequent updates and monitoring. The need to plan the generational change, with a view to process within a medium- to long-term horizon, is a preliminary aspect which cannot be postponed without endangering the very existence of the company. In other words, it should not be based on the establishment of strict objectives in a set time, since the variables are numerous and shifting, and they pertain to the unpredictable sphere of individual behavior. The relationships should be managed, bearing in mind the principle of autonomy of the firm from the family, influencing the way remuneration, financial needs and recruitment criteria are perceived. The opposite view that transfers family logics within the firm may have harmful effects on the organizational climate and corporate management; this is why the designation of the future leaders should take place, regardless of seniority, and depend on the attitude and the results actually achieved (Brockhaus 2004).

2.4.1   *Generational Change*

In family businesses, generational change can be defined as "*the process that, with the aim of ensuring business continuity, comes to a new ownership structure of the firm's capital headed by the successors, and to the takeover by all the latter or by some of them in the responsibilities of government and direction*".

Succession is a key step for the continuity of family businesses, that is, for the continuity of the tie between the enterprise and the founding family. In order to consider a process of successful generational change, it is necessary that two requirements are met: the firm's survival and the maintenance of capital control in the hands of the descendants of the owner family.

To ensure long-lasting functioning of the business, it may be necessary that the descendants' families lose the majority of capital that ensures their control of governance or hand over the entire capital of the company; in these cases, it can be stated that the process of generational change has a physiological conduct with regard to the enterprise; from the side of the family, the transfer of shares or stocks leads to the termination of the tie between the families descended from the founder and the enterprise.

The basic factor that determines the success or not of a succession, allowing for better management of these problems, is planning.

The issues to be dealt with promptly and systematically in order to process a succession are the inclusion of managers to whom decisions and responsibilities should be delegated, the distinction of ownership interests from business interests, the founder's shift from management to supervision roles, the inclusion of the heirs in the enterprise and the creation of a business culture independent from that of its founder. All this through the establishment of procedures to be followed in the decision-making process.

The training of the heir must be preceded by the definition of the minimum entry requirements, trying to be as objective as possible when identifying the adequate expertise of the individual who will manage the business. The successor should be placed both on the BoD and on the Management Committee, and assist his predecessor for a shorter or longer period of time (Brenes et al. 2011).

In the event that no family member has the capacity or is willing to take control of the enterprise, the current head of the company should, also with the help of intermediaries, identify a non-family manager who is able to continue to run the business and, in case transfer of ownership is required, identify a partner that can take over from the family as the main shareholder.

There may be cases in which the main shareholder is reluctant to release his succession intentions too early. The reasons may be different: to avoid the risk of creating possible disagreements and jealousies among the family members who are candidates for replacement; to exclude the possibility that some family members may feel demoralized or undervalued with a negative impact on efforts in the enterprise; to avoid influencing relationships with the company's stakeholders. All this can create a situation of ambiguity and uncertainty among family members.

At the strategic level, it is clear that the greatest difficulty lies in maintaining an approach in line with the evolution of the external environment in the phases of generational change. The continuity and survival of family businesses is, therefore, related to the outcome of processes of generational succession, and not only to aspects of competitive variables (Miller et al. 2003).

Other issues of great importance relating to succession are the specific economic and social situation and the particular phase of the firm's life cycle. Risks increase when the company is either in a phase of recession, or in situations of production conversion and entry into new markets, or is undergoing organizational restructuring. The advantages of a planned succession are clear and the fundamental elements of this phase are the management of the relationships between family and non-family members, the creation of a corporate culture, the training of successors, the progressive delegation of responsibilities, with the gradual separation from management and wise use of experts or external consultants.

2.4.2 *The Transfer Models*

In general, the transition process can take place within the family (*intra-familial transfer* or *succession*) or externally (*extra-familial transfer*) appearing as an assignment to managers, employees, third parties or through mergers and acquisitions. The goal is to plan the phenomenon of succession and guide the family businesses toward a generational change that will be configured as a new corporate structure. An undefined or incomplete succession threatens the continuity of the family business, as well as the lengthening or deferral in time of the leadership transfer that may cause disastrous effects for the management, compromising its own survival (Lambrecht 2005).

The possibility that the handover is done in a less problematic way depends on both the older generation handing over the helm carefully, and on the attitude and the characteristics of the emerging generation. In particular, the attitude of an entrepreneur when dealing with the issue of family succession within the firm may be related to two important variables: willingness to cooperate and delegate, and orientation to the future.

By crossing these two variables, the succession can either take the form of a complete transfer of all the skills necessary to continue the business (*succession without abdication*) or of a non-controlled transition (*succession with abdication*), or of a postponement of the transfer, preventing the planning and related transfer of tacit knowledge (*deferred or eluded succession*).

The behavior of the emerging generation, namely that of the children, can be studied with reference to two other variables: willingness to wait and innovativeness of skills. As for the analysis of the father's attitude, also in this case, the intersection of the two criteria can result in a *physiological* succession, by maintaining the firm in the previous situation in a perspective of continuity; *claimed,* with the intention of immediate takeover in search of self-assertion; *engaging,* when the transfer takes place gradually respecting each other's roles; *traumatic,* when, in the absence of gradualness, it is a source of generational conflicts.

Thus, it is possible to identify two types of transition that are completely opposite scenarios, without, however, considering the many situations that in reality could emerge by combining the characteristics of the entrepreneur and his successor.

Furthermore, it is possible to configure different situations characterizing the handover from the founder to the heirs. In particular, *hereditary* succession is tied to the death of the person, who may or may not have drawn up a will. It is divided, in turn, in: intestate succession, when the deceased did not leave a will, or when he did, but disposed only of a portion of his assets; and testate succession that allows a person to adjust his succession according to his will, and is revocable, personal, formal, unilateral and without proof of knowledge. The law considers only holographic wills and notary testaments, which can be either public or secret. The parties involved in the succession may decide tacitly or expressly to accept or renounce the inheritance (Brockhaus 2004).

In the case of *necessary* succession, the law provides for special protection for some individuals, who, by succeeding the deceased and accepting the inheritance, determine a state of accidental communion, in which each heir is assigned an abstract part of the inheritance assets. To remedy this situation, the inheritance is divided, by declaring the dissolution of the hereditary communion and the assignment of concrete portions owed to every heir. Responsible for this division can be either a testator (testator's division) or the parties in mutual agreement (contractual division) or, failing that, a judge (judicial division).

A process is started, defined as collation, if the deceased made donations while living. In this case, the law presumes that these donations are advances on the future succession, and as such should be included or conferred in the hereditary assets only to be divided according to the due shares. As regards the hereditary debts, the heirs are liable in proportion to their shares, and among them there is no passive solidarity.

The generational transfer is influenced by many variables related to the characteristics typical of the business and the characteristics of the family. The governance system plays an important role in the process of generational succession, and all of these elements together determine the context where it takes place.

According to the degree of managerial development, firms may be classified as:

- *conservative*, when the generational change appears to be difficult because the founder wants to transfer to his successor all the characteristics of the family business built in his image and likeness;
- *pragmatic*, when the transition process is driven by conflicting logics, one of high managerialization, and the other based on the division of the ownership, which favor the business view rather than the family view;
- *precursory*, when lower managerialization implies stability of control by the ownership, and facilitates the management of the successors' future;
- *forward-looking*, with a high degree of management development and stability of control, in which the generational change can be worked out in the best way.

The planning stages of the transition process go through the strategic analysis, the identification of the most suitable strategy and the choice of the strategy and its implementation. Internal strategies retain a closed system, providing for the maintenance of the ownership and management by the family. Mixed strategies imply that the ownership and management are transferred in part or in their entirety to a third party. Finally, mixed strategies are those that realize the succession of ownership and management outside the family. Internal solutions are reflected in the creation of a family holding company, the establishment of a trust, and with the donation or transfer of stocks and shares. Mixed and external solutions, instead, are accomplished through partial or total transfer of the firm with innovative financial solutions such as buyout, private equity or IPO.

2.4.3   *The Conclusion of the Succession Process*

The succession process ends with the transfer of the firm and of the leadership, and with the retirement of the predecessor. Following the choice

38   M. DEL GIUDICE

of the successor and his formal "proclamation", the next step is to take office. These phases end the transition period and, contrary to the initial stages (managed by the retiring entrepreneur), have the successor as the protagonist. For the transaction of power to be accomplished as smoothly as possible, there must be cooperation and coordination between the predecessor and the heir (Venter et al. 2005). The transfer takes the form of a progressive delegation of responsibilities, accordingly with the exit scheme previously defined for the predecessor, who may adopt a conservative attitude with attachment to the past, rebellious with rejection of the past or swinging with inconsistencies between past and present. His attitude is decisive for assessing the continuity of the business and may significantly influence its chances of success.

The sustainability of business development at the end of the succession process is linked to the transfer of tacit knowledge with the planning of organizational solutions that support the successor in understanding the business context and maintaining the condition of familiness. The success of the transition process, therefore, depends very much on the behavior of the successor who, if able to assert his leadership over time, through an innate ability to gain support and extend his influence over others, will open up new paths of development for the company. The possibility of developing a vision independently, an entrepreneurial identity or a management style, contributes to the so-called intergenerational innovation, which is decisive for the continuation of the family business.

2.5   GROWTH DYNAMICS AND CONTINUITY OF SUCCESS

Certain conditions regarding the firm's internal and external environment, although they are not sufficient to trigger a dimensional shift, determine the start of the growth process. The presence of a competent entrepreneur is the basis of this process, but there is also the need for investment programs in tangible, intangible and financial assets, as well as the strengthening of the existing management team.

A family prepared to sustain growth, a low level of debt, good profitability and a modest international presence are factors that make the internal environment conducive to growth. However, when the ownership structure is devoted to the solution of internal problems, some members belonging to the family unit envisage growth as a threat or, given the organization's complexity, decision-making is slow, so the firm's growth can be impeded (Chittoor and Das 2007).

It is, therefore, necessary to solve first these ownership related issues, and then focus on growth, even if the approach of generational change will entail, once again, the need for behavior and rules to maintain family cohesion.

Normally, the growth process starts when a business formula already provides good returns, else the focus will be more on its review rather than growth, or the entrepreneur will no longer be convinced, or it will be difficult to find financial resources when reliability is lost. International presence, instead, facilitates this process through the provision of another vector of development with additional managerial attitude and skills. Low level of debt is the result of a prudent attitude by entrepreneurs in relation to the owner family's resources, with some exceptions, such as a high debt model compared to considerable family resources, and a commitment to reducing the level of debt resulting in a low growth rate.

A favorable external environment is characterized by industries with much larger competitors, customer firms with strong growth potential, industries where there are companies for sale and others in which the market share held is relatively small with small-sized competitors. In these cases, the interpretation of the external environment by the entrepreneur and his collaborators will influence the growth process. With regard to the cases cited, the choice is between competing in a well-protected niche or starting a growth process, deciding whether or not to accommodate the tendency of customer companies to grow as sole providers, and deciding whether or not to participate in purchasing processes. Many of these conditions change according to the vision of the entrepreneur or of the management team, the geographic markets taken into account and the definition of industry used. The strategic decisions made will be contextually different, because the internal circumstances are different and, accordingly, the propensities for growth.

Dimensional shifts take place with the presence of entrepreneurs motivated by the desire to be recognized as someone who has contributed significantly to the history of their company, with both economic and social goals of supporting the development of their territory. This need appears with the generational issue, when the children have decided to follow their parents' work or when the founder-entrepreneur retires giving way to the next generation. Another necessary condition is the existence of a strong propensity to invest; in fact, the higher the growth rate, the higher are the investments that support it. It may occur that managers impede the growth process for fear of losing the positions acquired, or for lack of expertise; at other times, instead, growth is initiated precisely due to the presence of external managers with the introduction of production and commercial novelties.

Intense and successful growth is difficult to handle over an extended period, because various situations may occur, interrupting the growth process or even triggering a business crisis. It is important that firms decide the pace of growth and maintain it for a number of years, without having it imposed by the market or by the dynamics of the industry, so that they are able to accomplish the dimensional shift. In these firms, the learning process is continuous and there is controlled growth that does not allow much risk-taking in every single phase of the growth process, there is time to reflect and learn from experience, without having to use all the resources in continuous growth, to make the management team grow in line with the managerial and organizational change, and to prepare for confrontation with larger competitors. Growth is, therefore, a process consisting of several phases, designed periodically, which change the firm, while the dimensional shift is its conclusion. Besides, the early stages are decisive and their success is crucial for the entrepreneur's determination in continuing the growth process, for the ownership's trust in his abilities, for the reduction of the managers' resistance toward him, for the raising of financial resources to be used in the later stages, and for the visibility and attractiveness of the business. This process fuels resources and skills that may be used later. In case of failure, the line of action would be to recognize as soon as possible the mistake, acknowledging it and looking for a solution; and if this is not found, accepting the loss accrued.

The increase in the value of the enterprise, the possibility for the heirs to undertake only the role of owner or even that of manager, the expansion of the number of strategic options and the reduction of risks related to inaction and strategic displacement represent the advantages associated with the increase in the business size when growth is well managed (Chittoor and Das 2007).

The initiation and support of a profitable growth process require a cohesive ownership control structure, a united and periodically renewed management, high investments linked to the strategy and the market, a competitive strategy based on innovation and the ability to relate with funders. All this is combined with an ongoing commitment to improve productivity, even with international repositioning of the business, the ability to assess external growth paths through acquisitions, and control of the trend of profitability and financial balances.

2.6 Funding Management and Financial Structure of Family Businesses: A Look on Italy

The Italian management literature, acknowledging that family businesses are the essence of the Italian business fabric, have outlined over time, some of their distinctive traits. The element that more than any other was found to distinguish and differentiate them from non-family firms is the interaction between the family system and the enterprise system, summarized by the concept of family involvement, which is characterized by the presence of family members in the ownership and governance (Structure-based Approach), and by their ability of influencing long-term goals and decisions (Intention-based Approach) (Litz 1995; Westhead 1997). This feature is indicative of a number of advantages attributable to greater business flexibility, resulting from the high adaptability that characterizes the management; the predisposition to create a fertile ground" for the birth and development of interpersonal relationships; a strong orientation to attract both human and material key resources (Del Giudice et al. 2011); and high decision-making autonomy, linked to limited opening up of capital to third parties outside the family and to the tendency to self-financing. The financial structure of a firm encourages the growth process, but requires a dynamic balance with the structure of governance and control adopted by the company itself. Beyond the moments related to succession and to passing down the family business, with or without a designated leader, companies face daily decisions regarding the purchase or sale of shares of their own company. In relation to the latter, in fact, it is well-known that family businesses have a marked aversion to losing corporate control (Berger and Udell 1998), thus favoring, in the composition of the financial structure, which is both a propulsive and a depressant factor of business development potential, resorting to reinvestment of retained earnings. This choice, made possible by the small size that generally characterizes family businesses, allows them to enjoy a degree of economic independence and greater freedom of action, since they are free from external pressure arising from the stock market. Sometimes, this autonomy may be a disadvantage, when the family assets are insufficient to support the growth and development of the family business, so there appears to be a need to find additional sources of funding. In such circumstances, the use of risk capital is limited due, on the one hand, to the shortsightedness that characterizes the possible investors, which led them to measure the degree of reliability of a firm almost exclusively in terms of its available assets and income, leaving out the real entrepreneurial opportunities; on the other hand, to a reluctance by family capitalism to open up. Therefore, family firms mainly choose to confront financial issues and needs by increasing their debt exposure. In fact, the entry "debts" accounts for about 50% of liabilities and is mainly addressed to the banking system. It appears also unbalanced toward the short term and fractionated into a plurality of banking relationships; the medium-term portion prefers instead the form of mortgage, marginalizing the role of bonds. Therefore, there is the prevalence of a closed ownership model in which the entrepreneur's assets merge with those of the firm, and the financial structure becomes a tool used by the family to secure control over an extended set of activities. In order to meet their financial needs, it would seem that family businesses follow a hierarchical order (Pecking Order Theory) due to the existence of information asymmetries (Ang 1991; Watson and Wilson 2002; Hall et al. 2004). In fact, in pursuing the optimal financial structure, they rely on a precise hierarchical scheme, giving priority to internal financing and opting for external financing only when necessary, resorting first to debt and only in the last instance to share issuing. It is clear that the adoption of the theory of choice order in the identification of finance sources by family businesses does not imply the existence of an optimum combination of debt and equity, but it is best explained by the desire of the family to maintain the control and flexibility of the company. Family businesses, in fact, by experiencing higher transactional and behavioral costs in increasing external equity, show an aversion to the contribution of capital from the outside, also arising from fear of a hostile takeover. In conclusion, evidence suggests that Italian family businesses are undercapitalized and indebted mainly to the banking system and favor traditional finance sources involving the family assets, in terms of collateral. Sooner or later, every firm has to raise funds.[2] Indeed, whether small and medium-sized enterprises are adequately capitalized or not influences their success or failure. Therefore, it is necessary to make informed choices about the amount and type of capital required, the sources through which it can be obtained and how to apply. Funding management is certainly one of the most critical aspects for the development of family businesses. More and more often, in fact, businesses fail not because of a state of inefficiency or of incompetent corporate management, but due to illiquidity or unavailability of funds, causing a bottleneck in the cycle of net cash flows leading to business failure. These reasons of financial inadequacy, associated with globalized competitive dynamic factors and a particularly effective domestic fiscal policy affecting the operating income of businesses, involve a tightening of the competitive conduct which, combined with the characteristics of rigidity of family businesses, often lead to crisis. In this sense, the main role of the financial function is to prepare the financial means to support typical uses from current operations and investment policy. It follows that this function involves a global vision of business cash flows. In addition to the acquisition of financial resources, the following must also be considered:

- assessment of the factors that determine the firm's financial needs;
- identification of the most favorable forms of use of the capital obtained.

The optimization of the financial structure is achieved through the choice of a combination of finance sources that minimizes the cost of capital, and is consistent with the pattern of uses.

The current historical period makes the assessment of these policy options increasingly essential, common and complex. Actually, it is worth pointing out that if the family is able, thanks to a solid and balanced financial structure, to compete in terms of product quality and long-term sustainability of R&D investment required for this purpose, size is not characterized by need, urgency or strategic obligation. If family business as a whole allows a firm to maintain its competitive position in an evolutionary perspective, business size can follow a path of growth through internal means and does not necessarily face a dimensional discontinuity by takeover. Nevertheless, the choice of whether to sell or purchase assets is the element of entrepreneurial life. The main role of the financial function is to prepare the financial means to support typical uses from current operations and investment policy. It follows that this function involves a global vision of business cash flows.

The weakness of the financial structure of Italian businesses, and in particular that of SMEs, is a highly debated topic in the literature, which reveals vast empirical evidence playing a key role, as well as the point of departure for the analysis of the criticalities of the Italian banking system and of the difficulties experienced by businesses in raising financial resources (credit demand). Analyzing the issue from the point of view of family businesses, the financial structure is characterized by an excessive dependence on the banking channel with high levels of undercapitalization. The business financing model suffers from the weight of bank loans on the side of liabilities and is affected by a so-called pro-cyclical effect: the bank amplifies "faster" the offer in the positive cyclical phases and rations it (faster) in the downturn, increasing also its cost. Economic crises of the bank-centered system, and not always meritorious credit granting, have a greater impact on the current crisis, making the financial system even more unstable. In addition to the fortifications of the capital circuit, bank credit redevelopment is clearly necessary.

In this sense, the position of small-sized family firms, unfortunately, shows a serious backwardness. The causes are mainly to be found in:

- Cultural factors: mainly technical-productive training of small entrepreneurs. The mistake that small owner-entrepreneurs often make is to focus on strengthening specific production capabilities at the expense of a careful process of financial planning. They tend to overlook issues related to financial management, underestimating its incidence with respect to business profitability. Giving priority to growth by ignoring solvency protection may lead to breaking corporate balance;
- Attitude of the owner-entrepreneur: in small family businesses, this person tends to centralize control in all management areas. By doing so, even the financial decisions fall within his exclusive competence functions. The problem is that, most of the time, he does not have the appropriate skills to take on similar roles and decides on the basis of intuition or past experience.

The final result is that the finance function takes on a marginal position within small-sized family firms. This activity is treated indiscriminately by the administrative function and, often, in an approximate way. There is no clear financial strategy, aimed at achieving a balance between investments and related finance sources in accordance with a goal of profitability. The prevailing requirement is the satisfaction of daily needs, while the prospect of financial planning is still absent. The family is not used to providing accounting of its results and financial position, let alone fall back on pre-formed patterns for similar depictions. Therefore, a first problem is the choice of the entries that characterize the composition of family assets. The participation of the family in the business, in fact, involves their direct commitment from the operational, patrimonial and emotional point of view. This is reflected in the balance sheet, because shareholding becomes one of the components of the portfolio where the financial and real resources of the family itself are allocated. In this way, the investment held is comparable to any asset class, with its own risk and performance profile and the ability to increase/decrease family wealth over time. Placing shareholding within the family portfolio cannot ignore some considerations:

(a) owning a share of a firm requires that the family make a financial and asset planning by taking into account the risk profile of the company, which changes over time, in order to reduce dangerous correlations in terms of risk between the company's returns and other components of wealth;

(b) the family must consider possible induced effects for which in the future:
   – other components of its portfolio will probably have to be used in financial transactions with the company (such as debt or risk capital);
   – financial or real assets could probably be reserved as collateral to support the expansion of the firm's funding;

(c) family assets may undergo a "hostage" effect, for which there is the tendency to focus one's attention and resources on the share in the company, often neglecting the management of the remaining financial portfolio or, more generally, of the "residual" assets;

(d) the firm's shareholding must be managed with a long-term orientation, aimed at generating a stable value over time and increasing the family's wealth.

Usually, underlying an acquisition, the following actionable targets may be found:

- Increase in size;
- Entry into a new market;
- Expansion of geographic presence and, hence, internationalization;
- Expansion of production lines to reduce the break-even;
- Access to new technologies and new consolidated skills;
- Improvement of the supplier-customer chain;
- Better use of existing capabilities (production, marketing, etc.);
- Downstream and upstream integration of the production process.

Conversely, often the bases of the decision to divest or sell a business are the following reasons:

- Issues related to generational succession;
- Concentration on the core business;
- Improvement of the financial structure through an increase in equity;
- Creation of value through a sale procedure;
- Redistribution of value for shareholders from business to personal assets;
- Search for strategic partners for operational companies.

Family businesses can fund their growth through financial debt, both by resorting to bank debt and by issuing bonds. This is when the family business, with reference to growth, engages an additional layer of complexity: the relationship between the firm and the financial intermediaries.

Self-financing in first and second generation family structures is complex in terms of the number of family members involved in corporate life and the quality of interpersonal relationships; this can result in high conflict when it is required to make dividend policy decisions. It is clear, in fact, that the part of the family involved in the enterprise will tend to preserve within the firm the cash flows generated, in order to finance the enterprise, while those who play a role of mere shareholders may lean toward a more generous dividend policy.

Here is why the development process of a family business cannot do without a composite financial structure shared among multiple sources; however, it must be pointed out that the more structured, sophisticated and complex the firm's financial strategy is, the more an internal organization in charge of it is required.

In these activities, the relationship between the firm's main bank and the company itself is reinforced: very often, in fact, the opportunity to assist an entrepreneur in selling is established in the private dimension in the moments of succession planning. At the same time, of course, the opposite event may occur: when the corporate world assists an entrepreneur in merger and acquisition operations, private opportunities arise, for example, from managing the financial resources gathered by the entrepreneur, which result either from the stock market listing of an operational company, or from the sale of real estate, or from the collection of stock options.

2.6.1 A New Model of Finance for Knowledge Growth in Family Businesses: The Serial Family Entrepreneur

In the current economic evolution, the development of new ideas and creative projects is becoming increasingly important due to their ability to generate new wealth and "intellectual property" (patents, copyrights, trademarks, registered designs), and hence also support the economic development of a country (Lockett et al. 2005).

Digitization and computerization of knowledge, by means of the new computer and internet based technologies, have redefined in almost all areas the "rules of the game" of competition, resulting in: on the one hand, a gradual economic and financial literacy of consumers, which leads to a reconsideration of the competitive advantages arising from the so-called information biases, since the revenues from information asymmetry are minimized (and the effects of a bad customer management return like a boomerang with double effects); on the other hand, the need to redefine the competitive logic (redefining business models) to the extent that the technological dimension becomes the functional link to access new customers and enter new markets (Mattsson 2009).

Pursuant to the new scenario, the entry of new entrepreneurs and new ideas becomes, in fact, a vehicle for innovation in products and processes, fueling the process of interaction between people, ideas and capital, which enables the development and creation of new businesses, and the launch of virtuous cycles of accumulation of technological and organizational knowledge, which give new energy and perspective to the social and economic situation of a country (Rasmussen and Gulbrandsen 2012).

The launch and dissemination of a number of initiatives to encourage and facilitate the creation and development of new businesses is a fundamental tendency to support the recovery (and development) of the economies of industrialized countries, and in recent years, it has appeared with a certain strength also in emerging economies (Campanella et al. 2013b).

The phenomenon, better known in academic environments as spin-off, has typical macro-economic features in the modern capitalist contexts, and is involved at full capacity in the European and domestic planning policies, in order to introduce new job opportunities and encourage self-employment in stationary economies, where private and bank funding seem no longer capable (either due to the Basel Accords or to the high inherent risk that characterizes investment in innovation) to perform the function of support and credit assistance to new businesses, especially those characterized by a high immaterial and technological content.

For these reasons, in recent years, the interest of management experts has grown hyperbolically, to the point that there has been a gradual structuring of a specific entrepreneurship discipline, which analyzes in depth the research on the relationship that binds these institutions to the new entrepreneurship.

The many initiatives of collaboration with the production world and the national and international business realities have distinguished for years many of the universities engaged in the promotion of research, both in terms of quantity and quality, setting up specific offices for technology transfer, engaging directly in the training of potential entrepreneurs, and working toward the foundation of structures to support new businesses and the creation of spin-off companies. Hence, there is a process of continuous and progressive fertilization between the academic and the business world, which comes from the awareness that the two worlds cannot and should no longer be considered independent and self-referential, but the one serving the other (Della Peruta and Del Giudice 2013).

In this context of continuous transformation, especially with reference to the competitive environments, the convergence between public and private results, inevitably, in a very special combination, where university meets the family business world.

Specifically, it has been empirically shown that, more and more often, ambitious family business owners approach a university, in order to support and economically exploit the business ideas they cherish, among brilliant students, doctoral candidates or researchers (Del Giudice et al. 2013b).

In this sense, entrepreneurs seek to reap the benefits from positive spillovers. The idea is to enjoy differential margins compared to competitors, by emphasizing applied research. With the flair for business that only great entrepreneurs have, they are able to predict further, translating into innovation what emerged from research. Mutatis mutandis, in difficult territorial contexts, where firms are basically in a state of technological, financial and cultural backwardness, the gradual approach toward university is a strong catalyst not only for ideas, for the family entrepreneur, but also for knowledge, image and reputation, to the extent that the proximity of interaction between the place where knowledge is produced —University— and the place where it is exploited economically—the family business— becomes one of the most important intangibles of competitive advantage.

With the term "serial entrepreneur", management literature identifies an external party (private equity or incubator) that provides its own (financial and cognitive) resources to assist an entrepreneur in a particular moment of his life (start up or turnaround), or even entrepreneurs whose main activity consists in creating and selling companies continuously (make and sell), the business (and financial) success of which will be directly proportional to the difference between the initial investment produced and the economic value of the subsequent divestment (way-out).

The most interesting aspect that unites these two such heterogeneous categories, both for business purposes and operational procedures, is that, unlike what is generally supposed, they all follow a higher and deeper inner interest that goes beyond the mere accumulation of capital wealth.

The main motivation is the passion in doing business, in doing what they love most. While not neglecting, at least theoretically, the economic and financial aspect, namely profit maximization, what distinguishes these individuals is the vision, increasingly oriented to "doing business" for prestige and social recognition and not just to get richer and richer.

This finding becomes evident when considering that only a small part of all businesses and projects that serial entrepreneurs are engaged in can become successful businesses.

In fact, the people who challenge themselves are subject to the risk of failure that becomes particularly evident when the initiatives do not generate the expected results, or if the performance assumptions are ex-post overestimated, due to the serial entrepreneur's excessive emotional involvement.

However, contrary to what may be assumed, failures or defeats are the main "allies" for a serial entrepreneur, because they enrich his entrepreneurial track record, becoming invaluable scripts to encode unexpected events, useful to "adjust the aim" and better succeed in later attempts. It follows that *error and failure* do not always go hand in hand, hence must not be stigmatized, but rather assessed due to the experience they treasure, which can be transferred and taught. It is clear that it is difficult to identify in advance the parameters a serial entrepreneur may use to identify a new business, and new investment opportunities, often difficult to detect from the outside.

A quite different argument ensues when the spin-off comes from a family business.

In this case, his temperament and risk appetite are, in part, the result of experience and family background; in part, arise from the need to demonstrate entrepreneurial skills accumulated at family court and, finally, from the need to anticipate change, addressing the family assets to new competitive contexts, especially if the family business is on the decline.

In this case, the goal of the serial family entrepreneur is tempered by the "typical family need" to preserve the economic value accumulated, and at the same time can represent the initial phase of structural change rooted in corporate governance, which leads the family business to a new competitive dimension, where the generational transfer marks its change.

Already per se, the identification of an ideal type of serial entrepreneur is hardly possible, and it becomes even more difficult when the spin-off comes from a family business. For these reasons, numerous cases of new businesses, and new entrepreneurship, may be found: sometimes, even the very evolution of an existing business or corporate engineering, that is the construction of pyramidal groups or cascade enterprises, may be confused or understood as the birth of a new economic entity. Vallini (2005) identifies the phenomenon of the birth of a new company in the creation of a new system of relationships that is seen especially in a new strategic identity, a new business project and a new legal identity.

In this context, it is possible to make a distinction between different types of new businesses, on the basis of some typical traits of family entrepreneurs and in accordance with their previous educational and professional experiences.

According to this approach (Del Giudice et al. 2014), the birthing process of a new business varies *depending on the nature of its promoter*, which can take on the features of:

- *New entrepreneur—new family business*, when it is established together with the enterprise and starts up a business from scratch or reproduces existing businesses;
- *New entrepreneur—old family business*, when it starts up a new business, which replaces a previous one, the nature and object of which may be the same or different from those carried out in the past;
- *Family capitalist investor*, that is when the new initiative or serial purchase of companies or shareholdings is promoted by a family entrepreneur who acts according to a financial logic, the ultimate aim of which is to bet the family fortune on "good investments", in order to speculate and maximize value in a purely capitalist logic;
- *Serial family entrepreneur as an innovator*, who brings new business skills, new knowledge and expertise, trying to expose the family assets, as little as possible, to business risk, or by risking only his due share. This is the case of the new initiative being started up as a result of a

FAMILY BUSINESS BETWEEN FAMILY AND BUSINESS: THEORETICAL AND... 51

gradual approach of the entrepreneur to University, thanks to patenting and subsequent marketing of the results of applied scientific research.

The process of proliferation of any new business originates from the entrepreneur's ability to intercept new stimuli or unexpressed needs.

This external causal explanation comes along with another born inside the entrepreneur, and linked to the creative will of an individual (the promoter), who considers the firm as the instrument or mode to fulfill his own interests.

The genesis of new entrepreneurship, in fact, revolves around the figure of the *founder-entrepreneur*, to the extent that there is a perfect overlap between the two institutions.

In the embryonic stages of development, the strengths and weaknesses of the entrepreneur mix and mingle with the strengths and weaknesses of the future business: in fact, his personal characteristics, value system, motivations and (entrepreneurial, strategic and governance) skills, become the distinctive attributes of the new business, and will affect the immediate and future conditions of existence of the company.

As previously mentioned, in the midst of an economic and financial crisis, characterized by financial resources that are increasingly scarce and difficult to manage, the only source of an enduring competitive advantage, especially for family firms related to small business, is *knowledge*.

Thus, knowledge is to be understood both *in the broad sense,* as knowledge of the markets (in terms of suppliers and customers), of competitors or substitute products; and *in the strict sense,* as an integrated process of acquisition, management, transfer, sharing, control and protection of: skills, know-how, information, culture and values related to both technology and human capital.

According to the entrepreneurial or rather new entrepreneurship viewpoint, for family businesses, knowledge management becomes a condition for survival and the *quid pluris,* to nurture and bring out within the family, from a purely economic perspective, the "talents", so the assets are invested effectively and efficiently, avoiding impoverishment connected to "disoriented" management.

These elements, such as family connotation and knowledge, become fundamental characteristics for serial entrepreneurs, who have made business investment and divestment (make and sell) in new firms the core business of family assets, to the extent that the knowledge produced or regenerated in the enterprise becomes the most important "tool" to solve governance conflicts related to the *institutional overlap* between family and business.

In this view, the serial entrepreneur becomes for the family the liaison between the new demands of innovative and technological entrepreneurship, often linked to the new competitive logic of the entrepreneurs budding within the family (here understood as an evolution of business success), and the old ones, related to the patriarch's needs to accumulate and preserve the company's assets.

For these reasons, a serial entrepreneur will be able to arise from a family business, if and only if, aspects relating to family control and government match the motivational and personal profile the venture entrepreneur expects from the enterprise.

At this point in our analysis, by intersecting these two dimensions, four reasons emerge, that are the basis of a strategy of openness and diversification of family assets.

In particular, it is possible to distinguish:

(a) *an economic motivation*, related to the possibility of diversifying the systemic risk of business failure, when all the family investment is concentrated on a single business area. At the same time, the opening to new markets can enable the enterprise to seize the competitive opportunities related to cost and revenue synergies, that the new production process can generate, resulting in improved overall performance of the group;

(b) *a personal motivation*. What drives the entrepreneur in the choice of investing the family wealth in other or new businesses is personal success and prestige. In fact, prestige translates, within the firm, into charismatic leadership that allows the entrepreneur to gain consensus and succeed in family councils; externally, in social standing. This results in an improvement of reputation and image, and of the relationships with critical stakeholders, primarily the banks that support more easily the new initiatives, valuing them less risky;

(c) *a motivation of government and control*. Often next generation entrepreneurs spin-off one or more subsidiaries from the parent company, converting in fact the family business into a family group, strengthening the strategic focus onto the parent company and "liberating" the hidden economic value and the managerial autonomy of the subsidiaries, especially when innovation and

FAMILY BUSINESS BETWEEN FAMILY AND BUSINESS: THEORETICAL AND...   53

technology (i.e. knowledge) become precursors of diversification strategies within the family business;

(d) *a technological motivation*, linked to the aspects of influence and management of knowledge as the main intangible lever of competitive advantage, on which enterprise initiatives often depend in the modern hypercompetitive contexts.

For these reasons, the seriation processes can also be considered as the result of a delicate moment of generational transition, that is associated with "handing over the helm" to the "new captain", entrusted with the daunting task of managing and preserving the inherited family assets.

Sometimes, the initiative remains as if it were within the perimeter of the parent company; other times, the divestment (way-out) is performed, to highlight the different motivations of the entrepreneur, who aims at transferring it, in order to obtain a capital gain to be invested either in new industries or profitable initiatives (financial logic), or in industries the entrepreneur believes to be contiguous or complementary to his family core business (serial entrepreneur's strategic logic).

Prior to any process of new business creation is the elaboration of a concept of new business, expression of the combination of "creative will and entrepreneurial courage" and the characteristics of his business idea (Heck et al. 2008).

A key to interpretation that allows us to better specify the ways in which a serial entrepreneur can introduce himself to the audience of *family and non-family stakeholders* can be definitely led back to the methods of start-up funding, since the coverage of the physiological capital requirement to start up the business and enter the chosen industry-market is the most hostile and challenging moment for the new entrepreneur. This is particularly true in relation to firms operating in high growth industries, where the high dynamism determines in parallel an increase in domestic risk, which causes a decrease in creditworthiness, and a higher cost of finance, since the possibility of fundraising is more difficult.

Moreover, first and foremost, the fact that the financial allocations expressed by businesses in start-ups are often incomplete or otherwise inadequate compared to initial needs.

Secondly, the vision and the *modus operandi* of a traditional family business often result in a stiffening of the ownership structures toward new initiatives far from the core, causing an escalation in the condition of risk aversion that is accentuated more than proportionally with the increasing degree of innovation of the investment project and of the involvement of family assets. However, as it may be easily deduced from the previous statement, and from well-established rules governing the matter, in the construction stages of a business idea, the material and moral support and the source of finance of a start-upper are the family.

This phase known in the literature by the term, bootstrapping or family bootstrapping, is the time when the inventor and potential entrepreneur explains his project to a small circle of people he trusts, often enclosed in the family circle, imagining that they can endorse his initiative, by acting as financial supporters of the idea.

This concept is usually true when, within a family business, along the phase of generational change, a serial entrepreneur appears, and decides to open up the family wealth (and the firm) to new economic initiatives, which may emerge both within the enterprise and by searching outside. Often, the serial family entrepreneur is probably an entirely new figure, because he has not been acknowledged for a known position in academia. Nevertheless, the vast majority of the new ventures originate from a family business.

2.7   The Value of Family Business

The literature on the value and assessment of a business agrees that a constant monitoring of a firm's value and, therefore, the implementation of economic evaluation mechanisms, is essential in the development and control processes of the decisions of all companies, both in the case of extraordinary activities during the firm's life, and, in a perspective of continuity, as a strategic evaluation to support management.

The idea of some studies of identifying a correlation between the characteristics of the family business and its economic value leads to the conclusion that profit maximization is not the only objective pursued by this type of enterprise. Independence from the outside, long-term survival, high profitability, reduction of debt and increase of family wealth are the basic goals.

The concept of total value of a family business can be summarized as the sum of the company's market value, the individual economic objectives and the emotional value. The latter can derive both from private benefits received by the firm, such as reputation, and, with a negative meaning, from family feuds. Compared to the individual economic objectives, several studies have shown that family businesses have additional sources of income other than wages.

An attempt has been made to identify a methodology for the assessment of a family business that takes into account both its economic and non-economic value: the total firm value (TV) is, therefore, determined by the sum of the *"financial value"* (FV) and the *"emotional value"* (EV).

$$TV = FV + EV$$

Where:

- FV is the sum of the discounting of the expected cash-flows and the *"financial private benefits"*.[3] The latter consist of the control premium in the sale of stakes or in differences in control premiums between majority and minority stakeholders (Astrachan 1988). These premiums are one of the components in fixing the sale price of the stocks, both by the owner, and by the potential buyer.
- EV is the sum of the *"emotional returns"* (ER) and the *"emotional costs"* (EC). The former include the achievement of non-economic objectives such as respect, reputation, educational opportunities, the involvement of the family, solidarity; the latter can result from family conflicts, rivalry, stress, tensions, and may negatively affect the business dynamics and performance, resulting in failure to achieve the objectives.

Considering these variables, in the assessment of family businesses, two cases may occur:

1. if ER > EC, then the total value of the firm exceeds the economic value of the business so TV > FV. Furthermore, this positive difference can reduce the cost of capital, providing the family entrepreneur with greater flexibility in undertaking new activities, both in the economic and family perspective.
2. if ER < EC, then the traditional business assessment models overestimate the value of the family business, so, in that case, the total enterprise value, as perceived by the owner/founder, is lower (TV < FV). This may lead to a request by family members to release

the ownership, resulting in the need for liquidation of the stake, lawsuits or disadvantageous sale of the entire enterprise.

NOTES

1. In 2005, after becoming aware of the change in the national, European and international regulatory framework, the Italian Stock Exchange established the committee for corporate governance with the task of revising the principles of good governance and best practices. This led, in March 2006, to the approval of the new Code of Conduct (Preda Code), which identifies the primary objective of the directors as the shareholder value; distinguishes the duties of the directors between executive, non-executive and independent; suggests avoiding that one single person holds several offices concurrently and calls for respect of the principle of transparency.
2. According to data gathered by the European Commission in the BACH database, in Italy bank debt has almost twice the weight compared to France, Germany and Spain: 29% versus 15%.
3. The discount rate is generally calculated via the WACC, which for family businesses entails some problems, including the lack of a Beta for non-listed companies and the fact that family businesses do not typically make diversified investments.

REFERENCES

Ang, J. S. (1991). Small business uniqueness and the theory of financial management. *Journal of Small Business Finance, 1*(1), 1–13.

Astrachan, J. H. (1988). Family firm and community culture. *Family Business Review, 1*(2), 165–189.

Barnes, L. B., & Hershon, S. A. (1976). Transferring power in family business. *Harvard Business Review, 54*(4), 105–114.

Beckhard, R., & Dyer, W. G. (1983). Managing continuity in the family-owned business. *Organizational Dynamics, 12*(1), 5–12.

Bennedsen, M., & Foss, N. (2015). Family assets and liabilities in the innovation process. *California Management Review, 58*(1), 65–81.

Berger, A., & Udell, G. (1998). The economics of small business finance: The roles of private equity and debt markets in the financial growth cycle. *Journal of Banking and Finance, 22*(6/8), 613–673.

Brenes, E. R., Madrigal, K., & Requena, B. (2011). Corporate governance and family business performance. *Journal of Business Research, 64*(3), 280–285.

FAMILY BUSINESS BETWEEN FAMILY AND BUSINESS: THEORETICAL AND... 57

Breton-Miller, L., & Miller, D. (2006). Why do some family businesses out-compete? Governance, long-term orientations, and sustainable capability. *Entrepreneurship Theory and Practice, 30*(6), 731–746.

Brockhaus, R. H. (2004). Family business succession: Suggestions for future research. *Family Business Review, 17*(2), 165–177.

Brumana, M., De Massis, A., Discua Cruz, A., Minola, T., & Cassia, L. (2015). Transgenerational professionalization of family firms: The role of next generation leaders. In *Developing next generation leaders for transgenerational entrepreneurial family enterprises.* Cheltenham: Edward Elgar.

Cadieux, L., Lorrain, J., & Hugron, P. (2002). Succession in women-owned family businesses: A case study. *Family Business Review, 15*, 17–30.

Campanella, F., Del Giudice, M., & Della Peruta, M. R. (2013a). The role of information in the credit relationship. *Journal Of Innovation and Entrepreneurship, 2*, 17. doi:10.1186/2192-5372-2-17.

Campanella, F., Della Peruta, M. R., & Del Giudice, M. (2013b). Informational approach of family spin-offs in the funding process of innovative projects: An empirical verification. *Journal of Innovation and Entrepreneurship, 2*, 18. doi:10.1186/2192-5372-2-18.

Carney, M., Van Essen, M., Gedajlovic, E. R., & Heugens, P. P. (2015). What do we know about private family firms? A meta-analytical review. *Entrepreneurship Theory and Practice, 39*(3), 513–544.

Chittoor, R., & Das, R. (2007). Professionalization of management and succession performance—A vital linkage. *Family Business Review, 20*(1), 65–79.

Chua, J. H., Chrisman, J. J., & Sharma, P. (1999). Defining the family business by behavior. *Entrepreneurship: Theory and Practice, 23*(4), 19–40.

Cole, P. M. (1997). Women in family business. *Family Business Review, 10*(4), 353–371.

Corbetta, G., & Salvato, C. A. (2004). The board of directors in family firms: One size fits all? *Family Business Review, 17*(2), 119–134.

Curimbaba, F. (2002). The dynamics of women's roles as family business managers. *Family Business Review, 1*(5), 239–252.

Danco, L. A., & Jonovic, D. J. (1981). *Outside directors in the family owned business.* Cleveland: The University Press.

Danes, S. M., & Olson, P. D. (2003). Women's role involvement in family businesses, business tensions, and business success. *Family Business Review, 16*, 53–68.

Danes, S. M., Haberman, H. R., & McTavish, D. (2005). Gendered discourse about family business. *Family Relations, 54*(1), 116–130.

Danes, S. M., Stafford, K., & Loy, J. T. C. (2007). Family business performance: The effects of gender and management. *Journal of Business Research, 60*(10), 1058–1069.

58   M. DEL GIUDICE

Davis, P. (1983). Realizing the potential of the family business. *Organizational Dynamics, 12*(1), 47–56.

De Mik, L., Anderson, R. M., & Johnson, P. A. (1985). *The family in business.* San Francisco: Jossey-Bass Publishers.

Del Giudice, M., Della Peruta, M. R., & Carayannis, E. G. (2011). *Knowledge and family business. The governance and management of family firms in the new knowledge economy* (Innovation, technology and knowledge management series editor). New York: Springer. ISBN: 978-1-4419-7352-8.

Del Giudice, M., Della Peruta, M. R., & Maggioni, V. (2013a). Spontaneous processes of reproduction of family-based entrepreneurship: An empirical research on the cognitive nature of the spin-offs. *Journal of Innovation and Entrepreneurship, 2*, 12. doi:10.1186/2192-5372-2-12.

Del Giudice, M., Della Peruta, M. R., & Maggioni, V. (2013b). One man company or managed succession: The transfer of the family dream in Southern-Italian firms. *Journal of Organizational Change Management, 26*(4), 703–719.

Del Giudice, M., Della Peruta, M. R., & Carayannis, E. G. (2014). *Student entrepreneurship in the social knowledge'economy.* Cham: Springer.

Della Peruta, M. R., & Del Giudice, M. (2013). Knowledge accumulation and reuse for spinning off firms from learning organizations: An individual knowledge based perspective. *International Journal of Social Ecology and Sustainable Development (IJSESD), 4*(4), 20–29.

Donnelley, R. G. (1964). The family business. *Harvard Business Review, 42*(4), 93–105.

Dumas, C. (1989). Understanding of father-daughter and father-son dyads in family-owned businesses. *Family Business Review, 2*(1), 31–46.

Dumas, C. (1992). Integrating the daughter into family business management. *Entrepreneurship: Theory & Practice, 16*(4), 41–56.

Dyer, W. G. (1986). *Cultural change in family firms.* San Francisco: Jossey-Bass.

Gnan, L., Montemerlo, D., & Huse, M. (2015). Governance systems in family SMEs: The substitution effects between family councils and corporate governance mechanisms. *Journal of Small Business Management, 53*(2), 355–381.

Habbershon, T. G., Williams, M., & MacMillan, I. C. (2003). A unified systems perspective of family firm performance. *Journal of Business Venturing, 18*(4), 451–465.

Hall, G., Hutchinson, P., & Michaelas, N. (2004). *Determinants of the capital structure of European SMEs. Journal of Business Finance and Accounting, 31*(5), 711–728.

Harvey, M., & Evans, R. E. (1994). Family business and multiple levels of conflict. *Family Business Review, 7*(4), 331–348.

Heck, R. K., Hoy, F., Poutziouris, P. Z., & Steier, L. P. (2008). Emerging paths of family entrepreneurship research. *Journal of Small Business Management, 46*(3), 317–330.

FAMILY BUSINESS BETWEEN FAMILY AND BUSINESS: THEORETICAL AND... 59

Jaffe, D. T., & Lane, S. H. (2004). Sustaining a family dynasty: Key issues facing complex multigenerational business-and investment-owning families. *Family Business Review, 17*(1), 81–98.

James, H. S. (1999). Owner as manager, extended horizons and the family firm. *International Journal of the Economics of Business, 6*(1), 41–55.

Jensen, M. C., & Meckling, W. H. (1976). Theory of the firm. Managerial behavior, agency costs and ownership structure. *Journal of Financial Economics, 3*(4), 305–360.

Kepner, E. (1983). The family and the firm: A coevolutionary perspective. *Organizational Dynamics, 12*(1), 57–70.

Lambrecht, J. (2005). Multigenerational transition in family businesses: A new explanatory model. *Family Business Review, 18*(4), 267–282.

Levinson, H. (1971). Conflicts that plague family businesses. *Harvard Business Review, 49*(2), 90–98.

Litz, R. A. (1995). The family business: Toward definitional clarity. *Family Business Review, 8*(2), 71–82.

Lockett, A., Siegel, D., Wright, M., & Ensley, M. D. (2005). The creation of spin-off firms at public research institutions: Managerial and policy implications. *Research Policy, 34*(7), 981–993.

Martínez, J. I., Stöhr, B. S., & Quiroga, B. F. (2007). Family ownership and firm performance: Evidence from public companies in Chile. *Family Business Review, 20*(2), 83–94.

Mattsson, H. (2009). Innovating in cluster/cluster as innovation: The case of the biotechvalley cluster initiative. *European Planning Studies, 17*(11), 1625–1643.

Miller, D., Steier, L., & Le Breton-Miller, I. (2003). Lost in time: Intergenerational succession, change, and failure in family business. *Journal of Business Venturing, 18*(4), 513–531.

Rasmussen, E., & Gulbrandsen, M. (2012). Government support programmes to promote academic entrepreneurship: A principal–agent perspective. *European Planning Studies, 20*(4), 527–546.

Salvato, C. (2004). Predictors of entrepreneurship in family firms. *The Journal of Private Equity, 7*(3), 68–76.

Sciascia, S., & Mazzola, P. (2008). Family involvement in ownership and management: Exploring nonlinear effects on performance. *Family Business Review, 21*(4), 331–345.

Tricker, R. B. (2015). *Corporate governance: Principles, policies, and practices.* Oxford: Oxford University Press.

Vallini, C. (2005). Start-up 2004–2005 course notes. *Firenze: Università degli Studi di Firenze, Facoltà di Economia, corso di laurea specialistica in Governo di Impresa.*

60   M. DEL GIUDICE

Venter, E., Boshoff, C., & Maas, G. (2005). The influence of successor-related factors on the succession process in small and medium-sized family businesses. *Family Business Review, 18*(4), 283–303.

Vilaseca, A. (2002). The shareholder role in the family business: Conflict of interests and objectives between nonemployed shareholders and top management team. *Family Business Review, 15*(4), 299–320.

Von Bertalanffy, L. (1972). The history and status of general systems theory. *Academy of Management Journal, 15*(4), 407–426.

Ward, J. L. (2011). *Keeping the family business healthy: How to plan for continuing growth, profitability, and family leadership.* New York: Palgrave Macmillan.

Watson, R., & Wilson, N. (2002). Small and medium size enterprise financing: A note on some of the empirical implications of a pecking order. *Journal of Business Finance and Accounting, 29*(3–4), 557–578.

Westhead, P. (1997). *Ambitions, external environment and strategic factor differences between family and non-family companies. Entrepreneurship & Regional Development, 9*(2), 127–157.

Westhead, P., & Cowling, M. (1997). Performance contrasts between family and non-family unquoted companies in the UK. *International Journal of Entrepreneurial Behavior & Research, 3*(1), 30–52.

Young, M. N., Peng, M. W., Ahlstrom, D., Bruton, G. D., & Jiang, Y. (2008). Corporate governance in emerging economies: A review of the principal–principal perspective. *Journal of Management Studies, 45*(1), 196–220.

Zachary, R. K. (2011). The importance of the family system in family business. *Journal of Family Business Management, 1*(1), 26–36.

Zahra, S. A., & Sharma, P. (2004). Family business research: A strategic reflection. *Family Business Review, 17*(4), 331–346.

Zahra, S. A., Neubaum, D. O., & Huse, M. (2000). Entrepreneurship in medium-size companies: Exploring the effects of ownership and governance systems. *Journal of Management, 26*(5), 947–976.

Zellweger, T. M., Eddleston, K. A., & Kellermanns, F. W. (2010). Exploring the concept of familiness: Introducing family firm identity. *Journal of Family Business Strategy, 1*(1), 54–63.

CHAPTER 3

From Family Businesses to Business Groups

3.1 THE PROBLEM OF ENTERPRISE SIZE

Analysis of the size of enterprises embraces the structural characteristics of every single enterprise and the markets in which they operate, as well as intercompany relationships that are a method for increasing potential economic activity (Takayasu and Okuyama 1998). Company size is influenced by a great number of variables which have, both in quantity and quality, the necessary reciprocal coherence to guarantee management equilibrium. Investments, financing and production, therefore, determine size and are subordinate to the breadth and structures of the supply and output markets, as well as to those of the financial markets.

The notions of growth and development of the company system are erroneously interpreted as being the same thing. The first error is to connect the concept of development to development in size, when the latter merely refers to an increase in company size (Buzby 1975).

Considering the size variable alone means ignoring the more philosophical meaning, in which development is defined as "movement towards better", something that can come about not only by modifying or by amplifying the size of an enterprise, but also by leaving the same unchanged (Baylis et al. 1998). Development, therefore, is to be seen as the formation, within the enterprise as a whole, of solid prospects for future profitability and is connected to specific competences or to possible efficiency synergies among the various components of the enterprise (Evans 1987; Yasuda 2005). Growth, on the other hand, does not ensure development and

© The Author(s) 2017
M. Del Giudice, *Understanding Family-Owned Business Groups*,
DOI 10.1007/978-3-319-42243-5_3

constitutes the progressive enlargement of the base size of the enterprise, measurable by the incremental increase of some quantitative parameters (the sum of the technical tie-ins, the size of the workforce, the capital invested, etc.).

Furthermore, since it is influenced by the variability of the environment and the production process, the question of size is subject to "obsolescence". For this reason, any development plan for the enterprise must include possibilities that may lead to the expansion or the resizing of the company structure.

Deciding for growth is a fundamental choice of a strategic nature, carried out to contrast the effects of competitive pressure on the conditions of equilibrium or to exploit favorable opportunities that appear in the market of reference (Ramsden and Kiss-Haypal 2000). Such a decision must be pondered with great prudence, since an increase in size brings about considerable effects on the methods to be used for undertaking productive processes and on company organization. In fact, an increase in the size of a business that is not well-governed can induce a number of negative conditions that may tend to compromise its capacity for future profits (Terziovski and Samson 2000).

The economic motivations that determine the process of growth may be subdivided on the basis of the type of economic activity that the company intends to add to the ones it already carries out (Brooksbank 1991). Specifically:

- the quest for greater contractual power, exploiting economies of scale and experience leads the enterprise to increase its company size in the area of its existing activity (Sacchetti and Sugden 2003);
- benefits of economies of transaction, the quest for technological economies and the imperfections of the market lead the company to undertake activities that put it upstream or downstream with respect to its existing activities (Argyres and Liebeskind 1999);
- benefitting from economies of purpose and the diversification of risk, push the business toward developing activities that have the objective of the production and commercialization of new products (Schermerhorn 2009).

Besides economic forces that push toward the aggregation of new economic combinations, there are other forces that make disaggregation or maintaining the company size a good option (Salamon and Dhaliwal 1980; Boter and Lundström 2005):

- high organizational complexity, since businesses that exceed certain size limits find increasing difficulties in carrying out the tasks of coordination, communication and control;
- spending requirements of differentiation, since the union of very different economic activities within the same group can bring about problems when the enterprises do not adopt specific management policies and operational mechanisms for each of them;
- distinction of risks, because in the presence of an efficient capital market, every saver can diversify their own investment portfolio and may incur lower transition costs than those within a conglomerate enterprise.

In this case, the single units (of the business) pose an end to cooperation and decide to separate. Forms of disaggregation are outsourcing, spin-off, de-mergers and disincorporation (Quinn and Hilmer 1994; Fuguitt 1965; Corley and Gioia 2004). In these types the units separate themselves, or are separated, from common economic subject to become juridically autonomous.

As a definition, the size problem may take the form of oversized or undersized companies, and is to be resolved, in the first instance, through processes of company disaggregation and, in the second, through internal growth or processes of company aggregation.

One possible solution to both problems is represented by business groups and, in some cases, by other aggregation types (Yiu et al. 2007).

3.2 The Nature of Company Aggregations

Aggregations of businesses, aimed at guaranteeing their size development through external means, are distinguished on the basis of the juridical autonomy of the units, the community of economic subjects and the formalization of the relationships between the units (contractual, assets, organizational, shared knowledge) (Morck and Yeung 2003; Nohria and Eccles 1992).

Passing on to the analysis of the various types of aggregations that can be found in practice, these divide into intercompany, that is, aggregations between juridically independent companies that are linked by various

64 M. DEL GIUDICE

forms of relationships, and intracompany aggregations, that is, several economically interdependent units are constituted within the same company (single juridical subject) (Fu et al. 2005; De Fabritiis et al. 2003). Aggregations, in turn, may be divided into:

- *informal aggregations*, that is, characterized by a low formalization of the relationship. Their genesis is not connected to perfecting agreements that have a juridical value and that oblige the parts to respect agreed performances but, rather, to economic and financial relationships between the companies that benefit from exploiting synergies at an intercompany level. Some examples of these types of aggregation can be seen in sub-supply networks and in production constellations and districts (O'Gorman and Kautonen 2004). In particular, sub-supply networks foresee cooperation between juridically independent units, and the decentralization of production, that is, larger enterprises entrusting smaller enterprises with the predisposition of some parts of a final product or with carrying out of some phases of a production process. The constellations, instead, are characterized by the presence of a set of small and medium enterprises operating in mature sectors. The aggregations are formed by numerous enterprises of the same size that collaborate jointly for carrying out the different phases of the production process so as to obtain a single type of goods of service. The distinctive characteristic of constellations, unlike the networks of sub-supply, is the absence of large enterprises that constitute a pole of attraction for the smaller enterprises.
  Finally, the industrial district is composed of a geographically concentrated set of enterprises, in prevalence small and medium sized, specialized in one or more phases of a production process and integrated through a complex network of interrelations of an economic and social character:
- *formal aggregations*, or those based on contractual relationships (greater degree of formalization of the relationship). The juridical connection confers a greater degree of certainty and stability to formal aggregations, also supported by the free adhesion of the parties of the relationship. The different entities maintain their juridical autonomy but are closer from an economic point of view and the common contracts or structures have an impact on the ownership rights of each entity that is party to the aggregation. Among the formal types of aggregation, one recalls consortia, cartels, franchises, participatory associations, etc.

We define a consortium as the contract under which "several entrepreneurs set up a common organization for the discipline or for carrying out of specific phases of their respective enterprises". Participation in a consortium comprises carrying out an obligation, an obligation of "acting", that is, a common organization provided with powers of varying intensity is created. The provision of a supreme organ responsible for looking after the interests of the participating enterprises is a typical and distinctive characteristic of consortia, one that is not encountered as a binding characteristic for setting up cartels. The latter are identified as aggregations having the scope of guaranteeing limitations to and/or discipline of the market activity of each participating company. Such a type of aggregation has its origins in the stipulation of a formal contract, the observance of which produces juridical sanctions of various severities. Cartels are, therefore, agreements through which companies make reciprocal accords with respect to some limitations with the scope of regulating competition in favor of their common interest.

Franchising, instead, is a collaboration agreement between a party that is a company with a consolidated commercial formula (affiliating company or franchisor) and another party, company or juridical person (affiliated company, or franchisee) that adheres to this formula. It constitutes, therefore, a scheme of ongoing cooperation and intent for the production and commercialization of goods and services between the affiliating enterprise and one or more formally independent affiliated enterprises, with the connection formed by contractual stipulations.

Finally, we define participatory associations as contracts under which "the associate attributes to the associated participation in the profits of the associate enterprise or of one or more of its commercial activities, up to a consideration of a defined proportion". The premise, for the initiative to be successful, lies in the combined action between enterprises, with the scope of generating consistent levels of technico-productive integration. The general character of collaboration also implies respect for common policies or directives that redimension the level of autonomy of the associated enterprises in such a way as to facilitate the prosecution of a unitary objective:

- *association of assets (groups)*, is characterized by a greater formalization of the relationships, with respect to contracts and agreements, than those arising from the possession of participatory shareholdings. In this setting, the juridical entities, though remaining autonomous, are headed by a single economic subject and the relationships take a much stronger nature because they pertain to assets, that is, the relationship regarding risk capital.

Groups of family assets, trusts and company groups come under this series of aggregations.

After a process of growth and development that also interests the following generations, the family business may be configured as a managed group of family assets. Control of the operating company is first entrusted to the family holding of the founder and later to his/her heirs.

A trust, instead, is a juridical instrument that, in the interests of one or more beneficiaries or for a specific scope, allows various structurings of "juridical positions", based on fiduciary ties. The setting up of the trust is very similar to the form for company groups. While, in the trust, shares are transferred by the members to a connecting enterprise that has the power of assigning a single purpose to the overall management, in the group, the holding company itself is the promoter of the acquisition of significant quotas of capital able to guarantee the formal and substantial control of the participants. A deeper analysis of business groups shall be the subject under study in the next paragraph.

3.3   Toward a Definition of Business Groups

In the first place, it is necessary to introduce the concept of business group that represents the most widespread entity for the creation of equity type aggregations. This entity is difficult to define in an unequivocal way since there are various business interpretations of the same.

It is certain that the company business group has one characteristic that distinguishes it from other company configurations in business (Morck and Yeung 2003): in fact, it is constituted by a plurality of enterprises, most of which are autonomous, but at the same time, it has a leader company that holds control of all the enterprises making up the aggregation itself. The leader company features as a company that holds the majority of the shares of one or more operational companies (controlled) and carries out the function of control and coordination of the activities of such companies.

Possession of shares, held by the holding, in the capital of the controlled enterprises is a necessary presupposition for the relationships that link the different component entities of the business group to be recognized as asset aggregations. On the basis of their consistency it is possible to distinguish:

total participations, when the leader company holds the entire share capital of the controlled company, therefore, it is the reference for all the voting rights that may be exercised in the assemblies; participation with an absolute majority, in the case of possession of the majority of the business capital, for which the holding has the rightful power to determine the strategic aims and to manage the controlled enterprise directly, or indirectly through trusted administrators. Unlike for total participations, in the organs of governance of the controlled enterprise there are minority shareholders, holders of interests that may be in contrast to those of the economic subject of the controlling company, which keeps the power of determining the will of assemblies.

There are, besides, participation with a relative majority, when the leader company holds a minority of the business capital but is, in any case, the largest shareholder; and minority participation, where it represents the minority's interests, but is not able to influence the control of an enterprise, by right or by fact as it is controlled by other subjects.

Instead, on the basis of the connection created between the enterprises, participation may be distinguished into: direct, when the group leader holds the share capital of the controlled enterprise directly; indirect, if the controlling company holds the necessary capital for exercising control of an enterprise which, in turn, is able to control another enterprise; reciprocal, when there are established reciprocal ties of participation between two or more enterprises. Reciprocal participations are subject to a series of cautions/restrictions, in that they can become the means of reducing the capital of the companies.

The existence of the participation of the leader company in the other companies of the group can, in some cases, be considered a non-decisive element for the definition of the business group, because the power of direction and control may also come about through a contract, an established situation or from any factor that allows the exercise of such power. According to such an assumption, the concept of the group may be founded on circumstances according to which a company exercises management power over others, that is, a number of production combinations are shared by the same economic subject that, independent of the presence of a participatory relationship, imposes lines of common governance.

Another definition is one in which any business aggregation whatsoever, where the companies are connected in a formal or informal way, is considered to be a group, as long as the link between the units is strong, stable and long-lasting.

A series of actions, obligations and limits intended to protect third parties and the minority members of the controlled companies are connected to groups identified from a juridical point of view:

1. Preparation of the consolidated balance for the group leader, excepting for the cases with prescribed exceptions;
2. publicity and communications of their own status for the companies that are subject to the united management; for a controlled company, preparation of a prospective summary of the essential data of the last company balance or of the body that exercises the activity of management and coordination on it (to report in an integrated note);
3. indication, on the part of the administrators of the controlled company, of shared relationships with those exercising the activity of management and coordination and with other the companies that are subject to it, as well as the effect that such activities have had on the activity of the enterprise and on its results (to report in the management relation).

Overall, it is possible to define the business group as a "plurality" of productive units (of goods or services), with distinct juridical subjectivity (companies) or shared juridical subjectivity (divisions of a company), under the control of a single economic subject (physical person or group of physical persons), where control is intended as the power of the economic subject to manage the grouped units, irrespective of the concrete instruments used (e.g. participations, contracts, economic limitations).

At this point, it is necessary to distinguish between economic subjects and juridical subjects: the first is a subject that exercises the supreme decisional power in the company determining the main direction of the management and controlling the functioning of the company system. The juridical subject, instead, is the person or the group of persons or also the body in whose name/s the company acts and who are the end points of rights and obligations deriving from the constitution and the functioning of the company itself.

The business group must be run by the economic subject, that must pursue a common objective for all the companies that make up the group itself. The unified nature of the management and the economic subject provides elements for overcoming the juridical partitioning between the

FROM FAMILY BUSINESSES TO BUSINESS GROUPS 69

single units and identifying among them strong connections of an economic-business type. It is clear, in fact, that without the shared nature of these elements, the entities and activities would remain distinct not only on a juridical level, but also at the economic level. Therefore, the economic subject must have the purpose of governing the company, the managerial competences and must possess sufficient power (majority of votes) to impose its own decisions.[1]

3.3.1 Motivations for the Formation of Groups

The numerous forces that give impetus toward the creation of groups are dependent on the scopes pursued by the participating subjects that themselves determine the modalities of constitution and the characteristics of the groups created. In general, the most important motivations underlying the constitution of such aggregations are of an economic nature, that is, connected to the maintenance, improvement or return of conditions of long-term economic equilibrium for the companies involved, and extra-economic, that is, connected to attaining specific objectives and contingencies, not necessarily connected to the pursuit of savings (Yiu et al. 2007).

Specifically, among the economic forces there are:

- company restructuring to favor development or to address states of crisis;
- reduction of the risks of the enterprise;
- reduction of complexity;
- making savings.

Among the extra-economic motivations, instead, there are:

- increasing credit capital;
- exploiting share leverage and financial leverage;
- facilitating the running of the family business and the generational succession;
- quotation on the stock exchange of only specific activities;
- reduction of fiscal burden;
- creation of ad hoc production units;
- achieving hidden or illicit goals.

3.3.2 Modalities for the Formation of Business Groups

To better understand business groups, as particular organizational forms of production, and to investigate their characteristics fully, it is important to dwell on and analyze the modalities of their formation. The constitution of a business group derives from two main types of process: company aggregation and disaggregation.

The first process foresees the aggregation of several productive units that unify control, assigning it to a central unit: this latter formulates the strategies and policies, as well as orienting both the infra-group exchanges and the operational distribution of the processes. Concretely, the typical modality of constitution of the groups that are formed by aggregative processes are:

- the acquisition of controlling participation in other companies, consisting of the purchase, on the part of a preexisting or newly constituted company of the majority—absolute or relative—of the shares or quotas constituting the company capital of other companies. As an effect of the operation, technically defined as "takeover", the acquiring company becomes, to all intents and purposes, the leader company of the group, while the acquired companies take on the role of controlled companies. One considers, for example, three companies, named Alpha, Beta and Gamma, in which the members X,Y,Z, P, Q and S hold share participations (Fig. 3.1).

  If company Alpha decides to acquire the participation of member Z in company Beta (control quota equals 60%) and member P in company Beta (control quota equals 55%), the situation following the acquisition is as reported in Fig. 3.2, in which company Alpha becomes the family holding and exercises solid control on companies Beta and Gamma.

  This is the simplest form for creating a group and, for this reason, also the most widespread in practice. It is necessary, however, to distinguish between the fact that the "target" company may be: non-quoted (it is possible to carry out contracting among the parties and accumulation of shares liberally and without particular obligations) or quoted (in which case, there is the legal obligation of launching a public purchasing offer[2] for whoever, following acquisitions, holds a share package greater than 30% of the "target" company's capital).

FROM FAMILY BUSINESSES TO BUSINESS GROUPS 71

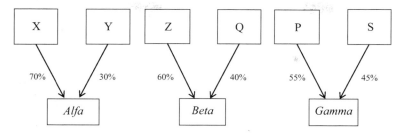

Fig. 3.1 Distribution of share participations before acquisition

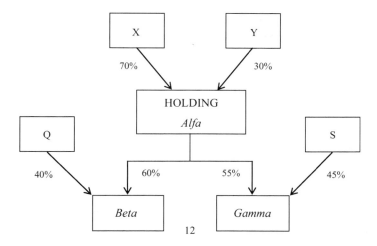

Fig. 3.2 Distribution of share participations after the acquisition

The acquisition of controlling participations allows the acquiring company to develop new economic activities without further burdening its own internal structure. The advantages deriving from such a procedure foresee short times of realization of the investment and activation of new activities and, in the case of operational non-success, the company can cede packages on the share market. On the contrary, possible resistance to the process of technico-economic integration of different companies (various working cultures, different organizational and production structures, informatics systems and non-homogeneous "languages") represents the main disadvantage of acquisition of controlling participation;

- the conferring of controlling participation, that occurs when the holder of the controlling packages of specific companies confer on a company (preexisting or newly constituted) such participation in exchange for shares or quotas of the new company. The creation of business groups through the conferring of participations is carried out both to constitute *ex-novo* business groups and for modifying the structure of already existing groups, through so-called backward development. The scheme of conferring under examination is especially used in the presence of family groups that, after many generations, have an extremely fragmentary company profile.
  In the situation described in Fig. 3.3, member Y holds the relative majority (35%) of the capital of company Alpha, in the hypothesis that if the company profile of Alpha were more fragmentary, the quota held by member Y could plausibly guarantee him/her the status of controlling shareholder.

In the case under examination, however, it appears clear that the remaining members could unite their own votes, and place member Y in the minority, in that, an eventual voting agreement would hold 65% of the company. To avoid this risk, member Y could make an agreement with one or more of the other members in such a way as to achieve an absolute majority of votes to the detriment of the other members (Fig. 3.4);

- filiation, that allows the creation, on the part of a company (parent company), of a new company with the totality of its shares or quotas or a limited participation up to a quota that allows control to be acquired by the parent company, at best making recourse to partners for the allocation of the remaining part of the capital. Filiation is an obligatory choice when it is not possible to acquire the control of a company already operating on the market, in that it is not available or only available at conditions unfavorable for the acquiring company. The creation of an *ex-novo* company, though limiting the risks typical of technico-operational integration of different companies and exploiting greater synergies in the relationships of the group, is not a simple operation, because it has a series of problems typical of the set-up phase: size profile, financing decisions, imposing the juridical form and identifying the most opportune placement.

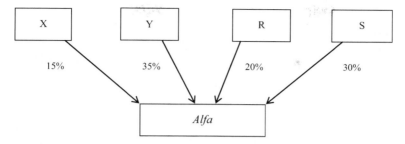

Fig. 3.3 Distribution of the quotas before conferring "backward development"

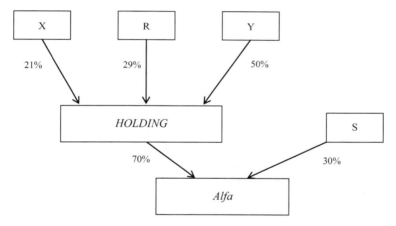

Fig. 3.4 Distribution of the shares after what is conferred

Unlike both formal and informal aggregations, where the union between enterprises derives from a plurality of juridical subjects that associate to each other, in some cases, the genesis of the group is a consequence of a process of disaggregation of an originating enterprise that finds it convenient to continue its own activity, concentrating on specific branches of activity or strategic business areas in bodies with separate juridical profiles. The conferring of branches of the company responds to a need for a separation of assets but, above all, to a juridical separation of the different activities, that remain, however, controlled by the preexisting economic subject. The discorporation consists of conferring, on the part of the existing company, its own business sectors (or branches of activity) to other, usually newly

74 M. DEL GIUDICE

constituted and juridically autonomous, companies in exchange for shares and quotas of company capital of the same. It can be: partial (the group leader takes on the role of an industrial holding that, as well as directly controlling some productive activities, financially manages the participations of the disincorporated companies) or total (the entire company is disincorporated; the group leader becomes a pure financial holding, while the newly constituted company is assigned the whole of the operational activity).

If, on the one hand, this procedure brings a notable complexity from an operational point of view, on the other, the disincorporated branches are "paid for" with quotas or shares of the beneficiary instead of with money (Gray et al. 1996).

3.3.3 Classification of Business Groups

The business group usually comes about because of the effects of the process of company expansion. In general, its formation means the opportunity of establishing a more convenient economic-financial structure by means of which the single companies, in the form of connections, seek the best economic combinations to "split the system of risks into partially coordinated systems" (Handler 1989, 1994; Hart 1995; Hirigoyen and Labaki 2012).

Considering the different morphologies that the business group can take, it may seem interesting to try to classify the different aggregation phenomena. A first distinction of business groups is based on the connections that exist between their constituent companies. Thus, one identifies:

- hierarchical or hegemonic groups, characterized by a vertical structure, in which a hierarchy is set up between the juridically distinct units thanks to, for example, relationships of control. The group leader exercises its own dominating influence on the controlled companies through its share participations, possibly combined with those detained by its directly controlled companies (hypothesis of direct or indirect control, by right or by fact);
- groups of equals, with horizontal structures with juridically distinct units on the same level. There is no group leader and the unitary direction is exercised by force of agreements between the companies, that lead to a common designation of the administrators or of a

management committee (joint control). The connections involving the enterprises of the group are normally of a contractual type.

The defining elements of the group (diversity of juridical subjects, economic unity) remain fixed, but in the first case, a formalized company structure is present, with holdings and controlled companies that are absent in the second case. Reality does not always follow the schemes in a rigid way: in fact, there are also intermediate situations, in which companies with a formalized hierarchy and companies directly referable to the economic subject coexist within the group, creating a hybrid configuration.

Making a deeper classification of the business groups means subdivision of the aspects to analyze into form and substance. The first refers to the characteristics given to the structure of the group as an effect of the management of the single companies. Taking into account this aspect, the possible structures where the phenomenon can be encountered and become an object for observation are:

- groups with a simple structure, characterized by the presence of relationships of direct control (A controls B)
- groups with complex structures, characterized by the presence of relationships of direct and indirect control. For example, cascade groups (pyramidal: A controls B, B controls C) and the groups with successive levels of grouping (A controls B and C, B controls D,E and F).
- groups with a chain structure, characterized by the presence of relationships of reciprocal participation among the various companies of the group. In particular, one distinguishes groups with a direct chain (bilateral relationship: A controls B and B controls A) and indirect chain (multilateral relationship: A controls B and C controls A).

Considering, instead, what comes under the definition of the elements of substance, reference is made to characteristics attributable to the groups on the basis of the nature of their production activities, the economic-productive relationships between the group companies, territorial affinities, nature of the juridical subjects and group size characteristics.

On the basis of the nature of the productive activities carried out by the companies making up the complex, groups may be classified into:

- economic, characterized by homogeneity of the productive activities that make processes of horizontal and vertical integration possible. Such groups tend to be stable and permit achieving economies of scale and specialization;
- financial, characterized by heterogeneity in the activities undertaken, making it impossible to set up forms of operational collaboration among the different bodies. Therefore, the assets and financial links deriving from the possession of participations acquire preeminent importance;
- mixed, that is, the result of intermediate configurations, that unite the characteristics of the economic and the financial groups.

However, considering the economic-production relationship among the companies or rather "the order of processes and the economic combinations carried out by the units of the group", it is usual to distinguish business groups into:

- horizontal, that arise from the development of enterprises that operate in the same economic sector, carry out analogous production processes and produce or distribute similar products and services. As well as for advantages of scale, the constitution of such groups is stimulated by advantages for supplies and by the aspiration of achieving stronger sales positions that permit exercising a certain influence on the markets themselves and, in part, permit reducing the competition;
- vertical, constituted by companies that, though operating in the same sector or in related sectors, carry out successive phases of the production process. A variegated series of advantages derive from the composition of the said group structure, like better exploitation of production factors, reduction of market risks and production continuity;
- conglomerate, in which the single units constituting the group operate in more or less different and distant sectors and the possibility of productive interrelationships are minimal, if not entirely absent (so-called polyfunctional groups). These may, in any case, present the characteristics of the types previously described. The diversification of the overall entrepreneurial risk is the main advantage of conglomerate groups.

With regard to the presence on the territory, that is the geographical area served by the set of units that form the aggregation, the groups are qualified as:

- national, that is, set up in companies operating in markets of reduced dimensions (local and regional), at most coinciding with the country of origin (national);
- international, in which the holding also has controlling participation in companies under foreign jurisdiction. They can take the form of multinationals, if the ownership and management of the group maintains a clear, non-single national identity, transnational groups, if the ownership and management of the group cannot be traced to the nationality of the parent company.

The nature of the juridical subject of the group leader company makes possible a further subdivision of groups into:

- public, when the juridical subject is a person under public law. The holding of the group, in fact, can be controlled by the State or by a public body (these are always groups under private law, but the economic subject is of a public nature);
- private, when the judicial subject is a person under private law. The control of the holding, in this case, is held by the physical person/s (or by a private juridical person, in turn controlled by a physical person).

Finally, there is the analysis of the size characteristics of the groups as a classification criterion for the same. In the course of its own development, any company tends toward some forecast size, projected into the future. However, determination of this size is not quantifiable in an absolute way. In the company the concept of size is, in itself, indeterminate and the identification of size parameters is subject to limitations of applicability. Nonetheless, such parameters are usually identified with reference to the entity of capital invested, the turnover, the number of employees and the production numbers and number of entities of the aggregation. The size characteristics of business groups is not a problem of little importance, and difficulties increase from the moment one tries to identify size parameters. The number of companies making up the aggregation may be believed to be one of the many parameters but, taken alone, it cannot act as the discriminatory element for size measurement. In the same way, identification of the size on the basis of the parameters listed above appears relatively insignificant. The size of the group, in a certain sense, can be seen as the result of investments and operations that bring the single company complexes under the guidance of the dominant economic subject; besides establishing whether the aggregation is small, medium or large, knowing and interpreting the contribution of size characteristics on savings appears to be economically relevant.

3.4 The Family Enterprise Structured as a Group: Peculiarities of Family Groups

The concept of the group, typical of multinational enterprises up to some years ago, is now more and more widespread, also in the simple family setting. It is being adapted better and better to the needs and the necessities of the different physical persons composing the family nucleus, often also permitting valid fiscal planning. In any case, it is essential to recall that some characteristics are inherent to family business groups, reiterating some particular previous views that concern individual family enterprises.

Groups with family control present problems similar to those of pyramidal groups controlled by holdings with a majority shareholder, with particular characteristics destined to have an impact on conflicts of interest with other stakeholders.

The characteristics of family groups involve the psychological sphere of interpersonal relationships since they are absolutely immaterial and have a subjective content that is hard to measure. Among the peculiar aspects, are the following:

- the innate sense of belonging that is generated by the family group often represents a stimulus to the natural incentive to exploit the private benefits of control, especially in the presence of personal goods assigned to the ownership of the company;
- relationships of an economic type (profit flows), ownership (passage of assets) and financial (cash flows) between the family and the family group are a precious source of self-financing or a loss of wealth for the group, according to the prevalence of flows from the family to the company, or vice versa;

FROM FAMILY BUSINESSES TO BUSINESS GROUPS   79

- the level of cohesion between the family shareholders that compose the controlling nucleus depends not only on considerations of economic opportunity, but also on complex psychological factors that take on particular relevance in family companies: solidarity, but also rivalry, emulation as a constructive stimulus but also as a source of envy, not always meritocratic selection of successors, sense of entrepreneurial tradition as a factor of stability and long-term vision, but also as satisfaction and a brake to innovation;
- the circulation of information on company affairs within the family is made easier by greater intimacy, that may, however, generate the erroneous conviction that the flow of information is superfluous;
- the risk of delegitimating or disincentivizing managers external to the family that derives from conferring work positions (generally as administrators or managers) to members of the family with low competences and poor entrepreneurial behavior;
- the divergence between the expectations of members of the family working in the company and those not involved (the first tend to privilege personal income rather than the dividends that go to everyone; the second can have an over-speculative vision of the company, even regarding it as a mere "family bancomat");
- the traditional conflicts of interest (agency costs) between managers and shareholders, typical of companies with dispersed shareholding, are reduced in the case of family businesses because of the tendency that the administrators are frequently family members. In some cases, during an assembly of shareholders, the family members not involved in management oversee the correctness of their administrator relatives (Donaldson and Davis 1991; Gomez-Mejia et al. 2001);
- reciprocal recognition between the members facilitates dialogue and dialectic confrontation both in the assemblies and in the board meetings, but at the same time, the frequent confusion of family and company roles can also be an obstacle;
- generational increase amplifies the horizons of choice for possible successors and brings about delicate problems of selection (if it is not possible to do this within the family beforehand, sooner or later the market chooses);
- in the absence or non-application of preemptive or of limiting clauses in family pacts, the succession of generations brings about the progressive fragmentation of the shareholder base and the loss of control of the company or of the group on the part of the family system;

- the successor phase is particularly delicate, especially in the presence of parents (pioneers-founders or successive generations) that also dominate their sons and daughters psychologically, not allowing them to grow, also through opportune external experiences, or to gradually take on increasing responsibility for the running and the strategic aims of the group.

3.5   Understanding the Family Holdings

From some studies, it has emerged that the constitution of a family holding appears to be the most frequent instrument used by family enterprises and groups in order to maintain cohesion among members.

In the specific case of family enterprises, the holding preestablishes management of the family's participation in the operating companies and, possibly, also of other family assets, but without entering into the management issues of the single controlled enterprises (Astrachan et al. 2002)

Share division among the family occurs at the level of the holding on the basis of the quotas of control of each family nucleus and, therefore, the evolution of the relationships among all the family members has a direct influence on the holding, but not on the productive and operational companies that, on the contrary, can be devolved to trusted external managers. All this is also reflected in the financial strategies, in the policies of indebtedness and the distribution of dividends from the operational companies to the holding and, from this, to the single family shareholders. So, in this sense, it is possible to quote the operating company while maintaining the family compact in the holding and exercising voting rights with respect to the operational company in a cohesive and agreed manner.

Thus, the holding carries out the function of separating the operational management of the family enterprise from the problems of ownership, thereby creating separation between the ownership role, the entrepreneurial role and the role of managerial control, the superposition of which is often the source of conflicts and misunderstandings.

In fact, making juridical distinctions between the various levels of ownership (represented in the holding) and the entrepreneurial and managerial levels (represented in the operational company) allows the conjunction of all the family members in a single subject. With this, the holding comes to represent the unique site in which:

- problems connected to divergences between family members (in particular, remuneration of the family members active in the operational company, the conditions to give to clients and suppliers etc.) can be discussed and eventually defined;
- the strategies of governance of the operational enterprises can be delineated without, however, decisions being taken on translating the objectives contained in the basic strategy lines into concrete actions.

3.5.1 *Types of Holdings*

The expression *family holding* indicates different types of companies and businesses; any reflection on the subject, therefore, cannot but ignore an initial assessment of the holding type at the vertex of the group. In fact four types of holding can be distinguished:

- financial holdings, that is, companies that act exclusively in guiding and in the coordination of the participating companies that do not have any operational structure but are limited solely to the "financial" activity of management of the share participations;
- industrial holdings, that is, companies that, as well as the management of the participations in other companies, carry out operational and entrepreneurial activities, and strategy-based activities that concern all the companies of the group;
- participation holdings, used at an intermediate level in the more complex pyramidal structures and in those on several levels, and appearing between the vertex holding and the operational companies. Often, this type of holding does not carry out business activities and is limited to holding financial participation in other companies of the group;
- asset holdings, the so-called family strong-boxes in which the asset interests of the family members converge. Such companies generally have no employees and do not carry out business activities but are limited to acquiring and selling participation in one or more controlled enterprises.

Such subdivisions demonstrate how the entity of the holding can be very diversified. In tracing the structure of the group most suitable for the family situation, a careful analysis of the discipline of the convenience companies cannot be overlooked, given that asset holdings and participation holdings (that come into the category of so-called pure holdings) run the risk of being qualified as convenience companies, constituted for the mere enjoyment of goods on the part of the members, with relative consequences for the issue of taxation (Melin et al. 2013).

Besides, it is necessary to make careful analysis of the ownership structure and the family business so as to understand what type of holding it is necessary to make use of, there being different needs in the case of a single family business or of several businesses that are diversified among themselves (Donckels and Fröhlich 1991). The simplest form that appears, following such an analysis, is certainly that of the dominant shareholder (usually this figure coincides with that of the founder or his/her consort), who exercises a sort of absolute control, holding the participations of the company that he/she wishes to pass down to his/her own children (so-called controlling owner). In this case, recourse to a holding does not appear necessary, it being possible to undertake unitary management and the planning of the generational handover through a family pact or through other business instruments.

A different case is represented by the *sibling partnership*, that comes about through the joint management of brothers and sisters, with the problem that no one is able to control the enterprise by themselves and, moreover, that the passage of the quotas to their respective heirs provokes further fragmentation of the company capital. In this case, to resolve possible conflicts without prejudicing the fate of the operational enterprise and planning for the generational change at the company vertex, it may be useful to make use of a holding that holds the entire company capital of the operational company. Though, in this case, the holding instrument does nothing to resolve the problem of fragmentation of the company capital and the possible loss of control with the transfer of participations to the heirs of the entrepreneurs.

A further case that is found in practice, one that can present various problematic aspects, that of the *cousin consortium*, that is, a company that has already arrived at the third generation and that sees various cousins involved in the management of the family business. In this case, having a single holding at the vertex of the group is the most convenient solution, because the more subjects that are involved in management, the greater is the difficulty of finding agreement and a common vision. To a certain extent, it being difficult to make the needs of each branch of the original family coincide, it may be opportune that each family branch confers its own

FROM FAMILY BUSINESSES TO BUSINESS GROUPS 83

components' participations to a family holding. In this way it is possible to reduce the number of members of the operational company, resolve conflicts and establish the succession rule within each holding (one thinks of the case of a group of cousins, children of three brothers; with the scope of simplifying the structure of the group, one may create three holdings—each of which groups together the heirs of one sibling—and each branch of the family may decide how to plan the succession within its own holding without having to mediate their decisions with the other relatives).

3.5.2 Juridical Forms of the Family Holding

The family holding can take on different juridical configurations that depend on the family structure and the needs that the entrepreneur wants to satisfy. The choice of juridical form must guarantee the continuity of the family enterprise, the certainty of a profitable return for family members and should facilitate the passage of ownership to children and not obtain temporary fiscal advantages that are often in contrast to the best civil law solutions.

In particular, the holding can take on four possible forms:

- shareholder company
- limited responsibility company
- limited partnership company
- private partnership.

In the case where there are several leaders in the family, the juridical forms of the shareholder company and the limited responsibility company seem the most appropriate, in that they allow a fair partitioning of roles and responsibilities (Amore et al. 2011).

Shareholder companies, though, certainly do not have the flexibility of limited responsibility companies, as we shall see later on. However, the possibility of choosing from three different systems of governance can offer some advantages. In particular, it is possible to take recourse to dual systems and nominate some components of the family as members of the management board and others as members of the surveillance board. Nominating the members of the family not directly involved in management as surveillance counselors allows them, therefore, to carry out the activity of vigilance of the board of auditors, to agree on approval of the company balance sheet and to take part—where there is a specific statutory provision in that sense—in deliberations concerning "the strategic operations and the industrial and financial plans of the company projected by the management board, albeit the latter having final responsibility for any actions undertaken".

The family links between the members of the management board and the members of the surveillance board do not represent an impediment to such a solution.

The adoption of this system of governance within a family enterprise could allow, for example, fostering the entrepreneurial capacity of some family members by nominating them as management board members and reserving the role of presiding over the day-to-day management and, above all, operations of an extraordinary character, for those family members not interested in the strategic management of the company, but rather only the conservation of ownership. In addition, wishing to use the dual system to ease the passage of generations, the younger components of the family could also be nominated as management board members, allowing them to start running the enterprise, while maintaining the older members of the family within the surveillance board, where their greater experience could reveal itself as fundamental for the correct management of the delicate passage of the company's life and for the adoption of deliberations concerning extraordinary operations. Theoretically, these are the advantages connected to the adoption of the dual system within the shareholder company that could push toward the adoption of the said company type for the family holding. However, it should be mentioned that such a system of governance has not had any success in Italy, and having been created under a very different juridical order. In other words, the dual system does not seem the best instrument for the management of a family holding; its decline is also demonstrated by the fact that companies that have taken recourse to this (in the first instance, banking institutions) have later returned to the traditional administrative system.

In contrast, limited responsibility companies offer greater flexibility and adaptability to the needs of individual families. A prime example of such flexibility allows the assembly to attribute, through a specific agreement contained in the constituting act, particular rights regarding the administration of the company and the distribution of its profits to one or more members. The exercise of such a faculty within a family company allows, for example, fair distribution of the company capital among the various

FROM FAMILY BUSINESSES TO BUSINESS GROUPS **85**

components of the family, while only conferring the power to nominate the administrative organ to someone demonstrating a greater ability for managing the company; or, allowing attribution of participation in the profits that differs from the capital quotas possessed, thereby rewarding family members personally involved in the management of the company with a greater quota of profits (in any case, not strictly connected to the ownership quotas) than that awarded to family members not directly involved in management, as remuneration for their commitment and work in running the enterprise. These provisions may also be used for managing the passive risk that the members not directly involved in the management of the company incur because of the decisions of family members that administer the company, for example, attributing veto power over specific decisions of the administration (power of veto meaning a particular right regarding the administration); in the same vein of thought is the juridical provision that allows members to reduce the power to decide on specific questions from the administrative organ—again through specific statutory clauses— assigning the competence on such decisions to all members. Exercising this faculty allows family members not directly involved in the management to maintain control of the most relevant acts and to agree on the strategic decisions for the life of the company. Finally, the ample power of inspection guaranteed to the members not involved in the administration also allows members of the family, extraneous to the business, to be constantly informed regarding the behavior of family members involved in the administration of the enterprise.

Recourse to a limited partnership company appears preferable when there is a single recognized leader in the family (or, in any case, a limited number of family leaders), since the full partners can be assigned roles of management responsibility for the holding, while the limited partners confine themselves to giving their financial and patrimonial contribution.

With such juridical forms, there are, besides, separate roles for the Administration Board and Assembly of Shareholders, thereby avoiding most of the potential conflicts. The limit of using such a company type derives from the unlimited responsibility that falls on the full partners, which makes it advisable to adopt a limited partnership company in the case of a pure holding and not for an industrial holding.

When there are no recognized leaders, the juridical form of a private partnership appears more appropriate. This represents a provisional solution (also of an exclusive type) suited to particular aims and for the short term. The advantages deriving from such a juridical form are the impossibility of entry of third parties external to the company and the lower management costs. On the other hand, the adoption of a private partnership as the family holding is inadvisable, because it sidelines the process of the formation of consensus through dialogue and discussion, and privileges the choices of a single family member, given the absence of mechanisms that formalize the decision-making processes that concern the company's life.

Following such reflections, it may be concluded that the company type most adaptable to the various needs is that of the limited responsibility company, that is, the one that allows the greatest flexibility in the drafting of the statute. In fact, it is not possible to resolve all the questions that arise from the administration of a family business at the statutory level, in particular, those connected to generational change and to the choice of family members of the successive generations to entrust with the management of the company. The criteria for management of generational change and the ways of overcoming the possibility of blocked situations that could come about because of the effect of a disagreement among family members are usually addressed by other business agreements.

3.5.3 Advantages and Disadvantages of the Family Holding

The creation of a family holding represents the most efficient solution for overcoming the risks of confounding ownership (Anderson and Reeb 2003). In fact, it may be the right business instrument to interpose between the family and the operational company in order to favor reorganization of the group and to give discipline of the participation of the members (family members) in ownership. To avoid the pursuit of family unity leading to a static and immobile company structure lacking entrepreneurial initiatives it is necessary to have mobility of the quotas of participation, something that may be obtained through setting up a family holding. The mobility of the quotas can not only be ensured, but also controlled, through most opportune choice of the juridical form to give to the holding for the management of quotas (preemptive statutory clauses, joint trusts, block voting agreements and similar).

Numerous and various advantages may derive from setting up a family holding. First of all, considering the fiscal setting, it is possible to optimize the overall taxation at the group level (for VAT and direct taxes), as well as that of the single physical persons that are members of the holding. The latter, in fact, will not be subject to taxation since the financial flows (dividends), received by the controlled operational companies will not be distributed to the persons themselves, but will be used to acquire goods (real estate, participations, bonds, etc.) in the name of the holding itself.

The interposition of the holding may also be greatly advantageous financially. After having gathered them from the various controlled operational companies and assessed the specific needs of self-financing, it can favor an ordered distribution of the profits to the members (family members). It allows rationalization of the financial structures, through a centralized treasury that does not have to refer to members for inter-company movements of resources or in their use for new investments.

To finish, through the creation of a family holding, it is possible: to effect policies of diversification of the family assets without contaminating the ownership of the operational companies; to make partnerships with other companies at an operational level and eventually to quote the holding or the operational company; to face the generation change with less difficulty since every single family nucleus can manage its own participation in the family holding, effectively managing its own overall family assets; to put into action a careful management policy, opening specific posts to subjects with specialist competences, even though they may be external to the family; and, to manage possible family disputes upstream of the operational structure.

Besides the undoubted advantages, there are, however, some critical issues in the use of a holding, like for example the obligation of drafting a consolidated balance sheet, the risk of coming under the juridical discipline for convenience of companies with the consequent minimum obligatory tax, a greater complexity in the management and governance of the holding because of the effect of the phenomenon of generational increase (the growing number of components of the family reduces the control quotas of each member), the possible relevance of costs of reorganization, a duplication of the company and administrative costs, the occurrence of greater operational rigidity within the group and potential institutional conflicts among the various operational companies belonging to the group.

3.6 DESIGNATION OF THE COMPANY ASSETS TO THE HOLDING COMPANY

In family businesses, the assets invested in the business exist alongside and sometimes overlap with the personal assets of the members (invested in buildings for habitation, jewelry and collections, bonds and currency, etc.).

The business assets, represented by the shares or quotas of the companies making up the family group, may be in the name of a holding or may be fragmented among the different family members, the latter making it more difficult to have unitary management of the business (Anderson and Reeb 2003).

Personal assets are only occasionally under the ownership of the holding (as in the case of buildings of non-business use put in the name of the holding or an ad hoc real estate company) and may also be connected to guarantees (the holding obtains financing from the banks guaranteed by the personal properties of the members, etc.).

Assets external to the business can be used to compensate the family members less involved in the company management, that is, they can receive more assets external to the family business in exchange for their reduced participation.

The company assets and the family assets evolve over time following paths that are sometimes parallel (especially in the initial phase of the business) and in some cases completely independent. The inter-temporal inter-change dynamic between the two asset groupings, the technical methods by which the financial flows pass from the company to the family and vice versa, and the analysis of the overall assets of the "business-family system" poses several problems, bearing in mind that the family assets have different technical characteristics to the company assets, since they are subdivided among the family members, owners of the single goods and can only be maintained united if there is a long-running non-codified consensus, while the business assets are a complex of goods systematically organized for running the enterprise and, as such, contained by the company structure.

A corollary that derives from the coordination of the goods that constitute the business is represented by the existence of immaterial elements (generically qualifiable with the start-up, in private partnerships often strictly connected to the persons of the members) that are lacking in the family assets and that, even though not quantifiable, contribute in a notable way to the overall determination of the value of the business assets.

3.7 The Family Holding: Tutelage Instruments of the Assets During the Generational Change

Over the years, the business sees the need for tutelage and management of its matured assets. Tutelage of assets means protecting it from possible aggression on the part of third parties, while managing them means optimizing them in such a way that the same can be used for the aims determined by the asset holders (Gallo et al. 2004; García-Meca and Sánchez-Ballesta 2009). At an international level, there are numerous instruments for the tutelage of assets (from the trusts, to family holdings) that are used with discrimination to best exploit their specific characteristics. On this occasion, we shall focus our attention on family holdings so as to understand how these can be a valid instrument for tutelage of assets.

Through the family holding, it is possible to attribute a definite separate role to the family assets, avoiding possible internal contrasts between family members, separating the interests of those that only have an eye for the dividends from those members that, on the contrary, have the abilities and the desire to participate actively in the management, operations and future activities of the family business.

Planning for generational change, using the instrument of the holding, must be carried out taking into account the needs, expectations and aptitudes of all the family members, without forgetting that the main objective is always that of preserving the value created by the entrepreneur over time. For this reason, one of the essential elements of the constitution of a family holding pertains to the choice of juridical form and the most appropriate models of governance for every single situation. Certainly, the structure of the company capital, as seen previously, is what offers the greatest guarantees for tutelage.

Besides, the separation between the ownership setting and the management setting, made though the holding, also allows considering the event of the succession under these duplicate aspects. In the family business, succession under the ownership aspect would mean, in fact, participating actively in the strategic management of the entrepreneurial activity, ensuring rapidity and functionality for this process (institutionally confined to the holding), while for the operational management of the company's activity, succession would mean being able to guarantee a professional approach and motivation at the right level for the tasks required by such activity (carried out, institutionally, solely in the operational units).

If necessary, external subjects able to bring additional financial resources may take over the running of the family holding, without this altering the unity of command. This possibility of acquiring external financial resources, without losing control of the operational enterprise, gives the family the possibility of pursuing one or more important principles of economic survival: diversification of risks to assets and income.

In fact, the liberation of financial resources that is obtained when ceding quotas to new external partners allows them to be used for other types of fixed or mobile investments, made in the same or in different combinations of product/market and placed in national or international markets.

The holding, therefore, can become an optimal instrument for allowing, in the setting of generation change, the attribution of operational management powers only to some members at the same time as the attribution of equal profits to all the members.

Foreseeing, for example, different participation types in the capital of the newly constituted holding and in the capital of the operational company for the offspring (physical persons), it is possible to determine that each heir holds the same percentage in the operational company and, therefore, in a mixed manner (direct and indirect participation), the same quota of profits (Masulis et al. 2011).

Besides, through greater participation in the capital of the holding, it is possible to attribute the control of the management of the operational company to the heir interested in management and therefore certainly more able to guarantee the profitable continuation of the business activity (Davis 1983).

On the contrary, in the case of succession before planning as reported above, the sharing of management on the part of the heirs could bring about serious problems to the operational company, putting its future life at risk.

3.8   THE PHENOMENON OF GENERATIONAL DRIFT

The problem of the so-called generational drift is as delicate in single family businesses as in family groups. Generational drift means the tendency toward a progressive increase in the number of heirs as the generations pass (Daily et al. 2003; Davis and Tagiuri 1989; Davis et al. 1997). The phenomenon is all the greater: the larger the family nucleus, the higher the birth rate.

This has negative repercussions for the development of the enterprise and, in particular, one may encounter:

- conflicts between family members, triggered by the fragmentation of the ownership among an elevated number of subjects with different objectives, aspirations, tasks and functions, and that may be damaging for the running of the enterprise;
- a progressive diminishing, over the generations, of effective connections among family members and of their identification with the enterprise. This problem tends be reduced in the presence of a strong company culture and a leader that represents both the objectives of the family and those of the business.

The effects such a phenomenon produces on the share leverage and on the control of the group shall be analyzed later.

3.8.1 The Effects of the Generational Drift on Share Leverage

Among the characteristic elements of the family group described above, particular relevance is taken on by the impact of generational drift on share leverage.

Share leverage of the group shows itself when the economic subject manages to maintain control with a more contained proportion of ownership capital, through leverage of the contributions of other subjects. Exploiting share leverage is particularly evident in the case of companies in regulated markets.

Share leverage feels the effects of the generational drift since the latter represents an element of inevitable disaggregation for the preconstituted shareholding majority. In the absence of an asymmetric division founded on compensatory owelty,[3] the generational drift brings about a repartitioning of the quotas, each of which immediately tends to decrease below the threshold of control (Aronoff and Ward 1996).

With the passing of generations, the multiplicative effect of the generational drift tends to become so high that it is difficult for the family business (often having become a group) to grow at a similarly rapid rate (Breton-Miller and Miller 2006). It follows that the number of recipients grows more, in proportion, than the growth of the dimensions of the "pie" (i.e. the company assets, on which the size of the assets external to the company depends to an increasing measure) and the single "slices" reduce.

Therefore, one element to keep under consideration really concerns the relationship between the growth rate of the company and the growth rate of heirs.

In such a context, the conflicts among heirs may have profound repercussions on the stability of the group, undermining the cohesion of the controlling group on which the share leverage is based.

The different level of interest that the heirs have with respect to the family group represents a further element of division: those working in the company have different ideas and motivations to those who consider it a mere financial investment.

Family groups can grow in a greater proportion than the generational drift only through continual innovation, projected toward seeking out new markets and business opportunities (Colarossi et al. 2008). The growing competition characterizing all economic sectors and the relevance of the immaterial components, such as factors of success in leadership (adaptability, culture, constancy, organizational capacity, innovative spirit, family traditions, etc.) makes the creation of value more and more outside the control of the family group that is undergoing a change of generations, in an evolutionary context where income from market position no longer represents a barrier against competitors.

An analysis of the problems highlighted above may permit the elaboration and implementation of strategies aimed at avoiding such consequences. These strategies may often be non-negligible because they can affect the process of succession at their base.

3.8.2 Reinforcing Control Through the Family Holding

Starting from the assumption that the objective to pursue is that of keeping family control of the company (Bartholomeusz and Tanewski 2006), it is possible to implement (jointly or disjointly) the following strategies:

- a process of "selection" that can attenuate or eliminate the generational drift, that is, some members of the family "inherit" control and others are indemnified with assets external to the company (that must be sufficiently large). The value of the bonds, goods and buildings making up such assets is normally more easily measurable than the value of the company investment, especially if the latter is not quoted. In this case, problems arise concerning measuring the overall assets;

- as long as the subdivision of the company assets does not prejudice the overall value, it is possible to proceed to eliminate some business activities, not entering the core business (non-instrumental properties, marginal operational activities, etc.), so as to share them out among a number of heirs;
- one can predispose statutes and family pacts, with stronger or weaker binding juridical contents, that foresee pre-emption clauses, voting trusts, and specially qualified majorities for safeguarding the minority participants etc.;
- favoring dynastic capitalism, share leverage can be developed and benefit taken from its effects. However, this may produce a boomerang effect, deriving from the fact that the more the share leverage increases, the more disrupting are the effects of possible share fragmentation.

Control of family groups can be exercised through share growth downstream or upstream of the holding, deriving from the natural fragmentation of share ownership, arising from the generational drift: "decreasing" (downstream) generational drift sees fragmentation of the group, while the "ascending" (upstream) generational drift foresees maintaining family control of the group, founded on delicate equilibria.

For greater clarity, one may consider, for example, a family holding, 100% controlled by the founding member, set at the vertex of a family group. The holding has the total control of three operational companies.

The group fragments the moment that the children of the founder do not want to continue the activity; ad hoc companies may be created on the basis of the number of children. The repercussions on the value of such a repartitioning varies from case to case (there are fewer synergies, but there are also more conflicts, etc.).

In the case of generational drift that develops upstream of the holding, the objective pursued is that of maintaining the enlarged family's control of the business group.

When the generational drift ramifies, guaranteeing control is pursued with a long-term view: the cohesion of the group can be pursued with appropriate juridical instruments (e.g. trusts, the constitution of the family strong box or a combination of both),[4] which must foresee exit clauses in favor of members that want to sell their participation, with a preemptive buying option in favor of the other family members (in the absence of which, the enlarged family could lose control) (Granovetter 1995).

Some family groups, not having enough internal financial resources, grow less than they could to avoid losing control.

In conclusion, therefore, it is possible to state that the constitution of a family holding represents a possible solution to the phenomenon of generational drift.

In addition, it is possible to involve external managers and professionals in the running of the capital, profits and professional resources to ensure impartial management and to "purify" the relationships among family members and the operational company (Corbetta 1995). In this latter case, the group leader company features as a "family holding with professional management" that aims at resolving family conflicts (Daily and Dollinger 1992).

3.9 The Value of the Business Group

Single enterprises and company groups tend to have objectives traceable to the creation of value, which is a different concept to that of maximization of profits. It is necessary, therefore, to look after the common good and the satisfaction of the needs of the collectivity. An enterprise structured in a group pursues these objectives with the production of wealth and of added value to be distributed among the subjects that have made a contribution to its formation. The group must produce value in a lasting way with capital investment, production of income and financial flows (Yiu et al. 2005).

The creation of value in business groups has some peculiar features with respect to the single company and this is due to the intrinsic characteristics of the group, synthetically summarized as follows:

- Groups allow the formation of synergies under an economic-financial profile, with consequent increases of profit margins and cash flows.
- Information asymmetries make it more difficult to observe and measure, in terms of performance, the efforts of agents in pursuing the objectives of the principals.
- The net assets, in a group view, are expressed, in synthesis, by the net consolidated assets, in part constituted by the net assets of third parties, whose remuneration could, in some cases, diverge from that of the net assets not belonging to third parties (pertaining to the majority shareholders).
- The incentives offered to protagonists of the creation of value are asymmetrically distributed in the group.

FROM FAMILY BUSINESSES TO BUSINESS GROUPS 95

- The spread of value among the stakeholders is distorted in the presence of private benefits of control and by phenomena of transfer pricing.[5]

Incentivizing of single stakeholders to produce wealth and renouncing unilateral benefits in the name of a greater overall benefit (so as to generate more than proportional unilateral benefits, *ex post*) makes the creation of value possible. The convergence of the stakeholders' interests is, therefore, a fundamental passage in the creation of value and can be pursued at a group level through coordination, but it is usually found to be much more complicated and difficult than the coordination of single companies (because the "bearers of interest" are more numerous and because they are "segmented" in the single companies), even though leverage of higher potential synergies may be exploited (Bae et al. 2002).

The managers and other employees that acquire professional skills through long-term investments in "human capital" have some limits of diversification and this entails the risk that in the long term their competences are not expendable in other enterprises. Also, in the enterprises where the managers and employees are trained and mature, their competences run the risk that the experience transfused into the employees is expropriated by other enterprises that attract the qualified workforce with better prospects in terms of remuneration, careers and other benefits.

In groups, the possibilities of job rotation are higher and this can bring about a slight reduction of the risk of lack of diversification. Instead, the risk of a "brain drain" is also present in groups and can be contrasted with policies of adequate remuneration and flexibility.

3.9.1   Asymmetries in the Spread of Value

The private benefits of the control of pyramidal groups are founded on share leverage and are characterized by asymmetries of the spread of value, that lead to advantages, with respect to their investment, for the majority shareholders of the holding (Almeida and Wolfenzon 2006; Bebchuk et al. 2000; Bianco and Nicodano 2006; Masulis et al. 2011). The spread of value, meant as the destination of value toward the final users, is connected to the creation and measurement of the same: if the value created is not spread, it automatically loses meaning and merely keeps potential value.

If there is an asymmetry between the creation and spread of value, meaning a loss of proportionality between the expectations and the effective benefits of those that have contributed to the formation of this value, then some mechanisms disincentivizing the creation of value on the part of the stakeholders come into play. The greater value that is attributed to some stakeholders (in particular, to the majority shareholders) is exactly counterbalanced by the lower value destined to the others. In practice, a boomerang effect may occur: since the spread of value is asymmetric with respect to expectations, the overall value created gets reduced. This not only damages outsider-stakeholders (who have few incentives, because asymmetrically remunerated), but also brings problems for the insider-stakeholders, who have rights to a proportionally larger "slice" of a "pie" that, for other reasons, is diminished in size.

The spread of value of the holding is facilitated (Koslowski 2000) if it presents itself on the market with a rational structure of participations, attends to the divulgation of clear and detailed information on its sectors of activity and strategic guidelines, to make visible the reference framework of new initiatives.

3.9.2 *Measurement of Value: Return of Capital and Evaluation of Group Performance*

The measurement of value allows quantification of the overall value created and spread. Different parameters to allow measurement of the value of the single companies have been elaborated and are sometimes applied to the group setting.

In this setting, particular importance is taken on by the return on capital, seen as the percentage of remuneration of the capital that the investor makes available to the company in various ways. This parameter allows the investor to make a comparison between bonds representing the debt or risk capital of the different issuers.

The comparison between the returns and costs of capital allows quantification, at a differential level, of one of the most relevant elements of the process of creation of value, since it dwells on the mechanism of formation of marginal income (operational or net), that is constantly compared with the debt and risk capital and later used for investments.

In a group setting, the measurement of its value can be made for single companies, or at a consolidated level, considering the entire group (Chang and Hong 2000; Thomsen and Pedersen 2000; Miles and Snow 1986). This leads to a comparison between:

- the returns (performance) of each company;
- the returns (performance) at an aggregate level;
- the returns (performance) at a consolidated level.

The investor can find comfort from this comparison, which allows him/her to analyze whether or not belonging to the group generates synergies that have a positive reflection on overall returns; such synergies are positive if the consolidated returns are higher than the aggregate returns (determined by summation of the returns of the single companies, without considering their belonging to the group).

The degree of spread of these synergies depends on the structure of the group and on the presence or absence of asymmetries in the propagation of value.

3.9.3 The Group Economic Value Added

One of the main indicators that compares returns with costs of capital, equating them to debt capital and overall risk capital is Economic Value Added (EVA).

EVA, elaborated by the American economist, Bennett Stewart (Stern Stewart & Co), is a methodology for determining the performance of a company correlated to the objective of maximizing value for its shareholders. It is used to measure the value created, or "the residual profits after having deducted the cost of capital invested to generate those profits" (Stern et al. 2001).

The need to develop a method of measuring the created value derives from the assumption that the determination of a company's performance merely through reading the accounting results has numerous implicit limits, principally due to the prudential nature and the incompleteness of the accounting system, that does not allow reflection of the real influence of the management activity.

EVA is founded on the premise that a company creates value when the profits are superior to the costs of the overall sources of financing. The annual measure of the value generated or destroyed by the company is given by the operational profits, net of taxes, with deduction of a figurative cost expressing the remuneration of invested capital.

The formula is as follows[6]:

$$EVA = \text{NOPAT} - (\text{WACC} \times CI)$$

where

- NOPAT = Net Operating Profit After Tax;
- WACC = Weighted Average Capital Cost;
- CI = net invested capital, taken from the last balance

The application of EVA corresponds to the following fundamental rules:

1. if EVA > 0 creation of value, sustainability of growth
2. if EVA < 0 destruction of value, growth not sustainable.

The original methodology of the calculation of EVA prescribes some corrections to the accounting values of NOPAT and invested capital. Such corrections are necessary to give a correct measurement, both of the capital effectively invested by the financiers of the enterprise and of the monetary returns available to the same. The advantage that can derive from the application of EVA consists of its being the most analytic indication of how value is formed and allowing a uniform view of the main objectives of management, integrating the long-term strategic vision with the expectations of the shareholders.

The passage from the EVA of the single enterprise to the EVA of the group requires reference to the consolidated balance sheet, so as to determine the relevant parameters for calculating the EVA (O'Byrne 1997; Ross 1999).

Considering NOPAT, if there are synergies deriving from belonging to the group, then the consolidated NOPAT is greater than that obtained by aggregating the NOPATs of the single companies not placed in the group setting. The consolidated invested capital is net of the inter-company debts and the part of the net assets of each company that corresponds to inter-company participations. The consolidated WACC reflects the centralization of the inter-company cash flows.

NOTES

1. However, there are cases where the existence of the economic subject is independent of the possession of the majority of votes in the assembly: controlled by quotas of capital less than 50%; control without direct or indirect investment of capital.

2. The OPA can be consensual (offer following previous private contracting that led to holding more than 30% of the voting rights of a company, imposes the formulation of an offer for the total shares still in circulation) or aggressive (irrevocable public offer for a minimum quantity of shares at a preestablished price with the scope of obtaining a majority share position in the "target" company). The offeror may envisage specific conditions—for example, reaching a minimum quantity of shares—that must be met for the offer not to be withdrawn. Besides OPAs, there are Offers of Public Exchange that foresee an exchange of shares carried out on the stock exchange. The offering company proposes to holders of shares in the "target" company, an exchange of those shares for its own shares; the Offer of Public Acquisition and Exchange that forsees payment for shares in the "target" company being made partly with money and partly with shares.

3. If the founder has 100% and there are only two heirs, neither of the two has control, unless they have a greater participation than their co-heir, who may have compensation through the assignation of family goods external to the company.

4. Recourse to a family holding allows safeguarding the control of the family business, through the creation of true "strongbox" of the family business assets, in which it is easier to regulate and, in certain cases, block the transfer of family participation. In cases where there is high fragmentation of the capital quotas possessed by family members, finding simple and effective methods that guarantee a unity of direction in governing the company is an indispensible condition for continuation of the family business.

5. Transfer pricing makes it possible to transfer resources from one company to another, at an international level, adding to the private benefits of control or, more simply, in multinational groups where the shareholders of the holding are widely dispersed, limited to making fiscal arbitration that in any case reduces the resources of the company in countries with higher levels of taxation.

100 M. DEL GIUDICE

6. Corrections can be made to the components of the EVA so as to identify a NOPAT and a CI exclusively connected to the operative activities, that is, purified of the sums that do not regard the characteristic management of the enterprise.

REFERENCES

Almeida, H. V., & Wolfenzon, D. (2006). A theory of pyramidal ownership and family business groups. *The Journal of Finance, 61*(6), 2637–2680.

Amore, M. D., Minichilli, A., & Corbetta, G. (2011). How do managerial successions shape corporate financial policies in family firms? *Journal of Corporate Finance, 17*(4), 1016–1027.

Anderson, R. C., & Reeb, D. M. (2003). Founding-family ownership and firm performance: Evidence from the S&P 500. *The Journal of Finance, 58*(3), 1301–1328.

Argyres, N. S., & Liebeskind, J. P. (1999). Contractual commitments, bargaining power, and governance inseparability: Incorporating history into transaction cost theory. *Academy of Management Review, 24*(1), 49–63.

Aronoff, C. E., & Ward, J. L. (1996). *Family business governance: Maximizing family and business potential* (No. 8). Marietta: Family Enterprise Publisher.

Astrachan, J. H., Klein, S. B., & Smyrnios, K. X. (2002). The F-PEC scale of family influence: A proposal for solving the family business definition problem. *Family Business Review, 15*(1), 45–58.

Bae, K. H., Kang, J. K., & Kim, J. M. (2002). Tunneling or value added? Evidence from mergers by Korean business groups. *The Journal of Finance, 57*(6), 2695–2740.

Bartholomeusz, S., & Tanewski, G. A. (2006). The relationship between family firms and corporate governance*. *Journal of Small Business Management, 44*(2), 245–267.

Baylis, R., Connell, L., & Flynn, A. (1998). Company size, environmental regulation and ecological modernization: Further analysis at the level of the firm. *Business Strategy and the Environment, 7*(5), 285–296.

Bebchuk, L. A., Kraakman, R., & Triantis, G. (2000). Stock pyramids, cross-ownership, and dual class equity: The mechanisms and agency costs of separating control from cash-flow rights. In *Concentrated corporate ownership* (pp. 295–318). Chicago: University of Chicago Press.

Bianco, M., & Nicodano, G. (2006). Pyramidal groups and debt. *European Economic Review, 50*(4), 937–961.

Boter, H., & Lundström, A. (2005). SME perspectives on business support services: The role of company size, industry and location. *Journal of Small Business and Enterprise Development, 12*(2), 244–258.

FROM FAMILY BUSINESSES TO BUSINESS GROUPS **101**

Breton-Miller, L., & Miller, D. (2006). Why do some family businesses out-compete? Governance, long-term orientations, and sustainable capability. *Entrepreneurship Theory and Practice, 30*(6), 731–746.

Brooksbank, R. (1991). Defining the small business: A new classification of company size. *Entrepreneurship & Regional Development, 3*(1), 17–31.

Buzby, S. L. (1975). Company size, listed versus unlisted stocks, and the extent of financial disclosure. *Journal of Accounting Research, 13*(1), 16–37.

Chang, S. J., & Hong, J. (2000). Economic performance of group-affiliated companies in Korea: Intragroup resource sharing and internal business transactions. *Academy of Management Journal, 43*(3), 429–448.

Colarossi, F., Giorgino, M., Steri, R., & Viviani, D. (2008). A corporate governance study on Italian family firms. *Corporate Ownership & Control, 5*(4), 93–103.

Corbetta, G. (1995). Patterns of development of family businesses in Italy. *Family Business Review, 8*(4), 255–265.

Corley, K. G., & Gioia, D. A. (2004). Identity ambiguity and change in the wake of a corporate spin-off. *Administrative Science Quarterly, 49*(2), 173–208.

Daily, C. M., & Dollinger, M. J. (1992). An empirical examination of ownership structure in family and professionally managed firms. *Family Business Review, 5* (2), 117–136.

Daily, C. M., Dalton, D. R., & Cannella, A. A. (2003). Corporate governance: Decades of dialogue and data. *Academy of Management Review, 28*(3), 371–382.

Davis, P. (1983). Realizing the potential of the family business. *Organizational Dynamics, 12*(1), 47–56.

Davis, J. A., & Tagiuri, R. (1989). The influence of life stage on father-son work relationships in family companies. *Family Business Review, 2*(1), 47–74.

Davis, J. H., Schoorman, F. D., & Donaldson, L. (1997). Toward a stewardship theory of management. *Academy of Management Review, 22*(1), 20–47.

De Fabritiis, G., Pammolli, F., & Riccaboni, M. (2003). On size and growth of business firms. *Physica A: Statistical Mechanics and Its Applications, 324*(1), 38–44.

Donaldson, L., & Davis, J. H. (1991). Stewardship theory or agency theory: CEO governance and shareholder returns. *Australian Journal of Management, 16*(1), 49–64.

Donckels, R., & Fröhlich, E. (1991). Are family businesses really different? European experiences from STRATOS. *Family Business Review, 4*(2), 149–160.

Evans, D. S. (1987). The relationship between firm growth, size, and age: Estimates for 100 manufacturing industries. *The Journal of Industrial Economics, 35*, 567–581.

Fu, D., Pammolli, F., Buldyrev, S. V., Riccaboni, M., Matia, K., Yamasaki, K., & Stanley, H. E. (2005). The growth of business firms: Theoretical framework and empirical evidence. *Proceedings of the National Academy of Sciences of the United States of America, 102*(52), 18801–18806.

102 M. DEL GIUDICE

Fuguitt, G. V. (1965). The growth and decline of small towns as a probability process. *American Sociological Review, 30*(3), 403–411.

Gallo, M. Á., Tàpies, J., & Cappuyns, K. (2004). Comparison of family and nonfamily business: Financial logic and personal preferences. *Family Business Review, 17*(4), 303–318.

García-Meca, E., & Sánchez-Ballesta, J. P. (2009). Corporate governance and earnings management: A meta-analysis. *Corporate Governance: An International Review, 17*(5), 594–610.

Gomez-Mejia, L. R., Nunez-Nickel, M., & Gutierrez, I. (2001). The role of family ties in agency contracts. *Academy of Management Journal, 44*(1), 81–95.

Granovetter, M. (1995). Coase revisited: Business groups in the modern economy. *Industrial and Corporate Change, 4*(1), 93–130.

Gray, R., Owen, D., & Adams, C. (1996). *Accounting & accountability: Changes and challenges in corporate social and environmental reporting.* London: Prentice Hall.

Handler, W. C. (1989). Methodological issues and considerations in studying family businesses. *Family Business Review, 2*(3), 257–276.

Handler, W. C. (1994). Succession in family business: A review of the research. *Family Business Review, 7*(2), 133–157.

Hart, O. (1995). *Firms, contracts, and financial structure.* New York, USA: Oxford University Press.

Hirigoyen, G., & Labaki, R. (2012). The role of regret in the owner-manager decision-making in the family business: A conceptual approach. *Journal of Family Business Strategy, 3*(2), 118–126.

Koslowski, P. (2000). The limits of shareholder value. *Journal of Business Ethics, 27*(1–2), 137–148.

Masulis, R. W., Pham, P. K., & Zein, J. (2011). Family business groups around the world: Financing advantages, control motivations, and organizational choices. *Review of Financial Studies, 24*(11), 3556–3600.

Melin, L., Nordqvist, M., & Sharma, P. (Eds.). (2013). *The SAGE handbook of family business.* Los Angeles: Sage.

Miles, R. E., & Snow, C. C. (1986). Organizations: New concepts for new forms. *California Management Review, 28*(3), 62–73.

Morck, R., & Yeung, B. (2003). Agency problems in large family business groups. *Entrepreneurship Theory and Practice, 27*(4), 367–382.

Nohria, N., & Eccles, R. G. (1992). *Networks and organizations: Structure, form, and action.* Boston: Harvard Business School Press.

O'Byrne, S. F. (1997). EVA and shareholder return. *Financial Practice and Education, 7*(1), 50–54.

O'Gorman, C., & Kautonen, M. (2004). Policies to promote new knowledge-intensive industrial agglomerations. *Entrepreneurship & Regional Development, 16*(6), 459–479.

FROM FAMILY BUSINESSES TO BUSINESS GROUPS **103**

Quinn, J. B., & Hilmer, F. G. (1994). Strategic outsourcing. *Sloan Management Review, 35*(4), 43.

Ramsden, J. J., & Kiss-Haypal, G. (2000). Company size distribution in different countries. *Physica A: Statistical Mechanics and Its Applications, 277*(1), 220–227.

Ross, I. (1999). The Stern Stewart performance 1000. *Journal of Applied Corporate Finance, 11*(4), 122–126.

Sacchetti, S., & Sugden, R. (2003). The governance of networks and economic power: The nature and impact of subcontracting relationships. *Journal of Economic Surveys, 17*(5), 669–692.

Salamon, G. L., & Dhaliwal, D. S. (1980). Company size and financial disclosure requirements with evidence from the segmental reporting issue. *Journal of Business Finance & Accounting, 7*(4), 555–568.

Schermerhorn Jr., J. R. (2009). *Exploring management.* Hoboken, New Jersey, USA: Wiley.

Stern, J. M., Shiely, J. S., & Ross, I. (2001). *The EVA challenge: Implementing value-added change in an organization.* New York: Wiley.

Takayasu, H., & Okuyama, K. (1998). Country dependence on company size distributions and a numerical model based on competition and cooperation. *Fractals, 6*(01), 67–79.

Terziovski, M., & Samson, D. (2000). The effect of company size on the relationship between TQM strategy and organisational performance. *The TQM Magazine, 12*(2), 144–149.

Thomsen, S., & Pedersen, T. (2000). Ownership structure and economic performance in the largest European companies. *Strategic Management Journal, 21*(6), 689–705.

Yasuda, T. (2005). Firm growth, size, age and behavior in Japanese manufacturing. *Small Business Economics, 24*(1), 1–15.

Yiu, D., Bruton, G. D., & Lu, Y. (2005). Understanding business group performance in an emerging economy: Acquiring resources and capabilities in order to prosper*. *Journal of Management Studies, 42*(1), 183–206.

Yiu, D. W., Lu, Y., Bruton, G. D., & Hoskisson, R. E. (2007). Business groups: An integrated model to focus future research. *Journal of Management Studies, 44*(8), 1551–1579.

CHAPTER 4

Emerging Markets: Institutional Problems and Entrepreneurial Models

4.1 Emerging Markets: A Variety of Definitions

Emerging economies are low-income, rapid-growth countries using economic liberalization as their primary engine of growth. They fall into two groups: developing countries in Asia, Latin America, Africa, and the Middle East and transition economies in the former Soviet Union and China. (Hoskisson et al. 2000, p. 249)

Of the 64 emerging economies identified by Hoskisson et al. (2000), 51 are rapidly growing developing countries and 13 are in transition from centrally planned economies (often called "transition economies"). (Wright et al. 2005, p. 1)

Emerging economies provide a unique, quasi-experimental setting for testing existing theories. However, too often, emerging economies are treated as a set uniform bloc. Emerging economies may share many similarities, but they also have distinctive characteristics. Each country's history, size, and munificence of their economies differ, as do their economic development paths. (Bruton et al. 2008, p. 7)

In contrast to the G-7, emerging economies have lower per capita income, on average higher inflation and inflation uncertainty, and higher nominal interest rates. (Bansal and Dahlquist 2000, p. 116)

© The Author(s) 2017
M. Del Giudice, *Understanding Family-Owned Business Groups,*
DOI 10.1007/978-3-319-42243-5_4

105

The expression "emerging economies" was coined by the International Finance Corporation in 1981, to launch a new fund with investments in developing countries. Since then, it has been used with various meanings, but essentially, it describes economies (or a countries) with low or modest *pro capita* earnings that also have strong economic growth (Eichengreen and Hausmann 2010; Li and Kozhikode 2009; Glick and Hutchison 2005). Many of these economies have emerged from long periods of authoritarian regimes and strong state intervention in the production system (Peng et al. 2008; Manolova et al. 2008; Meyer 2004; Amato and Gerlach 2002).

Other criteria have been proposed in an attempt to better specify this concept (Neumeyer and Perri 2005; Goldstein and Turner 1996; Delios and Henisz 2000; Han Kim and Singal 2000; Dharwadkar et al. 2000; Goldstein 2009; Asif and Muneer 2007; Edwards and Savastano 1999; Guillén and García-Canal 2009; Isobe et al. 2000; Gonçalves and Salles 2008; Laxton and Pesenti 2003; Walumbwa and Lawler 2003; Paun 2013). Among the many proposals, the one that is most useful for businesses considers the extent of the presence of infrastructure in the market, whether it is *hard* infrastructure (transport, ports, airports, railways and roads for the movement of goods from the producer to sales points at sustainable prices) or *soft* infrastructure (information about the markets, capital markets, functioning of the justice system, ratings agencies, logistics consultants). According to this criterion, an economy truly emerges when it passes a certain quality threshold in its infrastructure. The more solid the infrastructure, the more manageable and less risky is entry to these markets. Three deficiencies that are more frequently encountered than others in the infrastructure of emerging countries are: the lack of reliable information on demand trends; choices guided by politics and not by the economy (e.g. last ditch defense of employment); and inefficient judiciary systems (or rather the incapacity of giving executive force to contracts) (Meyer et al. 2009; Arellano 2008; Young et al. 2008; Edwards 2001; Reinhart and Rogoff 2010; Luo et al. 2009).

> It is predicted that by 2050, the economies of Brazil, Russia, India, and China (the "BRIC" economies) will be larger than that of the United States, Japan, Germany, U.K., France, and Italy (G6). (Bruton et al. 2008, p. 1 cite Wilson and Purushothaman 2003)

When speaking about emerging markets, the mind rushes to acronyms: BRIC (Brazil, Russia, India, China), STIM (South Africa, Turkey,

EMERGING MARKETS: INSTITUTIONAL PROBLEMS AND ENTREPRENEURIAL... 107

Indonesia, Mexico) and other less well-known acronyms like BRICI, obtained by adding Indonesia to the four most important emerging markets (Stajano 2009; Wilson and Purushothaman 2003; Wilson and Purushothaman 2003; Jain 2006; Gammeltoft 2008). These settings cannot be likened to a shared market like ASEAN or NAFTA: they are a set of very different markets for dimensions and for stages of development. Some are very populous, others less so: China and India have more than a billion inhabitants each, Brazil and Russia fewer than 200 million. Every market has its own identity; potential clients differ in their ethnic and cultural backgrounds. A first selection can be made starting from examining the products and services that are on sale there and looking for useful information to separate the many existing markets.

> These economies have also become more diversified along many dimensions—in their economic structure, trading patterns and the composition of their capital flows. On the other hand, recent growth in some EMDEs—*Emerging Market* and *Developing Economies*—has been supported by capital inflows, strong credit growth, and, for commodity exporters, by the continued strength of commodity prices. (Abiad et al. 2012, p. 5)

In the Bloomberg classification, China is placed in first place among the emerging markets, continuing to hold the key role for the world economic growth. Not all emerging markets are marked by the same qualities: their differences can determine the economic attractiveness and therefore the future of an entire region or nation.

Currently Emerging Markets
Since 2015, emerging markets have been considered to offer the most promising opportunities for investing in stock, especially due to a sharp drop (more than 50%) in the oil prices. South Korea tops Bloomberg Markets' fourth annual ranking as the most promising emerging markets for 2015, followed by Qatar at No. 2, China as No. 3 and the United Arab Emirates at No. 4. They benefit from low oil prices and relatively high economic growth, as well as weak currencies which make exported goods cheaper. (see the article: http://www.bloomberg.com/news/articles/2015-02-11/gulf-nations-defy-oil-rout-to-top-list-of-best-emerging-markets).

108 M. DEL GIUDICE

It is possible to make a classification of future emerging markets through the analysis of some variables like growth rate, inflation rate, government debt, price earning of the main shares index, volatility of the currency and an index that shows the ease of doing business in the country that is being analyzed.

Transition and Emerging Economies: Definition and Classifications

In general terms, the evolution of an economy from a centrally planned system to a market-based system is known as *transition economy* (TE) (Hoskisson et al. 2000; Svejnar 2002; Makhija 2003; Samoilenko and Osei-Bryson 2008). There are differences between transition economies and controlled and developed economies, because of the range of reforms and the rather undefined conclusions they reach. The effects of such reforms are a vast liberalization of prices and trade, the end of secure employment, the loss of traditional markets and intense privatizations (Svejnar 2002; Makhija 2003). In this context, firms face severe difficulties, since they have to survive in a state of uncertainty (Peng and Heath 1996; Peng 2003). Sometimes, reforms have aggravated this condition because they gave advantages to particular sectors and businesses to the detriment of others (Farashahi and Hafsi 2009). Thus, institutional contexts diversely oriented toward the market were created by different reforms at the domestic level, and by processes of change.

According to Van Agtmael (1984), there is a subgroup of developing economies that can be described as *emerging market economies.* Arnold and Quelch (1998) used this term with regard to countries or regions characterized by low absolute but rapidly increasing per capita income, and administrations for which economic liberalization is fundamental.

In developed countries, living standards are usually high, the economy grows constantly and the infrastructure is advanced; conversely, developing countries are usually distinguished by low living standards, while the industrial and commercial infrastructure is underdeveloped. Generally speaking, in most developing countries, qualified workers are almost absent, consumers do not spend enough, capital markets

(continued)

are thin and the infrastructure is weak. Developing countries, in fact, are characterized by a low per capita income, high levels of unemployment, lack of well-paid jobs and scarce demand for luxury goods; as a result, capital forms at a slow pace and personal savings never reach high levels (Hoskisson et al. 2000). All these characteristics that are typical of developing or emerging economies highly affect business investments and operations. Thus, for example, if a multinational corporation that is present in an emerging market economy is willing to sell its products also to the least affluent consumers of that country, it will be forced to take into account price affordability and will have to apply lower unit prices than those demanded in developed countries. It is possible that companies turn a blind eye on quality and use cheaper materials in the manufacturing process in order to obtain a price reduction. Moreover, due to the lack of available capital and qualified workers, it is hard for local firms to emerge and grow. At the same time, the underdeveloped infrastructure makes it difficult to market the products.

Emerging Economies in Detail
According to Roztocki and Weistroffer (2004, 2008), emerging economies, which are characterized by low economic development but very high growth rates, usually provide businesses with a highly dynamic but definitely unstable environment compared to developed economies or to countries with a lower development rate. The unbalance in the business setting is caused in part by the fact that emerging economies depend on capital flow from the developed countries and the trade with them. Thus, if there is a financial shock in developed countries, or even if demand varies slightly, this may cause an intense recession in emerging economies. Here, there is usually an increase in national demand for new products and services by the new middle class whose income is on the rise. Such demand is speeded up by consumer loans, since this is the only way people can aspire to catch up with the living standards that characterize the developed world. This opens up new business opportunities to domestic firms, and also multinational companies are attracted.

(continued)

However, as argued by Djankov and Murrell (2002), there is a variety and diversity among institutional contexts worldwide, so emerging economies cannot be considered homogeneous. As pointed out by Hoskisson et al. (2000), such institutional heterogeneity appears also among countries that belong to the same geographic region and even among countries that had a common origin, as in the case of the post-Soviet republics. In emerging economies, differently to developed ones, institutions are not usually supported by any formal market.

In a market economy, the effective functioning of market mechanisms is mainly guaranteed by institutions, such as regulatory regimes, property rights and the entire legal framework and its enforcement. This way, it is certain that undue costs or risks will not be endured by individuals and firms (North 1990; Lu et al. 2008). The strength of institutions depends on the support of the voluntary exchange on which an effective market mechanism is based. Conversely, if they cannot ensure effective markets or they even undermine them, as in the case of corrupt business practices, institutions can be deemed weak. In developed economies, strong institutions play an important role, but their visibility may be scarce. In a number of emerging economies, instead, in which market malfunctions are so common, institutions that support the market are almost absent (McMillan 2008). North (1990) stated that the institutional settings in which firms operate are diverse and function according to different "rules of the game". These determine the extent of business "marketization" (Nee 1992; Davies 1995), since positioning depends on: business autonomy; distance from the plan in relation to input acquisition, output sale, and price fixing; the amount of incentives; and the significance of profit. Hence, the difference between more and less marketized contexts is substantial.

For firms present in less marketized settings, there are internal and external measures of organizational effectiveness and performance; the former refer to the organizational slack ensured through copious provision of resources, while the latter relate to conformance with administratively set objectives. These companies are confronted with limited independence, reduced budget, administered prices and

(*continued*)

administrative allocation of funds and materials. On the contrary, businesses present in contexts with a higher level of marketization enjoy much more autonomy with regard to the product and market domains they hold, and resources are mainly provided by the customers responsible for the revenues gained. Performance of these companies is measured by sales and profit, which are essential for their survival. The market provides them with capital, labor and materials at market prices; however, although these factors are very significant, it is the customer who plays the key role, since the resources necessary for the company's survival will be provided only if it is certain that the revenues originated from customers will cover payments owed.

Transition Economies in Europe
Transition Economies of Central and Eastern Europe (TECEE) can be divided into two groups. The first consists of the countries that became part of the European Union in 2004, and are no longer in the phase of transition. The group includes the following eight countries: Estonia, Latvia, Lithuania, Czech Republic, Slovakia, Slovenia, Poland and Hungary. The second group, on the contrary, is formed by those countries that are still experiencing the process of transition, and in particular, Bulgaria, Romania, Croatia, Moldova, Belarus, Georgia, Ukraine and Russia. The countries included in the second group were selected from the list of TECEE in IMF (2000), by way of example. Further distinction considers the two groups divided into two categories, Leaders and Followers, respectively (Samoilenko and Osei-Bryson 2008; EU Legislation 2010).

4.2 The Rise of Emerging Markets

There has been a great transformation of the global economic scenario in the last decade: emerging economies have grown much more rapidly than developed economies, making a fundamental contribution to the global economy. Investments in emerging markets, previously perceived as high returns but high risk investments, made in financial markets characterized by levels of evolution lower than those of the developed countries, have become established as an interesting alternative from the point of view of

112   M. DEL GIUDICE

strategic *asset allocation*, favoring a growing influx of capital toward markets with high development potential like Asia, Eastern Europe and Latin America. Given the growing volatility of more consolidated markets, both in shares and in bonds, and the relatively low correlation with the traditional markets, these constitute an interesting instrument for diversification.

Globalization has contributed to freeing the potential of emerging countries, initiating a process of convergence, at elevated rhythms, toward the economic and financial standards of developed countries, and requiring a new evaluation of the risks and opportunities of emerging markets. Benefitting from improvements in productivity and increasing exports—distinctive characteristics of the first phase of economic development—emerging economies have taken on an increasingly significant role in the international political and economic scenario, though not without notable differences in their rhythms of development (Fig. 4.1).

During the financial-economic crisis of 2007–2009, most developed countries experienced a deep recession; in such a weak phase, emerging economies provided important support for world economic growth. The current sovereign debt crisis of developed countries constitutes a further element in favor of the remodulation of power relationships, both economic

---

The Global growth rate is estimated at 3.4% in 2016 and 3.6% in 2017.

We can observe, however, a divergent and challenging trend, positively depending especially by emerging market and developing economies growth rate as well.

In advanced economies, a modest and uneven recovery is expected to continue, with a gradual further narrowing of output gaps.

In 2015, global economic activity remained subdued: the growth rate of emerging market and developing economies—while still accounting for over 70% of global growth—declined for the fifth consecutive year, while a modest recovery continued in advanced economies. The slowdown and rebalancing of the "world economic equilibrium" could be converted by new economic or political shocks.

While estimated growth in advanced economies were expected to rise by 0.2 percentage point in 2016 to 2.1%, and hold steady in 2017, supported by easy financial conditions and due to business in the USA and stronger private consumption in the UE area, growth in emerging markets is projected to increase from 4% in 2015 to 4.3% and 4.7% in 2016 and 2017, respectively (see article: http://www.imf.org/external/pubs/ft/weo/2016/update/01/).

Fig. 4.1   Global growth (advanced economies vs emerging market and developing economies)

and political, to the advantage of emerging countries that are enjoying strong fiscal and financial indicators (Husain et al. 2005).

Developed countries are also encountering negative demographic dynamics and showing reduced liberalist trends, characterized by a stiffening of regulations, an increase in tax burdens and reinforcement of the influence of the State in the economy. Emerging economies, instead, are more and more directed toward policies of a capitalist orientation and in favor of intensification of trade relationships, redimensioning the risks of a protectionist involution in economic policies in the context of lower growth. The development of trade agreements, both with other emerging countries and with developed countries, provides a well-defined regulatory setting, guaranteeing long-term relationships between the countries involved.

4.3 A New Growth Model

To date, the emerging economies in general, and China in particular, have shown a growth model based on exports and characterized by strong demographic development (Fig. 4.2) and low wages.

This has determined a composition of GDP overbalanced toward fixed investments, at the expense of private consumers.

The International Monetary Fund's (IMF's) latest World Economic Outlook (WEO http://www.imf.org/external/pubs/ft/weo/2016/update/01/) anticipates a decrease in GDP growth for some of the key emerging markets in Asia over the next five to six years. The drop is likely due to macro-economic factors, over the crisis, such as aging populations and human capital (i.e. the labor force and its set of skills and abilities). Over the medium term, IMF forecasts show Emerging and Developing Asia's growth fluctuating around 6.5% in the next six years, compared to a 7.6% annual average since 2009. Demographics in the region emerge as a major roadblock to speedier development. The proportion of working population (from 15 to 64 years old) has been decreasing since 2011 in the developing economies of East Asia and the Pacific to reach 71.1% in 2013. Although this ratio is still increasing in South Asia, it was lower at 64.8% in 2013, and the region is likely to follow a similar trend as birth rates have been declining sharply, while the cohort aged over 64 years has been increasing steadily as a share of the total population. All these have resulted in deteriorating dependency ratios, expressed as the population aged over 64 years per 100 persons of working age.

Fig. 4.2 Demographics in Asian EMDEs

> The Gross Domestic Product (GDP) in China was worth 10354.80 billion US dollars in 2014. The GDP value of China represents 16.70% of the world economy. GDP in China averaged 1437.04 USD billion from 1960 until 2014, reaching an all-time high of 10354.80 USD billion in 2014 and a record low of 46.68 USD billion in 1962. GDP in China is reported by the World Bank Group. During this period, there were many data adjustments, with weighting factors undergoing significant changes along with each year's comparable price amendments; significant changes in statistical methods resulted in the substantial deviation. Even with science and technology as advanced as it is today, the single item survey is allowed at least ±3%, or a total of 6% deviation.

So, China finds itself dealing with the necessary transition phase from an exporting country to an economy driven by internal demand. The re-equilibrium process, though gradual, given the government's renewed attention to growth, benefits from strong supporting factors. Persistent economic growth favors an increase of salaries and therefore the formation and development of a middle class with elevated purchasing power. The increase of demand for high quality consumer goods supports the hypothesis of stable high internal consumption in the near future. Good development prospects for productivity, that should benefit from the emigration of the workforce from the primary sector and the formation of a more qualified workforce, should limit the negative impact of the increase in labor costs on production costs and inflation, and therefore on the competitiveness of the country.

Internal demand should also be favored by bringing infrastructure up to the level of modern industrialized countries. The phenomenon of urbanization and the growth of the population, in fact, give rise to the need for increased availability of services of public utility. So, the continuation of appreciable *pro capita* economic growth rates is predictable in the near future, also supported by the phenomenon of the so-called demographic dividend, which occurs when population of working age is large compared to the population of non-working age. The re-equilibrium process of the Chinese economy will favor the other economies of the Asian area, characterized by relevant trade links with the country, and, in general, those emerging economies that have enormous reserves of raw materials (Luo et al. 2010). As a consequence, the structural factors described redimension the risk of the natural effect of saturation of the growth dynamic of emerging economies.

4.4 The Importance of the Emerging Economies for Investors

The importance of the emerging markets is not a temporary phenomenon: on the contrary, it is a structural phenomenon, able to modify power relationships at a world level. The emerging economies have made great progress in making the rules of business governance more transparent and, in many cases, in order to safeguard investors they have introduced western standards in their respective judicial systems, favoring evolution from economies with a high growth rates to markets able to offer interesting investment opportunities. However, such areas continue to have higher risks in terms of corruption, state intervention in the economic system, inadequate protection of property rights and business management not always oriented toward the interests of the investors. Further progress is also necessary in the development of health systems and national pension schemes that guarantee social cohesion and that avoid putting the development model into question, or giving vigor to protests that may also be fuelled by the increase of concentrations of income. In fact, this phenomenon, normally characteristic of developing economies, creates notable problems if not effectively managed.

Moreover, empirical analysis also demonstrates that the economic processes rarely evolve along straight lines: predictions that are limited to extrapolating future trends from the dynamics of previous years' risk, not considering factors that may slow down growth. In emerging countries, therefore, constant analysis of the macro-economic and financial phenomena is an element of enormous interest for every investment decision, making trust in specialized management crucial.

The strong points of the emerging markets offer important arguments in favor of investment in this asset class. However, the importance of an approach based on diversification and on risk management is to be stressed. Evolution toward the status of developed economies is not, in fact, linear; the greater volatility of emerging financial markets is a synthesis of the greater risks that investors encounter. As a result, it is fundamental to trust qualified asset managers, who combine competence in macro-economic analysis and market analysis and experience of active management of portfolios specializing in emerging markets with the ability of identifying market inefficiencies and of using sophisticated technology in risk management.

4.5   The Relevance of Informal Institutions

A widely recognized definition of institutions has been proposed by Scott (1995): "institutions are those cognitive, normative and regulatory structures and activities that provide stability and direct social behavior. Institutions make use of several means (culture, structure and routine) and operate at several levels" (Scott 1995). The role of institutions in an economy is to reduce information and transaction costs through the reduction of uncertainty and the development of a structure that facilitates interaction.

An analysis shall now be made about how the shortcomings of formal institutions in the emerging markets influence the relationship between entrepreneurs and institutions, and how this relationship differs among the various countries. The analysis is concentrated on the environmental context and on the shortcomings of the formal institutions, such as those regarding the guarantee of the rights of private property, and explains how traditions and informal institutions have filled this gap (Puffer et al. 2010). A contrast of this type helps in examining the specific contexts of economies in transition, since entrepreneurship is defined as "a social process strictly dependent on the context through which individuals and social groups create well-being by creating unique combinations of resources or exploiting market opportunities" (Ireland et al. 2001). The definition, "dependent on the context", is particularly pertinent to the uniqueness of economies in transition, the circumstances of which differ greatly from those of the developed economies, that provide active support to entrepreneurs through their institutions. Such support can be described in terms of some basic conditions to create an environment favorable to entrepreneurship (Pennings 1982). Making reference to the analysis of Ahlstrom and Bruton (2006), who observed the use of informal institutions on the part of venture capitalists in different Asian markets, it may be seen that the entrepreneurial situation in Russia and China has a lot in common with venture capitalism, and that this may also be extended to entrepreneurs in those contexts. The study recognizes the need for entrepreneurs to base themselves on informal institutions, deriving from tradition and culture, to carry out their operations.

4.6 Institutional Vacuums

The ease of managing to match supply to demand is a very important characteristic of a market. In developed markets there are an ample number of intermediates that provide information and are occupied in the contracts necessary to close a transaction; in emerging markets, instead, there is neither the physical nor the institutional infrastructure necessary for the smooth functioning of the market itself. For sellers and buyers, in fact, it is difficult to manage to get into contact with each other and to have information to evaluate the quality of products and services.

The gaps created by the absence of intermediaries in a market are defined as institutional vacuums. They can have various forms and play an important role in defining the capital, labor and product markets. The absence or unreliability of information, an inefficient judicial system and uncertain legislation are the main causes of market failures and, for foreign and domestic companies, are a disincentive to investing large sums in the market.

In developed markets, businesses can trust various institutions, something that allows minimizing market failures, while in the emerging markets, despite the development of some informal institutions that aim to fill the institutional vacuums, such failures are frequent. In this type of context, businesses often have to compensate for these shortcomings, directly and actively.

The quality and quantity of the infrastructure determine economic growth and development, improving the functioning of the product, capital and labor markets, reducing the impact of distance on businesses and optimizing decisional processes and communications. According to Khanna and Palepu (2010), infrastructure refers to those fundamental services that make an economy work as it should, like roads, bridges, refineries, energy, social services and others. The authors stress the importance of both hard infrastructure and soft infrastructure, indicating that these are the backbone of every business environment, and point out that their absence can be seen as a means for businesses to invent alternatives or to adapt to what is available in the market context. The development of infrastructure, therefore, must be a priority for the emerging economies. Investigating the impact of communications infrastructure on economic growth shows the positive effects it has on every segment of society, from health to national defense. The development of telecommunications increases the demand for other goods and services and reduces the costs of coordinating business activities, through the reduction of research and information costs. For example, after liberalizing the telecommunications sector ten years ago, the government of the Philippines attracted massive investment that has translated into modern infrastructure. To improve infrastructure, it is also necessary to have a transparent normative picture. In Brazil, in fact, the prices of wind energy fell drastically after the government created a platform of online auctions based on maximum transparency. Also in China, it was necessary to provide for the drafting of new norms when consumer financing services were launched.

Despite the potential of infrastructure for economic growth and development, Prud'Homme et al. (2005) emphasizes characteristics of infrastructure that connect to market failures. The traditional forms of providing public goods, that reduce costs through externality of the network, provide a reason for justifying the public monopoly regime. Despite this, the role of public monopolies has failed in a lot of developed countries, or at least, the services provided have been insufficient and unreliable. Fishman and Khanna (2004) confirm the failure of the public sector in the provision of infrastructural services when analyzing the Nigerian telecommunications industry that, though controlled by the government, is totally inefficient.

The effects of the institutional shortcomings on the product, capital and labor markets are analyzed in the following section.

4.7   The Product Market

In developed markets, consumers can find their desired products, basing themselves on information provided by the companies through advertising, direct mailing, telemarketing, internet and other forms of communication. Also, distribution chains carry out a lot of functions typical to intermediaries: analyzing consumer preferences and offering products based on the attributes requested, carrying out quality controls, informing consumers of the attributes of products and allowing the return of products that are not satisfactory.

In a developed consumer market, all these mechanisms are supported by a network of material and immaterial infrastructure (hard and soft), but the public institutions play just as important a role.

When businesses decide to enter the market, before looking for solutions to institutional shortcomings, they have to study the local context to identify the same as precisely as possible, and they must also understand the importance of the market segments in emerging markets. The strategy

EMERGING MARKETS: INSTITUTIONAL PROBLEMS AND ENTREPRENEURIAL... 119

for dealing with institutional shortcomings positions multinationals and domestic businesses in different segments. These are not only distinct because of earnings and prices, but also for the needs, tastes and socio-demographic characteristics. The product markets in emerging markets can be divided into various segments:

- *global*, composed of consumers that wish to find products with the same attributes and quality of those found in developed markets and that are disposed to pay extra for these;
- *emerging middle class*, composed of consumers that require products or services having a combination of price, quality and characteristics between *local* and *global*;
- *local*, composed of consumers that are looking for products with a global quality or similar, but with characteristics and prices adapted to the local market;
- *bottom*, composed of those consumers that can only afford basic prices.

Understanding these segments can help multinationals (as well as national businesses) define their business models and growth strategies. Because of institutional shortcomings, multinationals find it difficult to serve other segments beyond the *global* segment, while local businesses, benefitting from their characteristics, can dominate the *local* segment. Knowledge of the market is fundamental for obtaining a competitive advantage in the *local* segment, both for adapting products and for getting around the institutional vacuums.

4.7.1 Capital Markets

The capital markets are also regulated by complicated mechanisms. Financial reporting enables communications to shareholders, which is made more credible and reliable by accounting standards and external audits. Financial intermediaries, like venture capitalists, commercial banks, insurance companies and investment funds help investors to channel their capital toward good investment opportunities and facilitate access to capital for entrepreneurs and businesses. Reducing the risks for investors, the institutions also enable the accumulation of capital for investment in new businesses.

An efficient financial sector allocates the resources saved by citizens, as well as those coming from abroad, in the most productive way possible. It channels resources toward the investment projects that have the highest capital return rates rather than on those that have political connections.

The use of resources for financing the workforce is made possible through the relationship between earnings and investment (Boskin 1984), which is the final objective of the financial sector of any economy. Businesses evaluate the market based on the availability and the costs of the financial services provided by the financial institutions (banking services, insurance, investment services, intermediation and consultancy, venture capitalist and private equity) and look for opportunities at a global level through expansion into other markets. The financial sector deals with feeding economic growth through the availability of capital and credit. The institutions deal with the availability and costs of the financial services, the ease of access to loans, financing through local capital, restrictions of capital flows, the solvency of the banks and the regulation of bonds and shares (Schwab 2010).

Institutional measures of development of the financial markets are the information on credit and on rights, both of which facilitate loans. In fact, providing information about credit can create great opportunities for enterprises that act as analysts (Khanna and Palepu 2010). There is a net contrast between the developed and developing countries: emerging markets are in the middle, trying to reform their own financial institutions so as to attract investors.

4.7.2 The Labor Market

In the labor market the education and training institutions not only help the development of human capital but also certify quality through qualifications and requirements for graduating. Placement agencies and headhunters help employers to find talent. Work contracts allow both workers and businesses to protect their own interests. Trades unions act as intermediaries between workers and large businesses, and the social safety net allows businesses to hire and fire on the basis of their needs. The main problems in emerging markets are:

- the lack of qualified personnel. The important growth of GDP in the last few years has given rise to a shortage of the competences requested by various sectors, since local schools and universities have not been able to satisfy the growing demand for specialization;

EMERGING MARKETS: INSTITUTIONAL PROBLEMS AND ENTREPRENEURIAL... 121

- turnover of personnel. The rate of turnover is very high for almost all jobs, from manual workers to middle management, and is influenced by geographical location. It is even higher for businesses that grow at rhythms higher than the mean, and probably the main cause of this phenomenon is rapid economic growth itself (with a demand for labor higher than the available supply, even small salary increases encourage people to change jobs);
- excessive responsibility. Local managers with relatively little experience have much greater responsibilities than their western counterparts. A lot of Asian businesses, for example, deal with problems of turnover by allowing the employees very rapid career advancement. This phenomenon often influences the efficiency of businesses.

Specifically, organizations that attempt to form tighter emotional bonds with their employees by being more solicitous of their well-being may be rewarded for doing so in a fast-changing industry—but most especially if they are family firms. The resulting motivation, dedication and cooperation among employees may represent a valuable competitive resource for high-technology family firms. The formation of connections with external providers of expertise, and social and financial capital, also appears to be an important source of advantage, and one more often used in FBs.

4.8   Methods for Overcoming Institutional Vacuums

In emerging markets the uncertain institutional contexts inhibit business opportunities and make entrepreneurial activity more risky and complex. An important part of the literature has believed it interesting to focus attention on the methods by which such contexts can create business opportunities (De Clercq et al. 2010; Ritchie 2010; Aidis 2005; Fogel et al. 2006; Luthans and Ibrayeva 2006; Manolova et al. 2008).

On the basis of recent developments in neo-institutional theory, one explores how entrepreneurs can make up for institutional shortcomings and create value, profiting from uncertainties in the emerging markets. In doing this, they often act as "institutional entrepreneurs", and their activity can be very important in the process of institutionalization of the markets (DiMaggio 1988; Beckert 1999). Specifically, entrepreneurs can identify and adopt different "pathways of action regarding the management of international structures for which businesses compete with the aim of obtaining resources" (Lawrence 1999). These institutional strategies are employed by entrepreneurs in emerging markets to start new businesses in "contexts that are composed of institutions that are not well-institutionalized" (Phillips et al. 2009).

Particular reference is made to:

- institutional intermediation, where the entrepreneurs start businesses that reduce the institutional uncertainty encountered by other businesses and provide them with a service in a specific organizational area;
- coverage of institutional vacuums, where the entrepreneurs start businesses to resolve problems in areas in which the level of institutionalization is low;
- reduction of institutional distance, that foresees the transfer and adaptation of solutions from other international contexts, through the work of the entrepreneurs;
- organization into business groups, through which businesses aggregate to create internal markets that substitute less developed external markets;
- by-passing the formal institutions, where businesses, especially those of a family character, invest in political relationships so as to obtain advantages independent of the institutional situation;
- loosening of institutional connections, done through repositioning production factors or capital in other countries, where the market is more efficient.

The implementation of such strategies deals with the management of institutional contexts of a given organizational field so as to create value. The fields characterized by a low level of institutionalization set complex challenges for entrepreneurs: the creation of new businesses without the support of formal institutions, such as working laws and a regulatory system, or even informal institutions, such as norms of shared sectors and widespread business practices, bring about high levels of risk (Peng 2000). It has been seen that, in these circumstances entrepreneurs in emerging economies are more disposed to adopt institutional strategies compared to those in developed economies.

So, institutional entrepreneurship in emerging markets requires a different set of skills to those required in developed markets, since the organizational areas are weakly institutionalized. As in all emerging fields, one key aspect of institutional entrepreneurs is their ability to build up alliances and networks, and to spread new sets of practices among other key actors in their own area (Garud et al. 2002). Besides, the fact that the institutions in some organizational fields are poorly rooted may often create more business opportunities.

In synthesis, the crux of the question is that some entrepreneurs in the emerging markets, rather than seeing the institutional uncertainties as an obstacle, try to start new businesses that can profit from such uncertainties, activating different strategies that do not aim at obtaining a competitive advantage based on the existing institutional structures, but aim at management of the institutional structures themselves.

In the following section, two of the above-mentioned strategies that aim at filling the institutional vacuums in emerging markets shall be examined in more depth: by-passing the formal institutions and organization of business groups.

4.8.1   By-Passing the Formal Institutions

The idea that creative actions of institutional entrepreneurs can lead to the dominion of a few business groups is in keeping with that of researchers who emphasize the exercise of power in the emerging and transition economies. They see the exercise of power as a local response to an external demand for institutional change that is often used to preserve the status quo and to maintain existing institutional regimes.

Emerging markets are characterized by a powerful presence of family businesses and extremely strong entrepreneurs. Given the scarcity of available capital, there is great rivalry between countries in growth and developed countries competing to access greater quotas of capital. Family businesses, therefore, have to make use of the instruments and resources necessary for success.

On this issue, to compete with the greatest global players and, therefore, be successful, a family business has to think long term and be the best in the sector. Its competitors are foreign businesses; therefore, the quality of its products and services offered must be superior to these external competitors. To make or establish a position in emerging markets, it is also necessary to have ambition, optimism and patience, to dispose of sufficient resources when "the game toughens" and to know how to reinvent a business when the evolution of the markets and the surrounding environment require it.

In the case of expansion abroad, family businesses tend to implement strategies that focus on their core business rather than attempting the arduous pathway of diversification. Collaboration with the right local partners and an excellent reputation represent further factors on which the family business may lever itself to achieve success. Emerging markets, therefore, offer great business opportunities to family businesses, but they must not be without strong collaboration with governments.

Morck and Yeung (2004) concentrate their studies on the role of the strategies of family businesses in attaining institutional and political objectives. Family businesses are less inclined to control externals compared to quoted businesses and to those controlled by management responsible toward their shareholders and that operate in a relatively transparent regulatory regime. Besides, by virtue of their own complex structures, families may act more discretely, since one group business can invest in political relationships, while another group business can benefit from this. Therefore, family businesses, thanks to opaque characteristics of corporate governance, have greater political skill and greater capacities in the quest for superior earnings.

Unlike professional chief executives, whose occupation rarely lasts more than five years, family businesses can invest large amounts with a longer-term view (Miller and Le Breton-Miller 2005), and their financial performances, especially in the closed and highly protected economies, may often depend more on political ability rather than on competitive virtues. Often the entrepreneurs try to camouflage the importance of political influence in nationalist rhetoric and legitimate their position by claiming that they facilitate the growth objectives of the state through their own operations.

However, there are proofs that indicate that family businesses effectively provide this national service (at least in their initial growth stages), but after passing through an extended period of importing technology and of imitation of foreign designs, they encounter difficulties in transforming themselves into innovative businesses and in developing superior managerial capacities (Whitley 1992; Church 1993; Aronoff and Ward 2011).

Thanks to State collaboration and promotion of entrepreneurs, the search for profits becomes more and more institutionalized and politically connected to asking for continuous State intervention and at the same time asking for restrictions of foreign investment, discouraging the entry of new actors in the economic system in exchange for safeguarding control of the most important domestic businesses.

4.8.2 Organization into Business Groups: Relying on Informal Institutions

The organization of businesses into business groups is a preeminent characteristic of emerging economies. "A commonly accepted definition of Business Groups does not exist in the economic or business literature, with already hinting at the fact that BGs should be located somewhere between markets and hierarchies" (Altomonte and Rungi 2013, p. 9).

The theory of transaction costs provides a widely accepted explanation for this trend, suggesting that the absence of institutions that make transactions safe and widespread market failures create considerable transaction costs for entrepreneurs. Really, market failures have been frequent thanks to the creation of business groups that have repeatedly established, among themselves, capital "markets", talent markets and mutual insurance (Khanna and Yafeh 2005), technology markets (Guillén 2000) and markets in communications infrastructure (Fishman and Khanna 2004) and in other resources that are expensive and inaccessible without market-assisted contracting. Generally, the aggregation of such business groups determines the creation of a competitive advantage that decreases over time and in relation to the development of the institutions.

Guillén (2000) claims that the business groups are particularly efficient when the government policies limit access to resources, both in the internal market and in international markets, and finds support for this notion from a sample of nine emerging markets. Siegel (2007) thinks that local businesses with political connections of particular importance in the current South Korean political context are greatly encouraged to undertake collaborations with American, European and Japanese businesses. In addition, he considers the effects of entering the New York Stock Exchange on business reputation.

In strategic terms, entrepreneurs respond to institutional shortcomings by internationalizing transactions with selected groups, thereby stabilizing an institutional micro-climate to save on transaction costs. Since the actors are known and deliberately create substitutes for market institutions, their actions can be seen as acts of institutional entrepreneurship to address the shortcomings.

Businesses can also aggregate into geographical clusters to provide incentives to private intermediaries specialized in developing in that given region, despite their not being present in the national market. Michael Porter

126 M. DEL GIUDICE

(1998) proposed the development of these clusters as a development strategy for emerging markets.

In any case, it is widely recognized that organization into business groups is a temporary phase of capitalist development (Lee et al. 2008). A lot of scholars believe that the motives at the basis of their existence are reduced once the institutional shortcomings are overcome and a solid market infrastructure comes about. A co-evolutionary perspective suggests a more complex dynamic (Carney 2008), in the sense that once business groups have become the dominant organizational model, the aggregate effects of their actions have repercussions on institutional effects, consolidating some practices and excluding others. For example, the presence of business groups that find it efficient to establish internal capital markets to allocate financial resources in competitive projects, simultaneously reduces liquidity and the development of external capital markets (Almeida and Wolfenzon 2006).

Besides, empirical evidence suggests that markets internal to business groups are characterized by earnings on an increasing scale (Khanna and Palepu 2006), that may arise from an equilibrium characterized by the formation of business groups that are large in relation to the dimensions of the market. In this state of stable equilibrium, less liquid and inefficient external capital markets inhibit the rate of start-ups of new businesses and the growth of independent businesses (Carney et al. 2009).

The consequence of the development of efficient internal markets is the reinforcement of the dominion of a few very large businesses creating, what Baumol et al. (2007) define as, oligarchic capitalism.

REFERENCES

Abiad, A., Bluedorn, J., Guajardo, J., & Topalova, P. (2012). *The rising resilience of emerging market and developing economies* (No. 12/300). Washington, DC: International Monetary Fund.

Ahlstrom, D., & Bruton, G. D. (2006). Venture capital in emerging economies: Networks and institutional change. *Entrepreneurship: Theory and Practice, 30,* 299–320.

Aidis, R. (2005). Institutional barriers to small and medium-sized enterprise operations in transition countries. *Small Business Economics, 25*(4), 305–317.

Almeida, H. V., & Wolfenzon, D. (2006). A theory of pyramidal ownership and family business groups. *The Journal of Finance, 61*(6), 2637–2680.

Altomonte, C., & Rungi, A. (2013). Business groups as hierarchies of firms. Determinants of vertical integration and performance. http://www.ecb.europa.eu or

EMERGING MARKETS: INSTITUTIONAL PROBLEMS AND ENTREPRENEURIAL... 127

from the Social Science Research Network electronic library at http://ssrn.com/abstract_id=2253222

Amato, J. D., & Gerlach, S. (2002). Inflation targeting in emerging market and transition economies: Lessons after a decade. *European Economic Review, 46*(4), 781–790.

Arellano, C. (2008). Default risk and income fluctuations in emerging economies. *The American Economic Review, 98*(3), 690–712.

Arnold, D. J., & Quelch, J. A. (1998). New strategies in emerging markets. *MIT Sloan Management Review, 40*(1), 7.

Aronoff, C. E., & Ward, J. L. (2011). *Preparing your family business for strategic change*. New York: Palgrave Macmillan.

Asif, M., & Muneer, T. (2007). Energy supply, its demand and security issues for developed and emerging economies. *Renewable and Sustainable Energy Reviews, 11*(7), 1388–1413.

Bansal, R., & Dahlquist, M. (2000). The forward premium puzzle: Different tales from developed and emerging economies. *Journal of International Economics, 51*(1), 115–144.

Baumol, W. J., Litan, R. E., & Schramm, C. J. (2007). *Good capitalism, bad capitalism, and the economics of growth and prosperity*. New Haven: Yale University Press.

Beckert, J. (1999). Agency, entrepreneurs, and institutional change. The role of strategic choice and institutionalized practices in organizations. *Organization Studies, 20*(5), 777–799.

Boskin, M. (1984). A longer term perspective on macroeconomics and distribution: Time, expectations, and incentives. In G. Feiwel (Ed.), *Issues in contemporary economics and distribution*. London, UK: The MacMillan Press.

Bruton, G. D., Ahlstrom, D., & Obloj, K. (2008). Entrepreneurship in emerging economies: Where are we today and where should the research go in the future. *Entrepreneurship Theory and Practice, 32*(1), 1–14.

Carney, M. (2008). *Asian business groups: Governance, context and performance*. Oxford: Chandos.

Carney, M., Gedajlovic, E., & Yang, X. (2009). Varieties of Asian capitalism: Toward an institutional theory of Asian enterprise. *Asia Pacific Journal of Management, 26*(3), 361–380.

Church, R. (1993). The family firm in industrial capitalism: International perspectives on hypotheses and history. *Business History, 35*(4), 17–43.

Davies, H. (1995). The nature of the firm in China. In H. Davies (Ed.), *China business: Context and issues* (pp. 137–154). Hong Kong: Longman.

De Clercq, D., Danis, W. M., & Dakhli, M. (2010). The moderating effect of institutional context on the relationship between associational activity and new business activity in emerging economies. *International Business Review, 19*(1), 85–101.

128   M. DEL GIUDICE

Delios, A., & Henisz, W. I. (2000). Japanese firms' investment strategies in emerging economies. *Academy of Management Journal, 43*(3), 305–323.

Dharwadkar, B., George, G., & Brandes, P. (2000). Privatization in emerging economies: An agency theory perspective. *Academy of Management Review, 25* (3), 650–669.

DiMaggio, P. (1988). Interest and agency in institutional theory. In L. G. E. Zucker (Ed.), *Institutional patterns and organizations: Culture and environment* (pp. 3–21). Cambridge: Ballinger.

Djankov, S., & Murrell, P. (2002). Enterprise restructuring in transition: A quantitative survey. *Journal of Economic Literature, 40*(3), 739–792.

Edwards, S. (2001). *Capital mobility and economic performance: Are emerging economies different?* (No. w8076). Cambridge, MA: National Bureau of Economic Research.

Edwards, S., & Savastano, M. A. (1999). *Exchange rates in emerging economies: What do we know? What do we need to know?* (No. w7228). Cambridge, MA: National Bureau of Economic Research.

Eichengreen, B., & Hausmann, R. (Eds.). (2010). *Other people's money: Debt denomination and financial instability in emerging market economies.* Chicago: University of Chicago Press.

EU Legislation. (2010). Enlargement 2004 and 2007. Retrieved October 4, 2010, from http://europa.eu/legislation_summaries/enlargement/2004_and_2007_enlargement/index_en.htm

Farashahi, M., & Hafsi, T. (2009). Strategy of firms in unstable institutional environments. *Asia Pacific Journal of Management, 26*(4), 643–666.

Fishman, R., & Khanna, T. (2004). Facilitating development: The role of business groups. *World Development, 32*(4), 609–628.

Fogel, K., Hawk, A., Morck, R., & Yeung, B. (2006). Institutional obstacles to entrepreneurship. In M. Casson, B. Yeung, A. Basu, & N. Wadeson (Eds.), *The Oxford handbook of entrepreneurship* (pp. 540–579). Oxford: Oxford University Press.

Gammeltoft, P. (2008). Emerging multinationals: Outward FDI from the BRICS countries. *International Journal of Technology and Globalisation, 4*(1), 5–22.

Garud, R., Jain, S., & Kumaraswamy, A. (2002). Institutional entrepreneurship in the sponsorship of common technological standards: The case of sun microsystems and java. *Academy of Management Journal, 45*(1), 196–214.

Glick, R., & Hutchison, M. (2005). Capital controls and exchange rate instability in developing economies. *Journal of International Money and Finance, 24*(3), 387–412.

Goldstein, A. (2009). Multinational companies from emerging economies composition, conceptualization & direction in the global economy. *Indian Journal of Industrial Relations, 45*, 137–147.

EMERGING MARKETS: INSTITUTIONAL PROBLEMS AND ENTREPRENEURIAL... 129

Goldstein, M., & Turner, P. (1996). Banking crises in emerging economies: Origins and policy options. In *BIS Economic Paper 46*. Bank for International Settlements, Monetary and Economic Department, Basle.

Gonçalves, C. E. S., & Salles, J. M. (2008). Inflation targeting in emerging economies: What do the data say? *Journal of Development Economics, 85*(1), 312–318.

Guillen, M. F. (2000). Business groups in emerging economies: A resource-based view. *Academy of Management Journal, 43*(3), 362–380.

Guillén, M. F., & García-Canal, E. (2009). The American model of the multinational firm and the "new" multinationals from emerging economies. *The Academy of Management Perspectives, 23*(2), 23–35.

Han Kim, E., & Singal, V. (2000). Stock market openings: Experience of emerging economies*. *The Journal of Business, 73*(1), 25–66.

Hermet, G., Hermet, G., Kazancigil, A., & Prud'homme, J. F. (2005). *La gouvernance: un concept et ses applications*. Paris: Karthala Editions.

Hoskisson, R. E., Eden, L., Lau, C. M., & Wright, M. (2000). Strategy in emerging economies. *Academy of Management Journal, 43*(3), 249–267.

Husain, A. M., Mody, A., & Rogoff, K. S. (2005). Exchange rate regime durability and performance in developing versus advanced economies. *Journal of Monetary Economics, 52*(1), 35–64.

Ireland, R. D., Hitt, M. A., Camp, S. M., & Sexton, D. L. (2001). Integrating entrepreneurship with strategic management actions to create firm wealth. *The Academy of Management Executive, 15*, 49–63.

Isobe, T., Makino, S., & Montgomery, D. B. (2000). Resource commitment, entry timing, and market performance of foreign direct investments in emerging economies: The case of Japanese international joint ventures in China. *Academy of Management Journal, 43*(3), 468–484.

Jain, S. C. (Ed.). (2006). *Emerging economies and the transformation of international business: Brazil, Russia, India and China (BRICs)*. Cheltenham/Northampton: Edward Elgar Publishing.

Khanna, T., & Palepu, K. G. (2006). Emerging giants: Building world class companies in developing countries. *Harvard Business Review, 84*(10), 60–69.

Khanna, T., & Palepu, K. G. (2010). *Winning in emerging markets: A road map for strategy and execution*. Boston: Massachuttes.

Khanna, T., & Yafeh, Y. (2005). Business groups and risk sharing around the world*. *The Journal of Business, 78*(1), 301–340.

Lawrence, T. B. (1999). Institutional strategy. *Journal of Management, 25*(2), 161–188.

Laxton, D., & Pesenti, P. (2003). Monetary rules for small, open, emerging economies. *Journal of Monetary Economics, 50*(5), 1109–1146.

Lee, K., Peng, M. W., & Lee, L. (2008). From diversification premium to diversification discount during institutional transitions. *Journal of World Business, 43*(1), 47–65.

130 M. DEL GIUDICE

Li, J., & Kozhikode, R. K. (2009). Developing new innovation models: Shifts in the innovation landscapes in emerging economies and implications for global R&D management. *Journal of International Management, 15*(3), 328–339.

Lu, Y., Tsang, E., & Peng, M. (2008). Knowledge management and innovation strategy in the Asia Pacific: Toward an institution-based view. *Asia Pacific Journal of Management, 25*(3), 361–374.

Luo, X., Chung, C. N., & Sobczak, M. (2009). How do corporate governance model differences affect foreign direct investment in emerging economies. *Journal of International Business Studies, 40*(3), 444–467.

Luo, Y., Xue, Q., & Han, B. (2010). How emerging market governments promote outward FDI: Experience from China. *Journal of World Business, 45*(1), 68–79.

Luthans, F., & Ibrayeva, E. S. (2006). Entrepreneurial self-efficacy in central Asian transition economies: Quantitative and qualitative analysis. *Journal of Business Studies, 37*(1), 92–110.

Makhija, M. (2003). Comparing the resource-based and market-based views of the firm: Empirical evidence from Czech privatization. *Strategic Management Journal, 24*, 433–451.

Manolova, T. S., Eunni, R. V., & Gyoshev, B. S. (2008). Institutional environments for entrepreneurship: Evidence from emerging economies in Eastern Europe. *Entrepreneurship Theory and Practice, 32*(1), 203–218.

McMillan, J. (2008). Market institutions. In S. Durlauf & L. Blume (Eds.), *The new Palgrave dictionary of economics* (Vol. 3, 2nd ed.). London: Palgrave Macmillan.

Meyer, K. E. (2004). Perspectives on multinational enterprises in emerging economies. *Journal of International Business Studies, 35*(4), 259–276.

Meyer, K. E., Estrin, S., Bhaumik, S. K., & Peng, M. W. (2009). Institutions, resources, and entry strategies in emerging economies. *Strategic Management Journal, 30*(1), 61–80.

Miller, D., & Le Breton-Miller, I. (2005). *Managing for the long run: Lessons in competitive advantage from great family business.* Boston: Harvard Business School Press.

Morck, R., & Yeung, B. (2004). Family control and the rent-seeking society. *Entrepreneurship Theory and Practice, 28*(4), 391–409.

Nee, V. (1992). Organizational dynamics of market transition: Hybrid forms, property rights, and mixed economy in China. *Administrative Science Quarterly, 37*, 1–27.

Neumeyer, P. A., & Perri, F. (2005). Business cycles in emerging economies: The role of interest rates. *Journal of Monetary Economics, 52*(2), 345–380.

North, D. C. (1990). *Institutions, institutional change and economic performance.* Cambridge/New York: Cambridge university press.

Paun, F. (2013). Technology push and market pull entrepreneurship. In *Encyclopedia of creativity, invention, innovation and entrepreneurship* (pp. 1808–1814). New York: Springer.

EMERGING MARKETS: INSTITUTIONAL PROBLEMS AND ENTREPRENEURIAL... 131

Peng, M. W. (2000). *Business strategies in transition economies.* Thousand Oaks: Sage.

Peng, M. W. (2003). Institutional transitions and strategic choices. *Academy of Management Review, 28*(2), 275–296.

Peng, M. W., & Heath, P. S. (1996). The growth of the firm in planned economies in transition: Institutions, organizations, and strategic choice. *Academy of Management Review, 21*(2), 492–528.

Peng, M. W., Wang, D. Y., & Jiang, Y. (2008). An institution-based view of international business strategy: A focus on emerging economies. *Journal of International Business Studies, 39*(5), 920–936.

Pennings, J. M. (1982). The urban quality of life and entrepreneurship. *Academy of Management Journal, 25*, 63–79.

Phillips, N., Tracey, P., & Karra, N. (2009). Rethinking institutional distance: Strengthening the tie between new institutional theory and international management. *Strategic Organization, 7*(3), 1–10.

Porter, M. (1998). *On Competition.* Boston: Harvard Business School Press.

Puffer, M. S., Mccarthy, D. J., & Boisot, M. (2010). Entrepreneurship in Russia and China: The impact of formal institutional voids. *Entrepreneurship: Theory and Practice, 34*(3), 441–467.

Reinhart, C. M., & Rogoff, K. S. (2010). Growth in a time of debt (digest summary). *American Economic Review, 100*(2), 573–578.

Ritchie, B. K. (2010). *Systemic vulnerability and sustainable economic growth: Skills and upgrading in Southeast Asia.* Cheltenham: Edward Elgar Publishing.

Roztocki, N., & Weistroffer, H. R. (2004). Evaluating information technology investments in developing economies using activity-based costing. *The Electronic Journal of Information Systems in Developing Countries, 19*(2), 1–6.

Roztocki, N., & Weistroffer, H. R. (2008). Information technology in transition economies. *Journal of Global Information Technology Management, 11*(4), 1–8.

Samoilenko, S., & Osei-Bryson, K. M. (2008). Determining strategies for telecoms to improve efficiency in the production of revenues: An empirical investigation in the context of transition economies. *Journal of Global Information Technology Management, 11, 7*, 56–75.

Schwab, K. (2010). *The global competitiveness report.* Geneva: World Economic Forum.

Scott, W. R. (1995). *Institutions and organizations.* Thousand Oaks: Sage.

Siegel, J. (2007). Contingent political capital and international alliances: Evidence from South Korea. *Administrative Science Quarterly, 52*(4), 621–666.

Stajano, A. (2009). Competitiveness of the European economy. In *Research, quality, competitiveness* (pp. 35–125). New York: Springer US.

Svejnar, J. (2002). Transition economies: Performance and challenges. *Journal of Economic Perspectives, 16*(1), 3–26.

132 M. DEL GIUDICE

Van Agtmael, A. W. (1984). *Emerging securities markets: Investment banking opportunities in the developing world*. London: Euromoney Publications.

Walumbwa, F. O., & Lawler, J. J. (2003). Building effective organizations: Transformational leadership, collectivist orientation, work-related attitudes and withdrawal behaviours in three emerging economies. *International Journal of Human Resource Management, 14*(7), 1083–1101.

Whitley, R. (Ed.). (1992). *European business systems: Firms and markets in their national contexts*. London/Newbury Park: Sage.

Wilson, D., & Purushothaman, R. (2003). *Dreaming with BRICs: The path to 2050* (Vol. 99). New York: Goldman, Sachs & Company.

Wright, M., Filatotchev, I., Hoskisson, R. E., & Peng, M. W. (2005). Strategy research in emerging economies: Challenging the conventional wisdom*. *Journal of Management Studies, 42*(1), 1–33.

Young, M. N., Peng, M. W., Ahlstrom, D., Bruton, G. D., & Jiang, Y. (2008). Corporate governance in emerging economies: A review of the principal–principal perspective. *Journal of Management Studies, 45*(1), 196–220.

CHAPTER 5

Business Groups in the Emerging Markets

5.1 Business Groups in the World

The prevalent organizational form in most **emerging markets** is **business groups.** (Yiu et al. 2005, p. 183)

In emerging markets, business groups share specific characteristics with groups present in the rest of the world, but also vary in terms of dimension, structure and ownership (Khanna and Yafeh 2005; Lins and Servaes 2002; Silva et al. 2006; Hoskisson et al. 2000; Guillen 2000; Khanna 2000; Khanna and Rivkin 2001; Khanna and Palepu 2000; Granovetter 1994). Khanna and Yafeh (2007) propose a taxonomy of groups in emerging economies, paying particular attention to two aspects overlooked in much of the literature: the circumstances in which the groups start and historical proof about some questions dealt with in recent studies. They claim that the business groups are responses to different economic conditions and, from a social point of view, some can be considered "parasites" and others "paragons". An analysis of a number of emerging economies (Brazil, Chile, China, India, Indonesia, South Korea, Mexico, Pakistan, Thailand, etc.) found a notable presence of diversified groups operating in non-correlated sectors. They are composed of juridically independent enterprises, linked either by relationships of an ownership character (equity) or informally (family). Table 5.1 suggests that, in all the countries for which data is available, the fraction of businesses classified by national sources as belonging to a group is quite substantial (about a fifth in Chile and two-thirds in

© The Author(s) 2017
M. Del Giudice, *Understanding Family-Owned Business Groups,*
DOI 10.1007/978-3-319-42243-5_5

133

134 M. DEL GIUDICE

Indonesia). The authors also indicate that, in almost all the emerging markets, affiliated enterprises tend to be relatively large and economically important. The main affiliate's system of connections with other group members is an essential means to update and improve continuously the affiliate's skills, practice and ideas. Furthermore, intragroup networks from which the ability to build R&D gains momentum are distinguished by a series of ties with integrative content and adequate network densities of particular kinds of connections. A group affiliate can benefit from the most significant innovative advantages related to its network ties, if it plays an important role in the purchaser-supplier network and is embedded in a dense director network and a sparse equity network. Business groups in the world act as internal capital markets, submitted by a high level of government intervention and an underdeveloped financial market. Business groups are able to support firm members to overcome constraints in raising equity. Compared to state-owned firms, business groups are more likely to support high-risk investments among private firms. Especially under the heading, country, Table 5.1 shows that the role of business groups in developing economies is focused primarily on risk sharing among affiliated firms, but according to Khanna and Yafeh (2007), we are capable of demonstrating that business group affiliation has a relative impact on firm profitability, especially for countries where there is a strong presence of state control.

In general, the business groups vary considerably based on the form they take: some are extremely diversified, while others are more concentrated; some groups have notable vertical integration and infra-group exchanges, others less so; involvement in banking and financial services distinguishes further group typologies. Some of these diversities are illustrated in Table 5.1, which shows partial data on the level of diversification, vertical integration and participation in financial companies, in business groups in nine emerging markets.[1]

The study finds a low degree of ownership concentration within firms affiliated to larger and corporate groups. At the same time, the affiliation to a group seems not to affect the diversification performance relationship. This leads us to confirm heterogeneity between business group and ownership structure.

Groups in Chile, for example, are more diversified than those in South Korea, which in turn are more diversified than groups in Taiwan; business groups from the Philippines have greater vertical integration than Indian groups and are more involved in financial services than groups in Thailand.

BUSINESS GROUPS IN THE EMERGING MARKETS 135

Table 5.1 Heterogeneity of groups in the world

Country	Group diversification	Group vertical integration	Group assets in financial firms
Brazil	1.4	0.04	N/A
Chile	5.1	0.06	0.24
India	4.2	0.04	0.05
Indonesia	2.1	0.04	0.45
South Korea	1.7	0.04	N/A
Mexico	2.7	0.02	0.05
Philippines	3.1	0.08	0.60
Taiwan	1.6	0.02	0.01
Thailand	3.5	0.04	0.35

Source: Khanna and Yafeh (2007)

Passing from structure to ownership and control, it is possible to show that some business groups are vertically controlled (pyramidal groups), while others are horizontally controlled through cross-participation (Karnani 2007; Prahalad 2005). The level of involvement of families varies greatly according to the aggregations. On a final note, in some countries, business groups enjoying close relationships with the government represent an important political force while, in others, the relationships between groups and government tend to be more turbulent.

Empirically, the ubiquity and the diversity of business groups outside the USA and the UK make the study of this organizational form fascinating and lay the foundations for new studies in various fields of the economy. Besides, comparative study of groups in emerging markets could bring clarity to some not dissimilar economic phenomena in developed markets.

Investigations on groups are common to the history of business, in which the unit of analysis is typically the history of a group (Roberts 1973) or of groups in a single country (Amsden 1989). Even if extended, the literature on business groups still leaves a lot of interesting questions without a reply. Despite the scarcity of data and econometric proofs regarding the origins of business groups, historical evidence in emerging countries suggests that such aggregations not only respond to the environment of reference, but also that they form and influence it.

In general, the background in which business groups form, in response to the economic and institutional contexts where they operate, is the fruit of the work of Akoi (2001) or Grief (2006), who stress that institutions should

136   M. DEL GIUDICE

be analyzed within a particular economic context. Since groups start for different reasons and in different settings, Khanna and Yafeh (2007) claim that their impact on social well-being is ambiguous, even though much of the existing literature suggests that they reduce economic well-being: groups can play a positive role, bridging institutional gaps, but may also be damaging for social well-being because of rent seeking[2] or monopoly power. Therefore, the verdict is not clear, as to the extent that groups must be considered "paragons" or "parasites", and the response may vary from country to country, from group to group and from time period to time period.

5.2   FAMILY GROUP VERSUS NON-FAMILY GROUP

Another classification criterion for business groups, based on ownership and control, regards the role of the family in the evolution and performance of the groups themselves.

On this issue, there have been many studies that admit an initial hypothesis: family-managed groups represent the most common organizational form in countries with scarce legal norms since the relationships with external members lead to higher costs. In some cases, even though it is not possible to improve their economic efficiency, these groups continue to exist for social reasons concerning the family.

Studies of La Porta et al. (1999) provided proofs about the relationships between the family, the prevalence of business groups and economic institutions. These register the elevated presence of family businesses (not necessarily groups) in countries where administration is difficult.

Using data about the largest business groups and individual enterprises in 40 countries, Fogel (2006) also suggests that family ownership is more common in economies with poor institutions. Analyzing these results, it emerges that family relationships and other links facilitate economic transactions and, more in general, that the groups are networks based on trust relationships that compensate for the incompleteness of contracts (Granovetter 2005). On the other hand, family ownership and control also represent the cause of economic and institutional underdevelopment (Morck et al. 2000).

In addition, there is a series of studies that report the prevalence of family groups in specific countries. Chung and Mahmood (2006) concentrate their studies on groups in Taiwan, showing a notable presence of family participation and involvement in management and a similar presence of pyramidal structures aimed at maintaining family control within the groups (Bianco and Nicodano 2006; Morck 2005; Morck and Yeung 2004; Gonenc et al. 2007). These concerns were raised by a number of government reports, and in particular that by Hazari (1966), which showed that entire sectors of the economy are widely controlled by a few large pyramidal groups (Morck 2005, p. 164). A common feature of businesses in Asia is pyramiding. This is particularly true in the case of China, where a single family, sometimes together with other family conglomerates, controls large businesses (Bebchuk et al. 1999).

Tsui-Auch (2006) suggests that about a third of the leading business groups in Singapore are family controlled, while the remaining two-thirds are connected to government. Family participation is often above 50% and the involvement of the family in business management is extremely high: in nine out of ten groups the president or the CEO is a family member. In Malaysia, 35 out of 50 groups are family owned, even though the number fell after the Asian financial crisis of 1997 (Gomez 2006); as in Singapore, the remaining non-family groups are connected to government. It is highly probable that, during a financial crisis, the priority of internal governance structure is altered due to the fact that principal-principal contrasts become the main issue at stake. In fact, firm value is often destroyed when minority shareholders are expropriated by firms with family CEOs, an event that is quite likely to occur in case of an economic shock (Jiang and Peng 2011, p. 33).

In addition to studies on the prevalence of family business groups in emerging markets, further research has been carried out to understand the influence that family businesses exert on growth and on the behavior of the groups themselves. The groups are seen as family organizations which have objectives connected to the social milieu (Bahl 1995; Dobbin 2007).

Besides economics and finance, the groups have attracted a lot of academic interest in the field of sociology, where they are seen as networks of social relevance and not only economic entities (Freyer 1992; Shah et al. 2001).

The importance of the non-economic functions of groups is confirmed by the diversity of structures that, together with factors like, succession, pride and national ideology, plays a fundamental role for groups in differing settings. The norms that regulate commercial exchanges, rather than the quest for a rational response to the markets and the shortcomings of economic institutions, create differences within the structures of the groups (Feenstra and Hamilton 2006).

Passing from sociology to economics, the issues concerning family businesses raised by the literature (like succession, the differences between enterprises controlled by the founder and enterprises controlled by the successor/s, the importance of family control and the trend toward using groups as a form of debt financing) and the impact that these have on performance seem relevant for understanding the connection between families and business groups. Such issues were examined systematically in a study by Bertrand et al. (2004) concerning groups of Thai enterprises. Using data of 70 groups, it was shown that the structure of the group is connected to the history of the family and the number of sons or brothers of the founder. In addition, Bertrand attempted to identify relationships between diversification and growth and the family, and to connect group performance to intra-family feuds.

Other studies identify problems connected to the family determining the structure of groups in Indonesia and describe family links and the dynamics of succession in Chinese groups and in those of other Asian countries. Chang (2006) reports the rapid decline in participation of the founding families of Hyundai and SK, while in other large family groups, the participants have remained stable. Chang and Shin (2005) show that the businesses of groups characterized by high family participation do not register better performances than other businesses affiliated to the same groups, in contrast to what is to be expected if tunneling[3] in the name of the controlling family takes place.

As a source of financing, family business groups tend to recur to debt rather than using equity, reflecting a desire not to dilute control of the business. So, in contrast to the possible negative effects on the share market, a lot of groups are great borrowers and important clients of banks. During the 1950s and 1960s, the Philippines were among the Southeast Asian economies with the highest growth rate and degree of industrialization. During the 1960s, the number of private banks increased considerably, and many of them became the central reference point of these family conglomerates (Pinches 1992, p. 390). However, it is not clear whether this trend is more pronounced in family controlled groups or in single family businesses.

Research about groups is considered highly promising, both with respect to the prevalence of family controlled groups in different settings and with respect to the relationships between the family, efficiency and performance of groups. A comparison between family controlled groups, government controlled groups (in China and Singapore) and groups controlled by a number of families (as has been happening for some time at LG in South

BUSINESS GROUPS IN THE EMERGING MARKETS **139**

Korea or like the joint venture between the Koc group and the Sabanci group in Turkey) would be very interesting. However, analyzing groups from this point of view is difficult for two main reasons. In the first place business performance may also influence the stability of the family pact and, therefore, the structure of the family interest (Bertrand et al. 2004). In the second phase, "equity contracts" may not be the most significant contracts in the system, where administration relationships predominate (Khanna and Thomas 2004).

5.3 THE ROLE OF FAMILY CONGLOMERATES IN EMERGING MARKETS

Although the role of small-sized firms had always been highly acknowledged, there was a duality in the Indian economy. Even if there were a huge number of small shopkeepers and local businesses, the economy was still monopolized by a limited number of enormous private sector conglomerates, such as the Tata and Birla groups, and several nationalized companies (Dossani and Kenney 2002, p. 230).

Family conglomerates are important actors in the scenario of emerging economies and are excellent partners for western companies. Kim et al. (2004) show the evolutionary models of family conglomerates and delineate the main driving forces of their growth, development, expansion and internationalization. Known as *chaebols* in South Korea, *business houses* in India, *holding companies* in Turkey and *grupos* in Latin America, family conglomerates represent a unique typology of aggregation in each country. Among family conglomerates in emerging markets, we can include groups that have reached very large size thresholds: for instance, Tata Motors, based in India, owner of the Land Rover and Jaguar brands, or alternatively the Korean groups, Hyundai and Daewoo in the automotive sector and LG and Samsung in the telecommunications and media market.

The role of such groups is substantial. For example, the 30 main conglomerates in South Korea generate more than 46% of the earnings of the sector and 47% of the entire national economy. Nevertheless, with regard to South Korea, most research has not considered one significant element: the employer role of the family conglomerates, the *chaebol* (Leggett and Bamber 1996). Andrade et al. (2001) describe the *grupos* as "the backbone of the economies in Latin America". In emerging markets, large family firms play the role of protagonists. In Latin America, they are called "grupos empresariales", meaning family conglomerates (Bianchi 2009).

In Latin America, most of the television networks are not subsidiaries of publicly traded corporations, but of private companies often entirely owned by a single individual or family. Among the latter, it is possible to mention RCN and Caracol in Colombia, TV Globo in Brazil and Venevisión in Venezuela: all these are owned by family conglomerates.

The origins and growth of such aggregations can be attributed to special relationships with the governments and with the economy itself.

Rather, the long-lasting presence of this specific type of business organization, and in particular specialized family businesses and modern family conglomerates, may be viewed as proof of its efficiency and rationality compared to a formalized institutional structure, and not as a failure (Suehiro and Wailerdsak 2004, p. 91).

Some aspects of the *family conglomerates* contribute to their relative success: the rapid decision making process, the strong shared values, the high level of loyalty of the workers, the low management turnover. Equally important is their deep understanding of local markets and consumers preferences, as well as close connections with the agencies of government and political parties that translate into strong competitive advantages.

Professionalization is an urgent need for family conglomerates in the Gulf Cooperation Council (GCC).

According to a report by Booz & Co, the management consulting division of PWC, it is necessary that the family conglomerates in the GCC redefine their focus, if they want to survive the next generational transfer.

GCC family firms are challenged by decreasing growth, also because of foreign competition in the area. Their lack of focus is due to what Booz & Co describes as "restless entrepreneur syndrome". The oil boom in Saudi Arabia and Kuwait had created new opportunities for family firms, but many founders and second-generation leaders accessed new industries randomly, avoiding rationalization and institutionalization of pre-existing businesses.

The report reveals that 48% of family conglomerates were present in more than five sectors, and an additional 40% in three or four. Only

(*continued*)

> 12% operated in one or two sectors. Between 2003 and 2007, GCC family firms concentrated on one or a few related sectors outperformed the others by 5.5% on a yearly basis.
>
> There will be an increasing difficulty in managing the widest range of interests, especially when ownership is transferred to the extended family. Moreover, at times, even if the original business is no longer profitable, divestment is not planned due to sentimental attachment.
>
> Thus, conditions for the survival of GCC family businesses are as follows: strong investment in the development of formalized management structures, hiring of external managers and divestment of underperforming units. The entire process should be overlooked by a change agent, who can be either a family member or a person close to the family.
>
> The annual growth rate of a typical GCC family business should be at least 18% in order to sustain the current standard of wealth across generations, but the creation of a family office could help lower this pressure.

Emerging markets have elevated growth potential, which is not only an opportunity but also a risk for western businesses. Their attractiveness resides not only in possession of raw materials and low labor costs, but also in their capacity to generate earnings. Emerging markets are not only providers but also purchasers of goods and services. These markets, as was previously stressed, are also characterized by high risks associated to inadequate infrastructure, poorly developed distribution systems, limited channels of communication, lack of regulatory discipline, market failures and political and economic instability. As a consequence strategic alliances are an important means of entry that can lower such obstacles. In fact, through alliances, western businesses are able to share risks and resources, acquire knowledge and obtain access to the emerging markets (Kock and Guillén 2001).

Typical family conglomerates are owned and controlled by a family (Ben-Porath 1980) and have a single founder who dominates, even if other family members may take on the role of directors in the different business areas. Usually, the family owns the majority of the controlling rights, therefore, family conglomerates differ from business groups, which are not necessarily owned by a family and can include businesses linked through personal relationships deriving from similar backgrounds. Family conglomerates also differ from family businesses despite having analogous characteristics: both are owned by a family and inherit similar behavior, like leadership and entrepreneurship. However, family conglomerates are vast networks of the most diversified businesses and have a greater dimension than family businesses. They invest in more sectors, use both internally generated capital and taking on debt (government loans) as sources of financing and their economic impact (employment, turnover, technology etc.) is much more consistent. Besides, although the members of the family may effectively work in the conglomerate, they are usually only members of the board.

The contributions of family conglomerates to national economies are noteworthy (Granovetter 1995; Kock and Guillen 2001; Nachum 1999). For example, the conglomerates in South Korea make significant contributions in terms of employment, financial tax revenue, generation of foreign currency and general economic growth (Hwang et al. 2000). To enter into new businesses, Hyundai, Samsung and Koc have all benefitted from the name of their group, obtaining more advantages. The positive reputation or image that surrounds the brand, even if limited to the local market, often symbolizes quality and consumer satisfaction (Khanna and Palepu 1999) and makes it competitive with well-established multinational brands (Prahalad and Lieberthal 1998). On the contrary, it is expensive for western businesses to build credible brand identities in markets with poor communications structures.

5.3.1 *The Formation of Family Conglomerates*

In many of the rapidly developing economies worldwide, and in particular in China, Brazil and India, the evolution of businesses has been distinguished by some interesting features. One of the most significant characteristics has been the development and success of business groups, which are often conglomerated family firms capable of developing precious, unique and inimitable competences in these environments, for example, swift diversification into unrelated product lines and repeated industry entry (Yaprak et al. 2006, p. 276).

A lot of factors seem to influence the formation of family conglomerates in emerging markets, but the most significant are the role of the founder and the specific characteristics of emerging countries.

Suehiro and Wailerdsak (2004, p. 85) investigated the way family businesses, before the financial shock, acted on their organizational structures in order to achieve the resources they needed to fund their growth both through financial institutions and the capital market, while the family never lost ownership and control. It is important to stress that the consequence is not the establishment of pure public companies. The founders and their families retain control by managing their businesses on a daily basis; they address policies and strategies, while retrieving new financial resources by using different instruments.

The founder has a predominant role within the family business or group. Within family businesses, founder families have a dominant role with regard to the set of decisions that deeply characterize the organization. The features of the founder family will probably have an impact on the effectiveness of those decisions, and hence on the institutionalization of the firm (Alpay et al. 2008, p. 436).

The culture, values and long-term objectives of the founder have a significant influence on the members of the family, their behavior and the relationships they have with the enterprise (or group) and the surrounding environment.

However, the desire to maintain control of the enterprise (or group) may also lead to the loss of interesting investment opportunities, lower growth or the lack of expansion into other markets. If the founders did not manage to reveal the true spirit underpinning the principles and practices they imposed, the descendants who are now in charge will probably consider them as a fact and follow them precisely. In this case, the firm is necessarily limited by the founder's legacy, and this determines a lower responsiveness to change, with the consequence of affecting business performance in a negative way (Venter and Kruger 2004, p. 5).

The "founder effect" expresses the complex of positive effects that are produced on management, organization and business performance that are attributable to the presence of the founder as the main shareholder and/or as a subject involved personally in the management of the business (Kelly et al. 2000; Horgos 2013). These positive effects would seem to derive from the ability of the founder to impress, on the business management, a winning entrepreneurial spirit based on intuition, talent and the abilities of an individual able to set up a business and make it competitive (Hewitt et al. 2012).

Not only this, the presence of the founder makes a decisive contribution to the formation of what has been defined as "culture", while the founder is

144 M. DEL GIUDICE

probably also the family member that most incisively carries out the functions of *resource provision* attributable to the family.

For the specific characteristics of emerging markets, every country is a unique environment, depending on the evolutionary phase of the economy, the political system, the influence of government, the work ethic and natural and financial resources (Kock and Guillen 2001; Nachum 1999). Some of these factors can cause decay of family businesses, while others may favor their growth (Khanna and Palepu 1999), according to the evolutionary phase that the business itself is passing through.

5.3.2 Drivers of Growth, Development and Expansion

The main drivers of growth, development and expansion for each evolutionary state (introduction, growth and maturity) of family conglomerates are outlined in Kim et al. (2004).

Family business groups dominate the economic scene of the most important emerging and developed economies as well. They represent excellent partners for largest corporations and Western companies. Nine critical factors seem to characterize the life-cicle process of development for family conglomerates. In this process, particular significance is ascribed to the role of entrepreneur, the country of origin factors and the venture capital contribution. If in the early stages of start-up, what is important are the innovative capacity and the entrepreneur's tenacity, as we start to growth and maturity stages, becoming more and more important are two other factors. In particular, the growth needs to be supported by a strong equity and financial capability, fundamental for supporting innovative and extensive investments. Conversely, in the maturity phase, the presence of specific domestic factors which support the strategic plan for a long period is necessary.

The following sections are organized in chronological order, that is, on the basis of the drivers that are relevant in the different phases of the development of conglomerates (Kandemir et al. 2004; Merchant 2007).

Early Mover Advantage
In every country, three evolutionary phases characterize conglomerates: establishment, growth and maturity. In the first stage, when it is time to decide whether to invest and establish a new business, it is important that conglomerates comprehend what consumers really want and need (Kurtović et al. 2013, p. 113).

BUSINESS GROUPS IN THE EMERGING MARKETS   145

In the initial phase, when it is necessary to make new investments and create new businesses, family conglomerates have to understand the needs and the expectations of consumers. They serve the local market, build strong brand equity before their competitors do and acquire market share. For example, Koc was the first producer of automobiles, washing machines and refrigerators in Turkey and played an important role in the industrialization of the country and in the development of these sectors. Hyundai Group, one of the main South Korean automobile producers, has the largest share in the country's automobile market (Guillén 2001). The pioneering and innovative role of their own enterprises establishes market position for a lot of family conglomerates that wish to expand into various sectors (Vecchi et al. 2014). Typical sectors for expansion are automobiles, electronics, informatics, construction, drinks, retail sales, etc.

Government Protection

In emerging markets, government is strongly involved in business decisions (Granovetter 1995; Kock and Guillen 2001; Steers et al. 1989; Wade 1990) and carries out a significant role for family conglomerates (as happened for the Siam Cement Group in Thailand and for Salim and Astra in Indonesia), especially in the growth phase of the business and less so in the initial and mature phases. For example, in the commercial banking sector after the war, a sort of process of "Mexicanization" occurred, when, with the help of state forces, foreign control was eliminated and powerful family conglomerates or holding groups were established around domestic private banks (Marois 2007, p. 5).

In South Africa, conglomerates have been unbundled, in part due to the economic and political pressure aiming at encouraging the creation of firms controlled by black people. Concurrently, pyramid structures are considered a way black business groups can control firms (Bebchuk et al. 1999, p. 35). Government protection can take on different forms: special loans, subventions, barriers to entry for competitors and tax incentives (e.g. the Indian government regulates prices, the importation of raw materials and business closures). In some Latin American countries such as Brazil, Mexico, Argentina, Colombia and Venezuela, a number of conglomerates that controlled a series of media outlets gave politicians the advantage of having to collude with a few important actors in order to gain absolute favorable coverage.

Together with the few large family conglomerates, the presence of the state in the economy is pervasive, and there is often a large state sector. The state usually owns the whole infrastructure and most of the heavy industry and the financial system.

Such protections tend to fall off when the enterprises enter into new business sectors.

Foreign Alliances

The internationalization of family businesses is influenced by the owning and managing families that act in a way that involves paternalism (when it is the founder who rules), nepotism (when relatives are favored) and personalism (when decisions are made by a single individual) (Kansikas et al. 2014).

The moment when a family business decides to internationalize depends on several factors: when external managers and board members trigger it, when new generations are born and network-relationships develop or when the "liability of outsidership" in relation to foreign networks is overcome. Social Emotional Wealth (SEW) preservation tendencies are guided by the desire of family principals to address the issue of risk related to their family assets; if they believe such a risk is high, they are willing to internationalize the company, so they do not have to limit their ambitions. These preservation tendencies also have an influence on the way the internationalization process of family businesses is carried out. Research shows that such a process is slower compared to non-family firms, but in the long term, the degree reached is almost the same. The explanation is simple: family principals are probably reluctant to create relationships in foreign networks and require higher levels of knowledge before opening up to international markets (Pukall and Calabrò 2014, p. 123).

International alliances are very relevant in the growth and mature phases of the business (Cavusgil et al. 2014): the need for expansion, access to resources and organizational learning lead to the formation of joint ventures and licensing agreements with western businesses (Kock and Guillen 2001). In the mature phase, they tend to make alliances aimed at improving managerial skills and at competing with enterprises that are more sophisticated from a management point of view. In the initial phase of the alliance, the conglomerates provide their partners with sales networks, information about the market, knowledge of institutions relating to local law and linguistic competence. Western partners also need local know-how to increase their own competitive strength. Through alliances, the businesses can co-invent and co-produce a product, uniting their forces and reducing the costs for the participants in such a way as to provide access to new business opportunities for all.

Expansion into Non-correlated Business Sectors

Businesses grow in different ways according to the entrepreneurial orientation of the owners, the business philosophy of the founder, financial solvency and the market of reference. In the initial phase, family conglomerates tend to implement strategies that focus on their core business, while in the growth and mature phases, they decide to expand into other business sectors. Diversification strategy has the objective of developing the competitive presence of an enterprise in a multitude of not necessarily correlated sectors, delineating useful organizational and operative conditions to that end. Therefore, a diversified enterprise makes a significant share of its own business volume in sectors differing from that of its origins which, in any case, is still considered its main sector. Sectors for expansion may be more or less pertinent to the core business of the enterprise.

Western companies and trade found in business conglomerates the main means to operate. Together with the state, they controlled the domestic market with regard to the access of foreign technology, new products and modern production. In Turkey, the conglomerates and essentially based in Istanbul adopted a policy of investment diversification into a number of industries and held most of the private industrial capital of the entire economy (Özcan and Turunç 2011, p. 63).

There are, therefore, two types of diversification: conglomerated, radically distancing from the core business; and correlated, in strategic vicinity to the core business. Some of the most important television networks, such as RCN in Colombia and Televisa in Mexico, initially were only radio broadcasters and still have significant holdings in this market. In other cases, such as the Argentinian Clarin and the Brazilian Globo, the first step was publishing, later followed by the diversification into both radio and television.

The objectives followed by family conglomerates that adopt such strategies are: growth, reduction of risk and increase in profitability. A strategy of diversification can be implemented in different ways: through internal development, through acquisitions, fusions and alliances. In their research on Chilean business groups, Khanna and Palepu (2000) hypothesize a curvilinear relationship between diversification and business value, the result showing interaction due to both the benefits and the costs of diversification. It has been shown that the profitability of enterprises increases at the same

148   M. DEL GIUDICE

rate as the level of production diversification, excepting a sudden decrease on overshooting a certain threshold.

For example, when there is an increase in the scale of financial institutions, the financial conglomerates can reinvest in other sectors of the economy, where income becomes increasingly distributed unequally due to the exercise of monopolistic power (Dar-Yeh and Wei-Hsiung 2007, 23). However, institutional shortcomings may also negatively influence such results.

Strong Work Ethic of Employees
A constant for South Korean family conglomerates seems to be the work ethic of their employees. For example, they are disposed to do overtime to reach the objectives assigned in a short period. Biggart (1991) describes this phenomenon as "institutionalized patrimonialism". This positive work ethic has contributed to conglomerates in most Asian countries.

According to research by Alpay et al. (2008, p. 445), measuring of qualitative performance is favorably affected by objectivity and fairness in employee relationships, and in particular correct evaluation, esteem and wage. This aspect of institutionalization enhances employees' predisposition toward the firm and hence behavior in the workplace. Thus, qualitative performance measures such as employee and customer satisfaction are favorably influenced by those positive attitudes and behaviors.

Competitive Intensity
In the growth and mature phases, family conglomerates have to satisfy even higher expectations of their clients, entering into other sectors and developing new technologies to beat the national and foreign competition (Kock and Guillen 2001). They implement diversification and internationalization strategies to obtain greater competitive advantage in the global economy. Having become part of the LG group, GoldStar enjoyed a strong competitive position in the electronics sector in South Korea until Daewoo and Samsung entered the market. Later, the fusion of GoldStar with Lucky was implemented so as to penetrate the North American market and in this way to contrast its competitors.

In the end, there is a relationship between conglomerates, government ties and market leadership. Competitive advantage is what businesses obtain from these three elements. Conglomerates have solid government ties and often have a strong presence in the national market. However, this set of relationships may even function in the opposite direction. For instance, a position of market leadership in an economic sector may be exploited to form government ties in order to achieve a licensing advantage and then proceed to development and expansion into diversified conglomerates (Kiattichai Kalasin 2011).

Access to Sources of Capital

Sources of capital play an important role in the formation of conglomerates, including government loans at very favorable interest rates (the result of close relationships with government) and special investment opportunities (e.g. terrain and/or real estate investments with very high annual earnings). All the family conglomerates analyzed in South Korea, as well as Koc and Sabanci in Turkey, Vitro in Mexico and Astra in Indonesia, have their own "financial arms" (e.g. insurance, banks and real estate intermediaries) that are sources of capital (Granovetter 1995). In the Philippines, commercial banks have a dominant role in the financial industry and at the same time are mainly owned by the diversified family conglomerates that continue to play a leading role in the entire economy (Hutchcroft 1999, p. 168). Conglomerates have different types of available financial resources, even though it is not always possible to identify the sources of capital for each conglomeration. Besides, the capital markets of each country contribute in various ways to the formation and growth of family conglomerates. Because of the less developed financial markets and the weaknesses of the institutions, family conglomerates need access to capital at a reasonable cost (Hitt et al. 2000). For instance, conglomerate expansion was made easier by bank-dominated financing and endemic moral hazard. Nowadays, the fact that banks, businesses connected to the government and deep-rooted conglomerates contract with one another leads to loss of creativity and capital deprivation of enterprises that may have good perspectives but do not have a well-established network of relations (Carney and Gedajlovic 2000, pp. 271–272).

Internationalization

Mature businesses try to use business opportunities outside the national market, undertaking a pathway that leads to internationalization (Kroeber 2006). With regard to such strategy, approaches diverge from enterprise to enterprise; in fact, some face new markets in a very rapid manner and others follow a more gradual approach. According to the nature of the company and the sector type in which the enterprise operates, internationalization is seen in different ways in different evolutionary phases. Despite companies

150   M. DEL GIUDICE

which are born "global" and internationalized, most of the companies faces a gradual and sequential process of expansion, especially if we consider a family-owned approach (Kim et al. 2004). Thus, depending on the nature of the company and the type of industry in which it is engaged, some will do business abroad in the introduction stage, and others will wait until the growth or maturity stage.

In the introduction stage, the principal activity involves importation of raw materials, followed in the growth stage by technology transfer, licensing and franchising from a foreign business partner, as a a consequence of developments in the domestic market (Sarkar and Cavusgil 1996). Late in the maturity stage, the conglomerate's structure may increase the level of resources committed abroad and change the mode of market servicing. In these cases, the switch from buying to making, through joint venture agreements, acquisitions and direct investments, becomes a crucial decision.

The choice of entry strategy must be made adopting a long-term perspective, not a short-term one. Enterprises invest in external production for various reasons that can be mainly traced to the following: extraction of raw materials, producing at low cost and serving the local market.

In the initial phase the main activity concerns the importation of raw materials, followed by the transfer of technology, licensing, franchising and by joint ventures typical of the growth phase (Sarkar and Cavusgil 1996). Johanson and Wiedersheim-Paul (1975) claim that internationalization is a consequence of the evolution of the market through which the family conglomerates accumulate skills that favor the transfer of technologies (Kock and Guillen 2001). The CEO of Vitro claims that international partnerships and exports helped the business to grow more rapidly and are crucial for future growth.

In the mature phase the conglomerates, rather than exporting products or giving up know-how through licensing, franchising and contract manufacturing, can decide to be present in a market with their own production establishments, their own distribution networks and their own research centers. Their presence is effectuated through targeted investments that give the enterprise management control of the operational unit. Hyundai, Daewoo and Samsung have a larger number of entirely controlled businesses in the foreign markets than Ayala has in the Philippines, Astra has in Indonesia and Siam Cement has in Thailand. Direct management of the retail distribution networks is aimed at avoiding the use of intermediaries, thereby maintaining profit margins but, above all, aims at creating a direct relationship with clients. Knowing directly what consumers ask for and

BUSINESS GROUPS IN THE EMERGING MARKETS 151

managing the accessory services to sales directly is an enormous competitive advantage. Direct management of research centers generally has three main purposes: to better understand what the market wants, to accelerate the time-to-market and to exploit the skills of local technicians and researchers at a cost generally much lower than that in developed markets.

Brennan (2013) thoroughly examined the limited research regarding the matter, and was able to show that, while Family Business Groups (FBG) internationalization strategies are affected by ownership and by the type of ties in so many different ways across clusters; the other key dimensions that distinguish FBGs tend to vary in accordance with them. Cultural embedment and cluster-dependency characterize those dimensions. To sum up, it can be stated that, according to Brennan's conclusions, there is a strict relationship between the evolution of family firms and their local economic context.

In Brazil, companies such as Camargo Corrèa and Odebrecht were leaders in carrying out projects that were essential for the expansion of the national economy; besides, in recent years, the state has considerably supported groups such as Gerdau and JBS-Friboi in their internalization strategies (Fernández Pérez 2016, p. 119).

Technology

Technology is not a main driver in the initial and growth phases of family conglomerates, because the initial focus is on production capacity, finalized to satisfying client demand. When there are only a few sources of capital available, new technology will be financed only in relation to the requirements of previously established social interests. This explains the disappointing levels of social spending on information technology and education in Latin America (Root 2006, p. 26).

When enterprises enter a foreign market, however, there is greater pressure, which brings about the adoption of new technologies so as to increase efficiency and to stay competitive. Family conglomerates look for knowhow and technology through licensing, agreements and joint ventures with foreign partners able to offer the most up-to-date technology. In the mature phase, family conglomerates, after having accumulated greater knowledge and developed their own research and development centers, can initiate projects characterized by a high level of technology (Amsden and Hikino 1994; Kock and Guillen 2001; Kurtovic et al. 2013). Businesses like Alfa, Koc and Mahindra & Mahindra approach the challenges of competitors through rapid modernization and expansion of their production

152   M. DEL GIUDICE

technologies. Samsung and Hyundai, on the other hand, concentrate on the high-tech sector.

Samsung has undergone an evolution that has led the company to overcome the family conglomerate structure. In the 1990s, thanks to Lee Kun-hee, its second-generation chairman, who started hiring foreigners and introduced a system of wages based on merit, Samsung's culture became globalized. Samsung has become much more concentrated if compared to the sprawling Japanese corporate model that initially influenced the company. Samsung Electronics, in particular, today represents about 75% of the group's market value, while half way through the 1990s it accounted for less than 50%. Also its profits are highly concentrated. In the first quarter of 2014, 76% of Samsung Electronics' operating profits came from mobile phones and tablets. (http://www.economist.com/news/special-report/21602829-state-firms-and-family-conglomerates-are-asias-favourite-kinds-companies-both-must)

With regard to vertical diversification, the GCC countries have heavily invested in refining, aluminum smelting, fertilizers and petrochemicals; in the future it would be advisable they aimed at technological transfer and upgrade, and created a network of connections with the entire economy. Also, conservative family conglomerates understood how important this was and began investing in the information technology sector. By the end of the 1980s, venture capitalism industry had already grown considerably (Cherif 2016, pp. 29–31)

The transfer of technology promotes economic efficiency, favors competitiveness, develops innovations, generates competition of products in the market and can bring about a further increase in research and development activity.

5.3.3   Evolution of the Family Conglomerate

The phenomenon of family conglomerates has received relatively scarce attention on the part of business scholars. This is surprising, given their economic pre-dominion in a lot of emerging markets. Kim et al. (2004) tried to fill this lacuna in part, providing evidence on the current and future roles of such organizations. The evolution of family conglomerates in emerging markets is still subject to much debate. According to an optimistic vision, the influence of the family of the founder will remain strong because of the accumulated wealth and the power of the shareholders (Chung 2000a, b; Hwang 2000).[4]

BUSINESS GROUPS IN THE EMERGING MARKETS 153

Although ownership tends to spread, since a single person is not able to control the entire conglomerate, it is very probable that the family will continue to exercise its power through cross-investments (as has happened in the Hyundai group). However, intra-family conflicts may weaken collective ownership and threaten the survival of such family organizations. The death of the founder or the transfer of ownership to successive generations marks the passage to more professional and participatory management, often characterized by the introduction of managers, external to the family nucleus, but with greater skills, into the business. "One may speculate that the management of family conglomerates will become more participative as well as more professional" (Sahin 2011, p. 13339). For example, Koc in Turkey and Vitro in Mexico include directors of western businesses on their administration boards.

In the pessimistic view, instead, increased pressures on the part of government, inefficiencies due to the lack of competent managers and an unplanned generational handover could provoke future redimensioning of family conglomerates down to small enterprises. The family can manage conglomerates until the business does not exceed a certain size and complexity. Moreover, ownership and management, which are concepts more related to the Western culture, can be hardly distinguished by Chinese managers. This is the reason why these businesses basically avoid sectors in which various different abilities need to be integrated (Buckley 2004, p. 266).

Therefore, to survive and prosper, conglomerates must adopt stronger governance models, that plan for a regular succession of power and diversification and internationalization strategies for expansion into new markets.

A collaboration partnership between western businesses and family conglomerates could provide the best solution, so that they may reduce the risks and increase the performance. In fact, conglomerates have a lot to offer western businesses (a network of local enterprises, government contacts, knowledge of the local markets, consolidated distribution channels, an agile decision-making process), but may also earn a lot from new business opportunities and the know-how that such businesses have available.[5]

5.4 Conclusions

In the last decade, emerging economies have grown much more rapidly than developed economies, providing a fundamental contribution to the global economy.

154 M. DEL GIUDICE

Analysis of emerging markets has revealed a characteristic that these countries have in common: institutional vacuums (lack of infrastructure, lack of reliable information on demand trends, choices guided by politics and not by the economy, inefficient judicial systems). The uncertain institutional contexts inhibit business opportunities and make entrepreneurial activity more risky and complex. In this scenario, businesses aggregate to create internal markets that substitute the poorly developed external markets and invest in political relationships so as to obtain advantages independent of the institutional situation.

The large amount of empirical evidence demonstrates, therefore, the importance that informal institutions take on in emerging countries: family businesses, thanks to their opaque characteristics of corporate governance, manage to by-pass formal institutions and have greater political capacity and the capacity to seek higher earnings. However, they encounter difficulties in transforming themselves into innovative businesses and in developing superior managerial skills; groups with family management are considered networks based on a relationship of trust that compensates the incompleteness of contracts and reduces transaction costs. Despite this, it is seen that family ownership and control also represents the cause of economic and institutional underdevelopment.

From this perspective, identification of the limiting factors and the propulsive factors of efficient strategic action, urge the need for greater understanding of the mechanisms that influence business governance and, in the last analysis, the performance of enterprises (or groups).

However, the results obtained from empirical investigations cannot be considered conclusive, since, for different reasons, the evidence offered is not always in agreement on the existence of a clear and meaningful difference between family and non-family businesses (or groups).

In conclusion, it is understandable how difficult it is to make a theoretical evaluation of the effects deriving from benefits and disadvantages attributable to family businesses or to business groups, because they depend on a variable set of elements and characteristics linked to specific characteristics of each business, to the development dynamics of the sector of relevance and, naturally, in the geo-political and economic-financial context of reference.

> Every business organization has a unique set of challenges and problems. The family business is no different. Many of these problems exist in corporate business environments, but can be exaggerated in a family business.

Notes

1. Diversification of groups is measured by the number of sectors the groups operate in (two digit International Standard Industrial Classification (ISIC) classification); vertical integration is measured as follows: businesses of the group are classified into two sectors (two digit ISIC classification) and, for each pair of businesses (x, y), the fractions of entry from sector x to y and vice versa are observed. In such a model, the higher value for each pair and the mean of all the pairs of the group give the index of vertical integration for the group itself; the inclusion of financial services is measured as the fraction of all the group activities in financial companies of the group itself. For further details on these measures, see Khanna and Yafeh (2005).
2. "Rent seeking" indicates the phenomenon that takes place when an individual, organization or business seeks to gain earnings through the acquisition of economic earnings, through the manipulation or exploitation of the economic environment rather than by executing economic transactions and the production of added value.
3. The term "tunneling" became popular after the studies of Johnson, La Porta et al. (1999) and refers to the expropriation of the minority shareholders in the Czech Republic.
4. Family firms dominate some of the fastest-emerging economies, and 70% of the firms are family controlled in India, Southeast Asia and Latin America. According to a recent study by McKinsey Quarterly, over 60% of emerging market companies with revenues of more \$1bn were family controlled, directly or indirectly. The estimated value of world's biggest family groups in 2025 will be more than 40%; especially for SALA (Southeast Asia and Latin America Africa), the data are particular significant. http://www.famcap.com/articles/2015/2/3/will-family-firms-continue-to-dominate-emerging-markets
5. When we consider the reasons for the good health of family business groups, we have to consider two main reasons. Firstly, because the main conflict between principals and agents that afflict shareholder-owned corporations is quite absent, the institutional overlapping between owners and managers resolve the problems related to the governance and control of the firms. Secondly, the role of the cultures in emerging markets is fundamental to prove that cordial and convivial environments stimulate entrepreneurial aggregations within and outside of the family that can exploit economies of proximity despite a

corporation, by adhering to the local economical reality, thus better performing than one in the surroundings areas. The comparison between Asia and South America shows a strong statistical significance in order to state the impact of these two critical factors on asset allocation on the market and, then the reason for the greater rate of speed of development for emerging economies. http://www.famcap. com/articles/2015/2/3/will-family-firms-continue-to-dominate-emerging-markets

References

Alpay, G., Bodur, M., Yılmaz, C., Çetinkaya, S., & Arıkan, L. (2008). Performance implications of institutionalization process in family-owned businesses: Evidence from an emerging economy. *Journal of World Business, 43*(4), 435–448.

Amsden, A. H. (1989). *Asia's next giant: South Korea and late industrialization.* New York/Oxford: Oxford University Press.

Amsden, A. H., & Hikino, T. (1994). Project execution capability, organizational know how and conglomerate corporate growth in late industrialization. *Industrial and Corporate Change, 3*(1), 111–147.

Andrade, L. F., Barra, I. M., & Klstrodt, H. P. (2001). All in the Family. *McKinsey Quarterly, 4.*

Aoki, M. (2001). *Toward a comparative institutional analysis, Comparative institutional analysis series.* Cambridge/London: MIT Press.

Bahl, S. (1995). Whither Asian public relations. *Media Asia: An Asian Mass Communication Quarterly, 22*(3), 136–143.

Bebchuk, L., Kraakman, R., & Triantis, G. (1999). *Stock pyramids, cross-ownership, and the dual class equity: The creation and agency costs of separating control from cash flow rights* (No. w6951). Cambridge, MA: National Bureau of Economic Research.

Ben-Porath, Y. (1980). The F-connection: Families, friends, and firms and the organization of exchange. *Population and Development Review, 6*(1), 1–30.

Bertrand, M., Johnson, S., Samphantharak, K., & Schoar, A. (2004). Mixing family with business: A study of Thai business groups and the families behind them, typescript.

Bianchi, C. (2009). Retail internationalisation from emerging markets: Case study evidence from Chile. *International Marketing Review, 26*(2), 221–243.

Bianco, M., & Nicodano, G. (2006). Pyramidal groups and debt. *European Economic Review, 50*(4), 937–961.

Biggart, N. (1991). Institutionalized patrimonialism in Korean business. In C. Calhoun (Ed.), *Comparative social research, Business institution* (Vol. vol. 12). Greenwich: JAI Press.

Brennan, L. (Ed.). (2013). *Enacting globalization: Multidisciplinary perspectives on international integration.* Basingstoke: Palgrave.

BUSINESS GROUPS IN THE EMERGING MARKETS   157

Buckley, P. J. (2004). Asian network firms: An analytical framework. *Asia Pacific Business Review, 10*(3–4), 254–271.

Carney, M., & Gedajlovic, E. (2000). East Asian financial systems and the transition from investment-driven to innovation-driven economic development. *International Journal of Innovation Management, 4*(03), 253–276.

Cavusgil, S. T., Knight, G., Riesenberger, J. R., Rammal, H. G., & Rose, E. L. (2014). *International business.* Melbourne: Pearson Australia.

Chang, S. (2006). Korean business groups: The financial crisis and the restructuring of chaebols. In S. Chang (Ed.), *Business groups in East Asia: Financial crisis, restructuring, and new growth* (pp. 52–69). Oxford: Oxford University Press.

Chang, J. J.,& Shin, H. H. (2005). Does the family portfolio perform better than the group portfolio? Evidence from Korean Conglomerates. Unpublished.

Cherif, R. (2016). *Breaking the oil spell.* Washington, DC: International Monetary Fund.

Chung, C. (2000a). Corporate governance system in Korea: What questions should we ask for future recommendations? Presented to the *Transforming Korean Business and Management Culture Conference*, Michigan State University, East Lansing.

Chung, Y. P. (2000b, September). Corporate governance system in Korea: What questions should we ask for future recommendations? In *Transforming Korean Business and Management Culture Conference*, Michigan State University, East Lansing.

Chung, C., & Mahmood, I. (2006). Taiwanese business groups: Steady growth in institutional transition. In S. Chang (Ed.), *Business groups in East Asia: Financial crisis, restructuring, and new growth* (pp. 70–93). Oxford: Oxford University Press.

Dar-Yeh, H., & Wei-Hsiung, W. (2007). Financial system reform in Taiwan. *Journal of Asian Economics, 18*, 21–41.

Dobbin, F. (2007). Economic sociology. In C. D. Bryant & D. L. Peck (Eds.), *Twenty-first century sociology: A reference handbook* (pp. 319–331). Thousand Oaks: Sage.

Dossani, R., & Kenney, M. (2002). Creating an environment for venture capital in India. *World Development, 30*(2), 227–253.

Feenstra, R. C., & Hamilton, G. G. (2006). *Emergent economies, divergent paths: Economic organization and international trade in South Korea and Taiwan, Structural analysis in the social sciences series* (Vol. 29). Cambridge/New York: Cambridge University Press.

Fogel, K. (2006). Oligarchic family control, social economic outcomes, and the quality of government. *Journal of International Business Studies, 37*(5), 603–622.

Freyer, T. (1992). *Regulating big business: Antitrust in great Britain and America, 1880–1990.* Cambridge/New York: Cambridge University Press.

158   M. DEL GIUDICE

Gomez, E. T. (2006). Malaysian business groups: The state and capital development in the post-currency crisis period. In S. Chang (Ed.), *Business groups in East Asia: Financial crisis, restructuring, and new growth* (pp. 119–146). Oxford: Oxford University Press.

Gonenc, H., Kan, O. B., & Karadagli, E. C. (2007). Business groups and internal capital markets. *Emerging Markets Finance and Trade, 43*(2), 63–81.

Granovetter, M. (1994). Business groups. Chapter 18. In N. Smelser & R. Swedberg (Eds.), *The handbook of economic sociology*. Princeton: Princeton University Press.

Granovetter, M. (1995). Coase revisited: Business groups in the modern economy. *Industrial and Corporate Change, 4*(1), 93–130.

Granovetter, M. (2005). Business groups and social organization. In N. Smelser & R. Swedberg (Eds.), *The handbook of economic sociology* (2nd ed., pp. 429–450). Princeton: Princeton University Press.

Greif, A. (2006). *Institutions and the path to the modern economy: Lessons from medieval trade.* Cambridge: Cambridge University Press.

Guillen, M. F. (2000). Business groups in emerging economies: A resource-based view. *Academy of Management Journal, 43*(3), 362–380.

Guillén, M. F. (2001). *The limits of convergence: Globalization and organizational change in Argentina, South Korea, and Spain.* Princeton: Princeton University Press.

Hazari, R. K. (1966). *The structure of the private corporate sector, A study of concentration, ownership and control.* Bombay: Asia Publishing House.

Hewitt, M. L., van Rensburg, L. J., & Ukpere, W. I. (2012). A measuring instrument to predict family succession commitment to family business. *African Journal of Business Management, 6*(49), 11865–11879.

Hitt, M. A., Dacin, M. T., Levitas, E., Arregle, J., & Borza, A. (2000). Partner selection in emerging and developed market contexts: Resource-based and organizational learning perspectives. *Academy of Management Journal, 43*(3), 449–467.

Horgos, D. (2013). Global sourcing: A family-firm's perspective. *Journal of Small Business & Entrepreneurship, 26*(3), 221–240.

Hoskisson, R. E., Eden, L., Lau, C. M., & Wright, M. (2000). Strategy in emerging economies. *Academy of Management Journal, 43*(3), 249–267.

Hutchcroft, P. D. (1999). Neither Dynamo nor Domino: Reforms and Crises in the Philippine Political Economy. In T. J. Pempel (Ed.), *The politics of the Asian economic crisis.* Ithaca: Cornell University Press.

Hwang, I. (2000). Diversification and restructuring of the Korean business groups. Presented to the *Transforming Korean Business and Management Culture Conference*, Michigan State University, East Lansing.

BUSINESS GROUPS IN THE EMERGING MARKETS 159

Hwang, I., Lee, I., Seo, C., Lee, B., & Han, H. (2000). *Chaebol structure and chaebol policy: Evaluation and recommendations.* Seoul: Korea Economic Research Institute.

Jiang, Y., & Peng, M. W. (2011). Are family ownership and control in large firms good, bad, or irrelevant? *Asia Pacific Journal of Management, 28*(1), 15–39.

Johanson, J., & Wiedersheim-Paul, F. (1975). The internationalization of the firm: Four Swedish case studies. *Journal of Management Studies, 12*(3), 305–322.

Kalasin, K. (2011). *The international expansion of emerging-economy firms: The influence of path-breaking change and its antecedents.* Business administration. HEC.

Kandemir, D., Daekwan, K., & Cavusgil, S. T. (2004). Family conglomerates: Key features relevant to multinationals. In B. Prasad & P. Ghauri (Eds.), *Global firms and emerging markets in the age of anxiety.* Westport: Praeger.

Kansikas, J., Huovinen, J., & Hyrsky, K. (2014). Family firm prerequisites for international business operations: A production and marketing capabilities approach. *World Review of Entrepreneurship, Management and Sustainable Development, 10*(4), 435–448.

Karnani, A. (2007). Fortune at the bottom of the pyramid: A mirage. *California Management Review, 49*(4), 90–111.

Kelly, L. M., Athanassiou, N., & Crittenden, W. F. (2000). Founder centrality and strategic behavior in the family-owned firm. *Entrepreneurship Theory and Practice, 25*(2), 27–42.

Khanna, T. (2000). Business groups and social welfare in emerging markets: Existing evidence and unanswered questions. *European Economic Review, 44* (4), 748–761.

Khanna, T., & Palepu, K. G. (1999). The right way to restructure conglomerates in emerging markets. *Harvard Business Review, 77*(4), 125–134.

Khanna, T., & Palepu, K. (2000). The future of business groups in emerging markets: Long-run evidence from Chile. *Academy of Management Journal, 43* (3), 268–285.

Khanna, T., & Rivkin, J. W. (2001). Estimating the performance effects of business groups in emerging markets. *Strategic Management Journal, 22*(1), 45–74.

Khanna, T., & Thomas, C. (2004). What type of control group causes stock price synchronicity? Unpublished.

Khanna, T., & Yafeh, Y. (2005). Business groups and risk sharing around the world*. *The Journal of Business, 78*(1), 301–340.

Khanna, T., & Yafeh, Y. (2007). Business groups in emerging markets: Paragons or parasites? *Journal of Economic Literature, 45*(2), 331–372.

Kim, D., Kandemir, D., & Cavusgil, S. T. (2004). The role of family conglomerates in emerging markets: What western companies should know. *Thunderbird International Business Review, 46*, 13–38.

160 M. DEL GIUDICE

Kock, C. J., & Guillen, M. F. (2001). Strategy and structure in developing countries: Business groups as an evolutionary response to opportunities for unrelated diversification. *Industrial and Corporate Change, 10*(1), 77–113.

Kroeber, A. (2006, May). China's industrial and foreign trade policies – What are they and how successful have they been? In *Conference on Capitalism with Chinese Characteristics: China's Political Economy in Comparative and Theoretical Perspective*, Kelley School of Business, Indiana University, Bloomington (pp. 19–20).

Kurtović, S., Siljković, B., & Dašić, B. (2013). Conglomerate companies as emerging markets phenomenon. *Retrieved September, 1*, 111–118.

La Porta, R., Lopez-De-Silanes, F., & Shleifer, A. (1999). Corporate ownership around the World. *Journal of Finance, 54*(2), 471–517.

Leggett, C. J., & Bamber, G. J. (1996). Asia-Pacific tiers of change. *Human Resource Management Journal, 6*(2), 7–19.

Lins, K. V., & Servaes, H. (2002). Is corporate diversification beneficial in emerging markets? *Financial Management, 31*, 5–31.

Marois, T. (2007, May). The lost logic of state-owned banks: Mexico, Turkey, and Neoliberalism. In *Canadian Political Science Association, 79th Annual Conference*, University of Saskatchewan (Vol. 31).

Merchant, H. (2007). *Competing in emerging markets: Cases and readings*. New York: Routledge.

Morck, R. (2005). How to eliminate pyramidal business groups the double taxation of inter-corporate dividends and other incisive uses of tax policy. In *Tax policy and the economy* (Vol. 19, pp. 135–179). Cambridge, MA: MIT Press.

Morck, R., & Yeung, B. (2004). Family control and the rent-seeking society. *Entrepreneurship Theory and Practice, 28*(4), 391–409.

Morck, R., Stangeland, D., & Yeung, B. (2000). Inherited wealth, corporate control, and economic growth: The Canadian disease? In R. Morck (Ed.), *Concentrated corporate ownership, NBER conference report series* (pp. 319–369). Chicago/London: University of Chicago Press.

Nachum, L. (1999). Diversification strategies of developing country firms. *Journal of International Management, 5*, 115–140.

Özcan, G. B., & Turunç, H. (2011). Economic liberalization and class dynamics in Turkey: New business groups and Islamic mobilization. *Insight Turkey, 13*(3), 63–86.

Pérez, P. F. (2016). Evolution of family business continuity and change in Latin America and Spain. Paloma Fernández Pérez (Ed.), University of Barcelona, Spain and Andrea Lluch, CONICET, Argentina and Los Andes University, Colombia.

Pinches, M. (1992). The Philippines: The regional exception. *The Pacific Review, 5*(4), 390–401.

Prahalad, C. K. (2005). *The fortune of the bottom of the pyramid*. Upper Saddle River: Wharton School Publishing.

Prahalad, C. K., & Lieberthal, K. (1998). The end of corporate imperialism. *Harvard Business Review, 76*(4), 68–79.

Pukall, T. J., & Calabrò, A. (2014). The internationalization of family firms a critical review and integrative model. *Family Business Review, 27*(2), 103–125.

Roberts, J. G. (1973). *Mitsui, three centuries of Japanese business.* New York: Weatherhill.

Root, H. L. (2006). Opening the doors of invention: Institutions, technology and developing nations. *International Public Management Review, 7*(1), 14–29.

Sahin, K. (2011). An investigation into why Turkish business groups resist the adoption of M-form in post-liberalization. *African Journal of Business Management, 5*(34), 13330–13343.

Sarkar, M., & Cavusgil, S. T. (1996). The trends in international business thought and literature: A review of international market entry mode research: Integration and synthesis. *International Executive, 38*(6), 825–848.

Shah, J., Ramachandran, J., Vaidyanathan, R., Jha, M., & Samanth, D. (2001). Role of community dominance of trade channels in India: Exploratory study. *IIM Bangalore Research Paper, 170.*

Silva, F., Majluf, N., & Paredes, R. D. (2006). Family ties, interlocking directors and performance of business groups in emerging countries: The case of Chile. *Journal of Business Research, 59*(3), 315–321.

Steers, R. M., Shin, Y. K., & Ungson, G. R. (1989). *The chaebol: Korea's new industrial might.* New York: Harper & Row.

Suehiro, A., & Wailerdsak, N. (2004). Family business in Thailand: Its management, governance, and future challenges. *ASEAN Economic Bulletin, 21*(1), 81–93.

Tsui-Auch, L. S. (2006). Singaporean business groups: The role of the state and capital in Singapore Inc. In S. Chang (Ed.), *Business groups in East Asia: Financial crisis, restructuring, and new growth* (pp. 94–115). Oxford: Oxford University Press.

Vecchi, A., Della Piana, B., & Cacia, C. (2014). Mapping family business groups from a cross-cultural perspective. In *Enacting globalization* (pp. 194–204). London, UK: Palgrave Macmillan UK.

Venter, W. P., & Kruger, S. (2004). The contribution of familiness' to the performance of family businesses. *Guidelines for Contributors to the Southern African Business Review 76, 8*(3), 1–20.

Wade, R. (1990). *Governing the market: Economic theory and the role of government in East Asian industrialisation.* Princeton: Princeton University Press.

Yaprak, A., Karademir, B., & Osborn, R. N. (2006). How do business groups function and evolve in emerging markets? The case of Turkish business groups. *Advances in International Marketing, 17*, 275–294.

Yiu, D., Bruton, G. D., & Lu, Y. (2005). Understanding business group performance in an emerging economy: Acquiring resources and capabilities in order to prosper*. *Journal of Management Studies, 42*(1), 183–206.

References

Abiad, A., Bluedorn, J., Guajardo, J., & Topalova, P. (2012). *The rising resilience of emerging market and developing economies* (No. 12/300). Washington, DC: International Monetary Fund.

Ahlstrom, D., & Bruton, G. D. (2006). Venture capital in emerging economies: Networks and institutional change. *Entrepreneurship: Theory and Practice, 30,* 299–320.

Aidis, R. (2005). Institutional barriers to small and medium-sized enterprise operations in transition countries. *Small Business Economics, 25*(4), 305–317.

Almeida, L. (2014). The level and structure of CEO compensation: Does ownership matter? *Revue d'économie politique, 124*(4), 653–666.

Almeida, H. V., & Wolfenzon, D. (2006). A theory of pyramidal ownership and family business groups. *The Journal of Finance, 61*(6), 2637–2680.

Altomonte, C., & Rungi, A. (2013). Business groups as hierarchies of firms. Determinants of vertical integration and performance. http://www.ecb.europa.eu or from the Social Science Research Network electronic library at http://ssrn.com/abstract_id=2253222

Amato, J. D., & Gerlach, S. (2002). Inflation targeting in emerging market and transition economies: Lessons after a decade. *European Economic Review, 46*(4), 781–790.

Amore, M. D., Minichilli, A., & Corbetta, G. (2011). How do managerial successions shape corporate financial policies in family firms? *Journal of Corporate Finance, 17*(4), 1016–1027.

Amsden, A. H. (1989). *Asia's next giant: South Korea and late industrialization.* New York/Oxford: Oxford University Press.

© The Author(s) 2017
M. Del Giudice, *Understanding Family-Owned Business Groups,*
DOI 10.1007/978-3-319-42243-5

164 REFERENCES

Amsden, A. H., & Hikino, T. (1994). Project execution capability, organizational know how and conglomerate corporate growth in late industrialization. *Industrial and Corporate Change, 3*(1), 111–147.

Anderson, R. C., & Reeb, D. M. (2003). Founding-family ownership and firm performance: Evidence from the S&P 500. *The Journal of Finance, 58*(3), 1301–1328.

Ang, J. S. (1991). Small business uniqueness and the theory of financial management. *Journal of Small Business Finance, 1*(1), 1–13.

Aoki, M. (2001). *Toward a comparative institutional analysis, Comparative institutional analysis series.* Cambridge/London: MIT Press.

Arellano, C. (2008). Default risk and income fluctuations in emerging economies. *The American Economic Review, 98*(3), 690–712.

Argyres, N. S., & Liebeskind, J. P. (1999). Contractual commitments, bargaining power, and governance inseparability: Incorporating history into transaction cost theory. *Academy of Management Review, 24*(1), 49–63.

Arnold, D. J., & Quelch, J. A. (1998). New strategies in emerging markets. *Sloan Management Review, 40*(1), 7–20.

Aronoff, C. (2004). Self-perpetuation family organization built on values: Necessary condition for long-term family business survival. *Family Business Review, 17*(1), 55–59.

Aronoff, C. E., & Ward, J. L. (1996). *Family business governance: Maximizing family and business potential* (No. 8). Marietta: Family Enterprise Publisher.

Aronoff, C. E., & Ward, J. L. (2011). *Preparing your family business for strategic change.* New York: Palgrave Macmillan.

Arregle, J. L., Hitt, M. A., Sirmon, D. G., & Very, P. (2007). The development of organizational social capital: Attributes of family firms*. *Journal of Management Studies, 44*(1), 73–95.

Asif, M., & Muneer, T. (2007). Energy supply, its demand and security issues for developed and emerging economies. *Renewable and Sustainable Energy Reviews, 11*(7), 1388–1413.

Astrachan, J. H. (1988). Family firm and community culture. *Family Business Review, 1*(2), 165–189.

Astrachan, J. H., & Jaskiewicz, P. (2008). Emotional returns and emotional costs in privately held family businesses: Advancing traditional business valuation. *Family Business Review, 21*(2), 139–149.

Astrachan, J. H., & Kolenko, T. A. (1994). A neglected factor explaining family business success: Human resource practices. *Family Business Review, 7*(3), 251–262.

Astrachan, J. H., & Shanker, M. C. (2003). Family businesses' contribution to the U.S. economy: A closer look. *Family Business Review, 16*(3), 211–219.

REFERENCES 165

Astrachan, J. H., Klein, S. B., & Smyrnios, K. X. (2002). The F-PEC scale of family influence: A proposal for solving the family business definition problem. *Family Business Review, 15*(1), 45–58.

Astrachan, J. H., Torsten, M. P., & Jaskiewicz, P. (2009). *Family business.* London: Edward Elgar Publishing Limited.

Aulakh, P. S., Rotate, M., & Teegen, H. (2000). Export strategies and performance of firms from emerging economies: Evidence from Brazil, Chile, and Mexico. *Academy of Management Journal, 43*(3), 342–361.

Bae, K. H., Kang, J. K., & Kim, J. M. (2002). Tunneling or value added? Evidence from mergers by Korean business groups. *The Journal of Finance, 57*(6), 2695–2740.

Bahl, S. (1995). Whither Asian public relations. *Media Asia: An Asian Mass Communication Quarterly, 22*(3), 136–143.

Bansal, R., & Dahlquist, M. (2000). The forward premium puzzle: Different tales from developed and emerging economies. *Journal of International Economics, 51*(1), 115–144.

Barnes, L. B., & Hershon, S. A. (1976). Transferring power in family business. *Harvard Business Review, 54*(4), 105–114.

Barry, B. (1975). The development of organization structure in the family firm. *Journal of General Management, 2*(3), 293–315.

Bartholomeusz, S., & Tanewski, G. A. (2006). The relationship between family firms and corporate governance*. *Journal of Small Business Management, 44*(2), 245–267.

Baumol, W. J., Litan, R. E., & Schramm, C. J. (2007). *Good capitalism, bad capitalism, and the economics of growth and prosperity.* New Haven: Yale University Press.

Baylis, R., Connell, L., & Flynn, A. (1998). Company size, environmental regulation and ecological modernization: Further analysis at the level of the firm. *Business Strategy and the Environment, 7*(5), 285–296.

Bebchuk, L., Kraakman, R., & Triantis, G. (1999). *Stock pyramids, cross-ownership, and the dual class equity: The creation and agency costs of separating control from cash flow rights* (No. w6951). Cambridge, MA: National Bureau of Economic Research.

Bebchuk, L. A., Kraakman, R., & Triantis, G. (2000). Stock pyramids, cross-ownership, and dual class equity: The mechanisms and agency costs of separating control from cash-flow rights. In *Concentrated corporate ownership* (pp. 295–318). Chicago: University of Chicago Press.

Beckert, J. (1999). Agency, entrepreneurs, and institutional change. The role of strategic choice and institutionalized practices in organizations. *Organization Studies, 20*(5), 777–799.

Beckhard, R., & Dyer, W. G. (1983). Managing continuity in the family-owned business. *Organizational Dynamics, 12*(1), 5–12.

166 REFERENCES

Ben-Porath, Y. (1980). The F-connection: Families, friends, and firms and the organization of exchange. *Population and Development Review, 6*(1), 1–30.

Bennedsen, M., & Foss, N. (2015). Family assets and liabilities in the innovation process. *California Management Review, 58*(1), 65–81.

Berger, A., & Udell, G. (1998). The economics of small business finance: The roles of private equity and debt markets in the financial growth cycle. *Journal of Banking and Finance, 22*(6/8), 613–673.

Bertrand, M., Mehta, P., & Mullainathan, S. (2000). *Ferreting out tunneling: An application to Indian business groups* (No. w7952). Cambridge, MA: National Bureau of Economic Research.

Bertrand, M., Samphantharak, S. J., & Schoar, A. (2004). Mixing family with business: A study of Thai business groups and the families behind them. Unpublished.

Bianchi, C. (2009). Retail internationalisation from emerging markets: Case study evidence from Chile. *International Marketing Review, 26*(2), 221–243.

Bianco, M., & Nicodano, G. (2006). Pyramidal groups and debt. *European Economic Review, 50*(4), 937–961.

Biggart, N. (1991). Institutionalized patrimonialism in Korean business. In C. Calhoun (Ed.), *Comparative social research, Business institution* (Vol. vol. 12). Greenwich: JAI Press.

Blanchard, O., Dornbusch, R., Krugman, P., Layard, R., & Summers, L. (1991). *Reform in Eastern Europe.* Cambridge, MA: MIT Press.

Boas, T. C. (2013). Mass media and politics in Latin America. In *Constructing democratic governance in Latin America.* (pp. 48–77). Baltimore, MD: Johns Hopkins University Press.

Boskin, M. (1984). A longer term perspective on macroeconomics and distribution: Time, expectations, and incentives. In G. Feiwel (Ed.), *Issues in contemporary economics and distribution.* London, UK: The MacMillan Press.

Boter, H., & Lundström, A. (2005). SME perspectives on business support services: The role of company size, industry and location. *Journal of Small Business and Enterprise Development, 12*(2), 244–258.

Brenes, E. R., Madrigal, K., & Requena, B. (2011). Corporate governance and family business performance. *Journal of Business Research, 64*(3), 280–285.

Brennan, L. (Ed.). (2013). *Enacting globalization: Multidisciplinary perspectives on international integration.* Basingstoke: Palgrave.

Breton-Miller, L., & Miller, D. (2006). Why do some family businesses out-compete? Governance, long-term orientations, and sustainable capability. *Entrepreneurship Theory and Practice, 30*(6), 731–746.

Brockhaus, R. H. (2004). Family business succession: Suggestions for future research. *Family Business Review, 17*(2), 165–177.

Brooksbank, R. (1991). Defining the small business: A new classification of company size. *Entrepreneurship & Regional Development, 3*(1), 17–31.

REFERENCES 167

Brumana, M., De Massis, A., Discua Cruz, A., Minola, T., & Cassia, L. (2015). Transgenerational professionalization of family firms: The role of next generation leaders. In *Developing next generation leaders for transgenerational entrepreneurial family enterprises.* Cheltenham: Edward Elgar.

Bruton, G. D., Ahlstrom, D., & Obloj, K. (2008). Entrepreneurship in emerging economies: Where are we today and where should the research go in the future. *Entrepreneurship Theory and Practice, 32*(1), 1–14.

Buckley, P. J. (2004). Asian network firms: An analytical framework. *Asia Pacific Business Review, 10*(3–4), 254–271.

Burkart, M., Panunzi, F., & Shleifer, A. (2003). Family firms. *Journal of Finance, 58*, 2167–2201.

Buzby, S. L. (1975). Company size, listed versus unlisted stocks, and the extent of financial disclosure. *Journal of Accounting Research, 13*(1), 16–37.

Cadieux, L., Lorrain, J., & Hugron, P. (2002). Succession in women-owned family businesses: A case study. *Family Business Review, 15*, 17–30.

Campanella, F., Del Giudice, M., & Della Peruta, M. R. (2013a). The role of information in the credit relationship. *Journal of Innovation and Entrepreneurship, 2*, 17. doi:10.1186/2192-5372-2-17.

Campanella, F., Della Peruta, M. R., & Del Giudice, M. (2013b). Informational approach of family spin-offs in the funding process of innovative projects: An empirical verification. *Journal of Innovation and Entrepreneurship, 2*, 18. doi:10.1186/2192-5372-2-18.

Carlock, R. S., & Ward, J. L. (2001). *Strategic planning for the family business. Parallel planning to unify the family and business.* Houndmills/New York: Palgrave.

Carney, M. (2005). Corporate governance and competitive advantage in family-controlled firms. *Entrepreneurship Theory and Practice, 29*(3), 249–265.

Carney, M. (2008). *Asian business groups: Governance, context and performance.* Oxford: Chandos.

Carney, M., & Gedajlovic, E. (2000). East Asian financial systems and the transition from investment-driven to innovation-driven economic development. *International Journal of Innovation Management, 4*(03), 253–276.

Carney, M., & Gedajlovic, E. (2002). The co-evolution of institutional environments and organizational strategies: The rise of family business groups in the ASEAN region. *Organization Studies, 23*(1), 1–29.

Carney, M., Gedajlovic, E., & Yang, X. (2009). Varieties of Asian capitalism: Toward an institutional theory of Asian enterprise. *Asia Pacific Journal of Management, 26*(3), 361–380.

Carney, M., Van Essen, M., Gedajlovic, E. R., & Heugens, P. P. (2015). What do we know about private family firms? A meta-analytical review. *Entrepreneurship Theory and Practice, 39*(3), 513–544.

168 REFERENCES

Cavusgil, S. T., Knight, G., Riesenberger, J. R., Rammal, H. G., & Rose, E. L. (2014). *International business*. Melbourne: Pearson Australia.

Chang, S. (2006). Korean business groups: The financial crisis and the restructuring of chaebols. In S. Chang (Ed.), *Business groups in East Asia: Financial crisis, restructuring, and new growth* (pp. 52–69). Oxford: Oxford University Press.

Chang, S. J., & Choi, U. (1988). Strategy, structure and performance of Korean business groups: A transactions cost approach. *The Journal of Industrial Economics, 37*, 141–158.

Chang, S. J., & Hong, J. (2000). Economic performance of group-affiliated companies in Korea: Intragroup resource sharing and internal business transactions. *Academy of Management Journal, 43*(3), 429–448.

Chang, J. J., & Shin, H. H. (2005). Does the family portfolio perform better than the group portfolio? Evidence from Korean Conglomerates. Unpublished.

Cherif, R. (2016). *Breaking the oil spell*. Washington, DC: International Monetary Fund.

Chittoor, R., & Das, R. (2007). Professionalization of management and succession performance – A vital linkage. *Family Business Review, 20*(1), 65–79.

Chrisman, J., Chua, J., & Steier, L. P. (2003). An introduction to theories of family business. *Journal of Business Venturing, 18*, 441–448.

Chu, W. (2009). The influence of family ownership on SME performance: Evidence from public firms in Taiwan. *Small Business Economics, 33*(3), 353–373.

Chua, J. H., Chrisman, J. J., & Sharma, P. (1999). Defining the family business by behavior. *Entrepreneurship: Theory and Practice, 23*(4), 19–40.

Chua, J. H., Chrisman, J. J., & Steier, L. P. (2003). Extending the theoretical horizons of family business research. *Entrepreneurship Theory and Practice, 27*(4), 331–338.

Chung, C. (2000a). Corporate governance system in Korea: What questions should we ask for future recommendations? Presented to the *Transforming Korean Business and Management Culture Conference*, Michigan State University, East Lansing.

Chung, Y. P. (2000b, September). Corporate governance system in Korea: What questions should we ask for future recommendations? In *Transforming Korean Business and Management Culture Conference*, Michigan State University, East Lansing.

Chung, C., & Mahmood, I. (2006). Taiwanese business groups: Steady growth in institutional transition. In S. Chang (Ed.), *Business groups in East Asia: Financial crisis, restructuring, and new growth* (pp. 70–93). Oxford: Oxford University Press.

Church, R. (1993). The family firm in industrial capitalism: International perspectives on hypotheses and history. *Business History, 35*(4), 17–43.

REFERENCES **169**

Claessens, S., Djankov, S., Fan, J., & Lang, L. (2002). Disentangling the incentive and entrenchment effects of large shareholdings. *Journal of Finance, 57,* 2741–2771.

Colarossi, F., Giorgino, M., Steri, R., & Viviani, D. (2008). A corporate governance study on Italian family firms. *Corporate Ownership & Control, 5*(4), 93–103.

Cole, P. M. (1997). Women in family business. *Family Business Review, 10*(4), 353–371.

Corbetta, G. (1995). Patterns of development of family businesses in Italy. *Family Business Review, 8*(4), 255–265.

Corbetta, G., & Salvato, C. A. (2004). The board of directors in family firms: One size fits all? *Family Business Review, 17*(2), 119–134.

Corley, K. G., & Gioia, D. A. (2004). Identity ambiguity and change in the wake of a corporate spin-off. *Administrative Science Quarterly, 49*(2), 173–208.

Craig, J. B. L., & Moores, K. (2006). A 10-year longitudinal investigation of strategy, systems, and environment on innovation in family firms. *Family Business Review, 19,* 1–10.

Cronqvist, H., & Nilsson, M. (2003). Agency costs of controlling minority shareholders. *Journal of Financial and Quantitative Analysis, 38,* 695–719.

Curimbaba, F. (2002). The dynamics of women's roles as family business managers. *Family Business Review, 1*(5), 239–252.

Daily, C. M., & Dollinger, M. J. (1992). An empirical examination of ownership structure in family and professionally managed firms. *Family Business Review, 5*(2), 117–136.

Daily, C. M., Dalton, D. R., & Cannella, A. A. (2003). Corporate governance: Decades of dialogue and data. *Academy of Management Review, 28*(3), 371–382.

Danco, L. A., & Jonovic, D. J. (1981). *Outside directors in the family owned business.* Cleveland: The University Press.

Danes, S. M., & Olson, P. D. (2003). Women's role involvement in family businesses, business tensions, and business success. *Family Business Review, 16,* 53–68.

Danes, S. M., Haberman, H. R., & McTavish, D. (2005). Gendered discourse about family business. *Family Relations, 54*(1), 116–130.

Danes, S. M., Stafford, K., & Loy, J. T. C. (2007). Family business performance: The effects of gender and management. *Journal of Business Research, 60*(10), 1058–1069.

Dar-Yeh, H., & Wei-Hsiung, W. (2007). Financial system reform in Taiwan. *Journal of Asian Economics, 18,* 21–41.

Davies, H. (1995). The nature of the firm in China. In H. Davies (Ed.), *China business: Context and issues* (pp. 137–154). Hong Kong: Longman.

Davis, P. (1983). Realizing the potential of the family business. *Organizational Dynamics, 12*(1), 47–56.

170 REFERENCES

Davis, J. A., & Tagiuri, R. (1989). The influence of life stage on father-son work relationships in family companies. *Family Business Review, 2*(1), 47–74.

Davis, J. H., Schoorman, F. D., & Donaldson, L. (1997). Toward a stewardship theory of management. *Academy of Management Review, 22*(1), 20–47.

De Clercq, D., Danis, W. M., & Dakhli, M. (2010). The moderating effect of institutional context on the relationship between associational activity and new business activity in emerging economies. *International Business Review, 19*(1), 85–101.

De Fabritiis, G., Pammolli, F., & Riccaboni, M. (2003). On size and growth of business firms. *Physica A: Statistical Mechanics and Its Applications, 324*(1), 38–44.

De Massis, A., Chua, J., & Chrisman, J. (2008). Factors preventing intra-family succession. *Family Business Review, 21*(2), 183–199.

De Mik, L., Anderson, R. M., & Johnson, P. A. (1985). *The family in business.* San Francisco: Jossey-Bass Publishers.

Del Giudice, M., Della Peruta, M. R., & Carayannis, E. G. (2011). *Knowledge and family business. The governance and management of family firms in the new knowledge economy* (Innovation, technology and knowledge management series editor). New York: Springer. ISBN: 978-1-4419-7352-8.

Del Giudice, M., Della Peruta, M. R., & Carayannis, E. G. (2014). *Student entrepreneurship in the social knowledge economy.* Cham: Springer.

Del Giudice, M., Della Peruta, M. R., & Maggioni, V. (2013a). Spontaneous processes of reproduction of family-based entrepreneurship: An empirical research on the cognitive nature of the spin-offs. *Journal of Innovation and Entrepreneurship, 2*, 12. doi:10.1186/2192-5372-2-12.

Del Giudice, M., Della Peruta, M. R., & Maggioni, V. (2013b). One man company or managed succession: The transfer of the family dream in Southern-Italian firms. *Journal of Organizational Change Management, 26*(4), 703–719.

Delios, A., & Henisz, W. I. (2000). Japanese firms' investment strategies in emerging economies. *Academy of Management Journal, 43*(3), 305–323.

Della Peruta, M. R., & Del Giudice, M. (2013). Knowledge accumulation and reuse for spinning off firms from learning organizations: An individual knowledge based perspective. *International Journal of Social Ecology and Sustainable Development (IJSESD), 4*(4), 20–29.

Demsetz, H., & Lehn, K. (1985). The structure of corporate ownership: Causes and consequences. *Journal of political Economy, 93*(6), 1155-77.

Dent, C. M., & Randerson, C. (1997). Enter the chaebol: The escalation of Korean direct investment in Europe. *European Business Journal, 9*(4), 31.

Dharwadkar, B., George, G., & Brandes, P. (2000). Privatization in emerging economies: An agency theory perspective. *Academy of Management Review, 25*(3), 650–669.

REFERENCES 171

DiMaggio, P. (1988). Interest and agency in institutional theory. In L. G. E. Zucker (Ed.), *Institutional patterns and organizations: Culture and environment* (pp. 3–21). Cambridge: Ballinger.

Djankov, S., & Murrell, P. (2002). Enterprise restructuring in transition: A quantitative survey. *Journal of Economic Literature, 40*(3), 739–792.

Dobbin, F. (2007). Economic sociology. In C. D. Bryant & D. L. Peck (Eds.), *Twenty-first century sociology: A reference handbook* (pp. 319–331). Thousand Oaks: Sage.

Donaldson, L., & Davis, J. H. (1991). Stewardship theory or agency theory: CEO governance and shareholder returns. *Australian Journal of Management, 16*(1), 49–64.

Donckels, R., & Fröhlich, E. (1991). Are family businesses really different? European experiences from STRATOS. *Family Business Review, 4*(2), 149–160.

Donnelley, R. G. (1964). The family business. *Harvard Business Review, 42*(4), 93–105.

Dossani, R., & Kenney, M. (2002). Creating an environment for venture capital in India. *World Development, 30*(2), 227–253.

Dumas, C. (1989). Understanding of father-daughter and father-son dyads in family-owned businesses. *Family Business Review, 2*(1), 31–46.

Dumas, C. (1992). Integrating the daughter into family business management. *Entrepreneurship: Theory & Practice, 16*(4), 41–56.

Dumas, C., & Blodgett, M. (1999). Articulating values to inform decision making: Lessons from family firms around the world. *International Journal of Value-Based Management, 12*(3), 209–221.

Dyer, W. G. (1983). Managing change in the family firm. Issues and strategies. *Sloan Management Review, 24*, 59–65.

Dyer, W. G. (1986). *Cultural change in family firms.* San Francisco: Jossey-Bass.

Edwards, S. (2001). *Capital mobility and economic performance: Are emerging economies different?* (No. w8076). Cambridge, MA: National Bureau of Economic Research.

Edwards, S., & Savastano, M. A. (1999). *Exchange rates in emerging economies: What do we know? What do we need to know?* (No. w7228). Cambridge, MA: National Bureau of Economic Research.

Eichengreen, B., & Hausmann, R. (Eds.). (2010). *Other people's money: Debt denomination and financial instability in emerging market economies.* Chicago: University of Chicago Press.

Eisenhardt, K. M. (1989). Building theories from case study research. *Academy of Management Review, 14*(4), 532–550.

EU Legislation. (2010). Enlargement 2004 and 2007. Retrieved October 4, 2010, from http://europa.eu/legislation_summaries/enlargement/2004_and_2007_enlargement/index_en.htm

172 REFERENCES

Evans, D. S. (1987). The relationship between firm growth, size, and age: Estimates for 100 manufacturing industries. *The Journal of Industrial Economics, 35,* 567–581.

Fama, E. F., & Jensen, M. C. (1983). Separation of ownership and control. *Journal of Law and Economics, 26*(2), 301–25.

Fama, E. F., & Jensen, M. C. (1985). Organizational forms and investment decisions. *Journal of Financial Economics, 14,* 101–119.

Farashahi, M., & Hafsi, T. (2009). Strategy of firms in unstable institutional environments. *Asia Pacific Journal of Management, 26*(4), 643–666.

Feenstra, R. C., & Hamilton, G. G. (2006). *Emergent economies, divergent paths: Economic organization and international trade in South Korea and Taiwan, Structural analysis in the social sciences series* (Vol. 29). Cambridge/New York: Cambridge University Press.

Fernández, Z., & Nieto, M. J. (2005). Internationalization strategy of small and medium-sized family businesses: Some influential factors. *Family Business Review, 18*(1), 77–89.

Fishman, A. (2009). *9 elements of family business success.* New York: McGraw-Hill.

Fishman, R., & Khanna, T. (2004). Facilitating development: The role of business groups. *World Development, 32*(4), 609–628.

Florin, J. M., Lubatkin, M. H., & Schulze, W. S. (2003). A social capital model of new venture performance. *The Academy of Management Journal, 46,* 374–384.

Fogel, K. (2006). Oligarchic family control, social economic outcomes, and the quality of government. *Journal of International Business Studies, 37*(5), 603–622.

Fogel, K., Hawk, A., Morck, R., & Yeung, B. (2006). Institutional obstacles to entrepreneurship. In M. Casson, B. Yeung, A. Basu, & N. Wadeson (Eds.), *The Oxford handbook of entrepreneurship* (pp. 540–579). Oxford: Oxford University Press.

Freyer, T. (1992). *Regulating big business: Antitrust in great Britain and America, 1880–1990.* Cambridge/New York: Cambridge University Press.

Fu, D., Pammolli, F., Buldyrev, S. V., Riccaboni, M., Matia, K., Yamasaki, K., & Stanley, H. E. (2005). The growth of business firms: Theoretical framework and empirical evidence. *Proceedings of the National Academy of Sciences of the United States of America, 102*(52), 18801–18806.

Fuguitt, G. V. (1965). The growth and decline of small towns as a probability process. *American Sociological Review, 30*(3), 403–411.

Gallo, M. Á., Tàpies, J., & Cappuyns, K. (2004). Comparison of family and nonfamily business: Financial logic and personal preferences. *Family Business Review, 17*(4), 303–318.

Gammeltoft, P. (2008). Emerging multinationals: Outward FDI from the BRICS countries. *International Journal of Technology and Globalisation, 4*(1), 5–22.

REFERENCES 173

García-Álvarez, E., & López-Sintas, J. (2001). A taxonomy of founders based on values: The root of family business heterogeneity. *Family Business Review, 14*(3), 209–230.

García-Meca, E., & Sánchez-Ballesta, J. P. (2009). Corporate governance and earnings management: A meta-analysis. *Corporate Governance: An International Review, 17*(5), 594–610.

Garud, R., Jain, S., & Kumaraswamy, A. (2002). Institutional entrepreneurship in the sponsorship of common technological standards: The case of sun microsystems and java. *Academy of Management Journal, 45*(1), 196–214.

Gerlach, M. L. (1992). *Alliance capitalism: The social organization of Japanese business.* Berkeley/Oxford: University of California Press.

Gimeno, A., Baulenas, G., & Com-Cros, J. (2010). *Family business models.* Basingstoke: Macmillan.

Glick, R., & Hutchison, M. (2005). Capital controls and exchange rate instability in developing economies. *Journal of International Money and Finance, 24*(3), 387–412.

Gnan, L., Montemerlo, D., & Huse, M. (2015). Governance systems in family SMEs: The substitution effects between family councils and corporate governance mechanisms. *Journal of Small Business Management, 53*(2), 355–381.

Goldstein, A. (2009). Multinational companies from emerging economies composition, conceptualization & direction in the global economy. *Indian Journal of Industrial Relations, 45,* 137–147.

Goldstein, M., & Turner, P. (1996). Banking crises in emerging economies: Origins and policy options. In *BIS Economic Paper 46.* Bank for International Settlements, Monetary and Economic Department, Basle.

Gomez, E. T. (2006). Malaysian business groups: The state and capital development in the post-currency crisis period. In S. Chang (Ed.), *Business groups in East Asia: Financial crisis, restructuring, and new growth* (pp. 119–146). Oxford: Oxford University Press.

Gomez-Mejia, L. R., Nunez-Nickel, M., & Gutierrez, I. (2001). The role of family ties in agency contracts. *Academy of Management Journal, 44*(1), 81–95.

Gonçalves, C. E. S., & Salles, J. M. (2008). Inflation targeting in emerging economies: What do the data say? *Journal of Development Economics, 85*(1), 312–318.

Gonenc, H., Kan, O. B., & Karadagli, E. C. (2007). Business groups and internal capital markets. *Emerging Markets Finance and Trade, 43*(2), 63–81.

Granovetter, M. (1994). Business groups. Chapter 18. In N. Smelser & R. Swedberg (Eds.), *The handbook of economic sociology.* Princeton: Princeton University Press.

Granovetter, M. (1995). Coase revisited: Business groups in the modern economy. *Industrial and Corporate Change, 4*(1), 93–130.

174 REFERENCES

Granovetter, M. (2005). Business groups and social organization. In N. Smelser & R. Swedberg (Eds.), *The handbook of economic sociology* (2nd ed., pp. 429–450). Princeton: Princeton University Press.

Graves, C. (2006). Internationalization of Australian family businesses: A managerial capabilities perspective. *Family Business Review, 19*(3), 207–224.

Gray, R., Owen, D., & Adams, C. (1996). *Accounting & accountability: Changes and challenges in corporate social and environmental reporting*. London: Prentice Hall.

Green, M. T. (2011). *Inside the multi-generational family business: Nine symptoms of generational stack-up and how to cure them*. New York: Palgrave Macmillan.

Greif, A. (2006). *Institutions and the path to the modern economy: Lessons from medieval trade*. Cambridge: Cambridge University Press.

Griffith, H. (2009). *Family wealth transition planning*. New York: Bloomberg press.

Gubitta, P., & Gianecchini, M. (2002). Governance and flexibility in family-owned SMEs. *Family Business Review, 15*(4), 277–297.

Guillen, M. F. (2000). Business groups in emerging economies: A resource-based view. *Academy of Management Journal, 43*(3), 362–380.

Guillén, M. F. (2001). *The limits of convergence: Globalization and organizational change in Argentina, South Korea, and Spain*. Princeton: Princeton University Press.

Guillén, M. F., & García-Canal, E. (2009). The American model of the multinational firm and the "new" multinationals from emerging economies. *The Academy of Management Perspectives, 23*(2), 23–35.

Habbershon, T. G., & Pistrui, J. (2002). Enterprising families domain: Family-influenced ownership groups in pursuit of transgenerational wealth. *Family Business Review, 15*(3), 223–237.

Habbershon, T. G., Williams, M., & MacMillan, I. C. (2003). A unified systems perspective of family firm performance. *Journal of Business Venturing, 18*(4), 451–465.

Haberman, H., & Danes, S. M. (2007). Father-daughter and father-son family business management transfer comparison: Family FIRO model application. *Family Business Review, 20*, 163–184.

Hall, A., Melin, L., & Nordqvist, M. (2001). Entrepreneurship as radical change in the family business: Exploring the role of cultural patterns. *Family Business Review, 14*(3), 193–208.

Hall, G., Hutchinson, P., & Michaelas, N. (2004). *Determinants of the capital structure of European SMEs. Journal of Business Finance and Accounting, 31*(5), 711–728.

Han Kim, E., & Singal, V. (2000). Stock market openings: Experience of emerging economies*. *The Journal of Business, 73*(1), 25–66.

Handler, W. C. (1989). Methodological issues and considerations in studying family businesses. *Family Business Review, 2*(3), 257–276.

REFERENCES 175

Handler, W. C. (1994). Succession in family business: A review of the research. *Family Business Review, 7*(2), 133–157.

Hart, O. (1995). *Firms, contracts, and financial structure.* New York: Oxford University Press.

Hartley, B. B., & Griffith, G. (2010). *Family wealth transition planning: Advising families with small businesses.* (Vol. 35). Hoboken, New Jersey: Wiley.

Harvey, M., & Evans, R. E. (1994). Family business and multiple levels of conflict. *Family Business Review, 7*(4), 331–348.

Hauser, B. (2011). *International family governance: A guide for families and their advisors.* New York: Palgrave Macmillan.

Heck, R. K., Hoy, F., Poutziouris, P. Z., & Steier, L. P. (2008). Emerging paths of family entrepreneurship research. *Journal of Small Business Management, 46*(3), 317–330.

Hewitt, M. L., van Rensburg, L. J., & Ukpere, W. I. (2012). A measuring instrument to predict family succession commitment to family business. *African Journal of Business Management, 6*(49), 11865–11879.

Hirigoyen, G., & Labaki, R. (2012). The role of regret in the owner-manager decision-making in the family business: A conceptual approach. *Journal of Family Business Strategy, 3*(2), 118–126.

Hitt, M. A., Dacin, M. T., Levitas, E., Arregle, J., & Borza, A. (2000). Partner selection in emerging and developed market contexts: Resource-based and organizational learning perspectives. *Academy of Management Journal, 43*(3), 449–467.

Horgos, D. (2013). Global sourcing: A family-firm's perspective. *Journal of Small Business & Entrepreneurship, 26*(3), 221–240.

Hoskisson, R. E., Eden, L., Lau, C. M., & Wright, M. (2000). Strategy in emerging economies. *Academy of Management Journal, 43*(3), 249–267.

Husain, A. M., Mody, A., & Rogoff, K. S. (2005). Exchange rate regime durability and performance in developing versus advanced economies. *Journal of Monetary Economics, 52*(1), 35–64.

Hutchcroft, P. D. (1999). Neither Dynamo nor Domino: Reforms and Crises in the Philippine Political Economy. In T. J. Pempel (Ed.), *The politics of the Asian economic crisis.* Ithaca: Cornell University Press.

Hwang, I. (2000). Diversification and restructuring of the Korean business groups. Presented to the *Transforming Korean Business and Management Culture Conference*, Michigan State University, East Lansing.

Hwang, I., Lee, I., Seo, C., Lee, B., & Han, H. (2000). *Chaebol structure and chaebol policy: Evaluation and recommendations.* Seoul: Korea Economic Research Institute.

International Finance Corporation–World Bank Group, *Family Business Governance Handbook.* Edition 2010.

176 REFERENCES

Ireland, R. D., Hitt, M. A., Camp, S. M., & Sexton, D. L. (2001). Integrating entrepreneurship with strategic management actions to create firm wealth. *The Academy of Management Executive, 15*, 49–63.

Isobe, T., Makino, S., & Montgomery, D. B. (2000). Resource commitment, entry timing, and market performance of foreign direct investments in emerging economies: The case of Japanese international joint ventures in China. *Academy of Management Journal, 43*(3), 468–484.

Jaffe, D. T., & Lane, S. H. (2004). Sustaining a family dynasty: Key issues facing complex multigenerational business-and investment-owning families. *Family Business Review, 17*(1), 81–98.

Jain, S. C. (Ed.). (2006). *Emerging economies and the transformation of international business: Brazil, Russia, India and China (BRICs)*. Cheltenham/Northampton: Edward Elgar Publishing.

James, H. S. (1999). Owner as manager, extended horizons and the family firm. *International Journal of the Economics of Business, 6*(1), 41–55.

Jensen, M. C., & Meckling, W. H. (1976). Theory of the firm. Managerial behavior, agency costs and ownership structure. *Journal of Financial Economics, 3*(4), 305–360.

Jiang, Y., & Peng, M. W. (2011). Are family ownership and control in large firms good, bad, or irrelevant? *Asia Pacific Journal of Management, 28*(1), 15–39.

Johanson, J., & Wiedersheim-Paul, F. (1975). The internationalization of the firm: Four Swedish case studies. *Journal of Management Studies, 12*(3), 305–322.

Kalasin, K. (2011). *The international expansion of emerging-economy firms: The influence of path-breaking change and its antecedents*. Business administration. HEC.

Kandemir, D., Daekwan, K., & Cavusgil, S. T. (2004). Family conglomerates: Key features relevant to multinationals. In B. Prasad & P. Ghauri (Eds.), *Global firms and emerging markets in the age of anxiety*. Westport: Praeger.

Kansikas, J., Huovinen, J., & Hyrsky, K. (2014). Family firm prerequisites for international business operations: A production and marketing capabilities approach. *World Review of Entrepreneurship, Management and Sustainable Development, 10*(4), 435–448.

Karnani, A. (2007). Fortune at the bottom of the pyramid: A mirage. *California Management Review, 49*(4), 90–111.

Kelly, L. M., Athanassiou, N., & Crittenden, W. F. (2000). Founder centrality and strategic behavior in the family-owned firm. *Entrepreneurship Theory and Practice, 25*(2), 27–42.

Kepner, E. (1983). The family and the firm: A coevolutionary perspective. *Organizational Dynamics, 12*(1), 57–70.

Khanna, T. (2000). Business groups and social welfare in emerging markets: Existing evidence and unanswered questions. *European Economic Review, 44*(4), 748–761.

Khanna, T., & Palepu, K. G. (1999). The right way to restructure conglomerates in emerging markets. *Harvard Business Review, 77*(4), 125–134.

REFERENCES 177

Khanna, T., & Palepu, K. (2000). The future of business groups in emerging markets: Long-run evidence from Chile. *Academy of Management Journal, 43* (3), 268–285.

Khanna, T., & Palepu, K. G. (2006). Emerging giants: Building world class companies in developing countries. *Harvard Business Review, 84*(10), 60–69.

Khanna, T., & Palepu, K. G. (2010). *Winning in emerging markets: A road map for strategy and execution.* Boston: Massachuttes.

Khanna, T., & Rivkin, J. W. (2001). Estimating the performance effects of business groups in emerging markets. *Strategic Management Journal, 22*(1), 45–74.

Khanna, T., & Thomas, C. (2004). What type of control group causes stock price synchronicity? Unpublished.

Khanna, T., & Yafeh, Y. (2005). Business groups and risk sharing around the world*. *The Journal of Business, 78*(1), 301–340.

Khanna, T., & Yafeh, Y. (2007). Business groups in emerging markets: Paragons or parasites? *Journal of Economic Literature, 45*(2), 331–372.

Kim, D., Kandemir, D., & Cavusgil, S. T. (2004). The role of family conglomerates in emerging markets: What western companies should know. *Thunderbird International Business Review, 46*, 13–38.

Klein, S. B., & Bell, F. A. (2007). Non family executives in family business: A literature review. *Electronic Journal of Family Business, 1*(1), 19–37.

Kock, C. J., & Guillen, M. F. (2001). Strategy and structure in developing countries: Business groups as an evolutionary response to opportunities for unrelated diversification. *Industrial and Corporate Change, 10*(1), 77–113.

Koiranen, M. (2002). Over 100 years of age but still entrepreneurially active in business: Exploring the values and family characteristics of old Finnish family firms. *Family Business Review, 15*(3), 175–187.

Koslowski, P. (2000). The limits of shareholder value. *Journal of Business Ethics, 27*(1–2), 137–148.

Kroeber, A. (2006, May). China's industrial and foreign trade policies – What are they and how successful have they been? In *Conference on Capitalism with Chinese Characteristics: China's Political Economy in Comparative and Theoretical Perspective*, Kelley School of Business, Indiana University, Bloomington (pp. 19–20).

Kurtović, S., Siljković, B., & Dašić, B. (2013). Conglomerate companies as emerging markets phenomenon. *Retrieved September, 1*, 111–118.

La Porta, R., Lopez-De-Silanes, F., & Shleifer, A. (1999). Corporate ownership around the World. *Journal of Finance, 54*(2), 471–517.

Lambrecht, J. (2005). Multigenerational transition in family businesses: A new explanatory model. *Family Business Review, 18*(4), 267–282.

178 REFERENCES

Lang, A. G., & Ward, J. L. (2000). Governing the business-owning family. *Family Business Newsletter*.

Lansberg, I. S. (1983). Managing human resources in family firms: The problem of institutional overlap. *Organizational Dynamics, 12*(1), 39–46.

Lawrence, T. B. (1999). Institutional strategy. *Journal of Management, 25*(2), 161–188.

Laxton, D., & Pesenti, P. (2003). Monetary rules for small, open, emerging economies. *Journal of Monetary Economics, 50*(5), 1109–1146.

Lee, K., Peng, M. W., & Lee, L. (2008). From diversification premium to diversification discount during institutional transitions. *Journal of World Business, 43*(1), 47–65.

Leggett, C. J., & Bamber, G. J. (1996). Asia-Pacific tiers of change. *Human Resource Management Journal, 6*(2), 7–19.

Levinson, H. (1971). Conflicts that plague family businesses. *Harvard Business Review, 49*(2), 90–98.

Li, J., & Kozhikode, R. K. (2009). Developing new innovation models: Shifts in the innovation landscapes in emerging economies and implications for global R&D management. *Journal of International Management, 15*(3), 328–339.

Lins, K. V., & Servaes, H. (2002). Is corporate diversification beneficial in emerging markets? *Financial Management, 31*, 5–31.

Litz, R. A. (1995). The family business: Toward definitional clarity. *Family Business Review, 8*(2), 71–82.

Litz, R. (2000). Your old men shall dream dreams, your young men will see visions. A conceptualization of innovation in family firms, In *Canadian Council for Small Business & Entrepreneurship 17th Annual Conference*, Ottawa, Ontario.

Litz, R. A., & Kleysen, R. F. (2001). Your old men shall dream dreams, your young men shall see visions. Toward a theory of family firm innovation with help from the Brubeck family. *Family Business Review, 14*(4), 335–352.

Lockett, A., Siegel, D., Wright, M., & Ensley, M. D. (2005). The creation of spin-off firms at public research institutions: Managerial and policy implications. *Research Policy, 34*(7), 981–993.

Lu, Y., Tsang, E., & Peng, M. (2008). Knowledge management and innovation strategy in the Asia Pacific: Toward an institution-based view. *Asia Pacific Journal of Management, 25*(3), 361–374.

Luo, X., Chung, C. N., & Sobczak, M. (2009). How do corporate governance model differences affect foreign direct investment in emerging economies. *Journal of International Business Studies, 40*(3), 444–467.

Luo, Y., Xue, Q., & Han, B. (2010). How emerging market governments promote outward FDI: Experience from China. *Journal of World Business, 45*(1), 68–79.

REFERENCES 179

Luthans, F., & Ibrayeva, E. S. (2006). Entrepreneurial self-efficacy in central Asian transition economies: Quantitative and qualitative analysis. *Journal of Business Studies,* 37(1), 92–110.

Mace, M. L. (1971). *Directors: Myth and reality.* Cambridge, MA: Harvard University Press.

Makhija, M. (2003). Comparing the resource-based and market-based views of the firm: Empirical evidence from Czech privatization. *Strategic Management Journal,* 24, 433–451.

Manolova, T. S., Eunni, R. V., & Gyoshev, B. S. (2008). Institutional environments for entrepreneurship: Evidence from emerging economies in Eastern Europe. *Entrepreneurship Theory and Practice,* 32(1), 203–218.

Marois, T. (2007, May). The lost logic of state-owned banks: Mexico, Turkey, and Neoliberalism. In *Canadian Political Science Association, 79th Annual Conference,* University of Saskatchewan (Vol. 31).

Martínez, J. I., Stöhr, B. S., & Quiroga, B. F. (2007). Family ownership and firm performance: Evidence from public companies in Chile. *Family Business Review,* 20(2), 83–94.

Masulis, R. W., Pham, P. K., & Zein, J. (2011). Family business groups around the world: Financing advantages, control motivations, and organizational choices. *Review of Financial Studies,* 24(11), 3556–3600.

Mattsson, H. (2009). Innovating in cluster/cluster as innovation: The case of the Biotechvalley cluster initiative. *European Planning Studies,* 17(11), 1625–1643.

Maury, B., & Pajuste, A. (2005). Multiple large shareholders and firm value. *Journal of Banking and Finance,* 29, 1813–1834.

McMillan, J. (2008). Market institutions. In S. Durlauf & L. Blume (Eds.), *The new Palgrave dictionary of economics* (Vol. 3, 2nd ed.). London: Palgrave Macmillan.

Megginson, W. L. (1997). *Corporate finance theory.* Reading: Addison-Wesley Longman.

Melin, L., Nordqvist, M., & Sharma, P. (Eds.). (2013). *The SAGE handbook of family business.* Los Angeles: Sage.

Merchant, H. (2007). *Competing in emerging markets: Cases and readings.* New York: Routledge.

Meyer, K. E. (2004). Perspectives on multinational enterprises in emerging economies. *Journal of International Business Studies,* 35(4), 259–276.

Meyer, K. E., Estrin, S., Bhaumik, S. K., & Peng, M. W. (2009). Institutions, resources, and entry strategies in emerging economies. *Strategic Management Journal,* 30(1), 61–80.

Miles, R. E., & Snow, C. C. (1986). Organizations: New concepts for new forms. *California Management Review,* 28(3), 62–73.

180 REFERENCES

Miller, D., & Le Breton-Miller, I. (2005). *Managing for the long run: Lessons in competitive advantage from great family business.* Boston: Harvard Business School Press.

Miller, D., Steier, L., & Le Breton-Miller, I. (2003). Lost in time: Intergenerational succession, change, and failure in family business. *Journal of Business Venturing, 18*(4), 513–531.

Morck, R. (2005). How to eliminate pyramidal business groups the double taxation of inter-corporate dividends and other incisive uses of tax policy. In *Tax policy and the economy* (Vol. 19, pp. 135–179). Cambridge, MA: MIT Press.

Morck, R., & Yeung, B. (2003). Agency problems in large family business groups. *Entrepreneurship Theory and Practice, 27*(4), 367–382.

Morck, R., & Yeung, B. (2004). Family control and the rent-seeking society. *Entrepreneurship Theory and Practice, 28*(4), 391–409.

Morck, R., Stangeland, D., & Yeung, B. (2000). Inherited wealth, corporate control, and economic growth: The Canadian disease? In R. Morck (Ed.), *Concentrated corporate ownership, NBER conference report series* (pp. 319–369). Chicago/London: University of Chicago Press.

Nachum, L. (1999). Diversification strategies of developing country firms. *Journal of International Management, 5*, 115–140.

Nee, V. (1992). Organizational dynamics of market transition: Hybrid forms, property rights, and mixed economy in China. *Administrative Science Quarterly, 37*, 1–27.

Neumeyer, P. A., & Perri, F. (2005). Business cycles in emerging economies: The role of interest rates. *Journal of Monetary Economics, 52*(2), 345–380.

Newman, K. L. (2000). *Organizational transformation during institutional upheaval, Academy of Management Review, 25*(3), 602-619.

Nohria, N., & Eccles, R. G. (1992). *Networks and organizations: Structure, form, and action.* Boston: Harvard Business School Press.

North, D. C. (1990). *Institutions, institutional change and economic performance.* Cambridge/New York: Cambridge university press.

O'Byrne, S. F. (1997). EVA and shareholder return. *Financial Practice and Education, 7*(1), 50–54.

O'Gorman, C., & Kautonen, M. (2004). Policies to promote new knowledge-intensive industrial agglomerations. *Entrepreneurship & Regional Development, 16*(6), 459–479.

Orrù, M., Biggart, N. W., & Hamilton, G. G. (1997). *The economic organization of East Asian capitalism.* Thousand Oaks/London/New Delhi: Sage Publications.

Özcan, G. B., & Turunç, H. (2011). Economic liberalization and class dynamics in Turkey: New business groups and Islamic mobilization. *Insight Turkey, 13*(3), 63–86.

REFERENCES 181

Paun, F. (2013). Technology push and market pull entrepreneurship. In *Encyclopedia of creativity, invention, innovation and entrepreneurship* (pp. 1808–1814). New York: Springer.

Peng, M. W. (2000). *Business strategies in transition economies.* Thousand Oaks: Sage.

Peng, M. W. (2003). Institutional transitions and strategic choices. *Academy of Management Review, 28*(2), 275–296.

Peng, M. W., & Heath, P. S. (1996). The growth of the firm in planned economies in transition: Institutions, organizations, and strategic choice. *Academy of Management Review, 21*(2), 492–528.

Peng, M. W., Wang, D. Y., & Jiang, Y. (2008). An institution-based view of international business strategy: A focus on emerging economies. *Journal of International Business Studies, 39*(5), 920–936.

Pennings, J. M. (1982). The urban quality of life and entrepreneurship. *Academy of Management Journal, 25*, 63–79.

Pérez, P. F. (2016). Evolution of family business continuity and change in Latin America and Spain. Paloma Fernández Pérez (Ed.), University of Barcelona, Spain and Andrea Lluch, CONICET, Argentina and Los Andes University, Colombia.

Phillips, N., Tracey, P., & Karra, N. (2009). Rethinking institutional distance: Strengthening the tie between new institutional theory and international management. *Strategic Organization, 7*(3), 1–10.

Pinches, M. (1992). The Philippines: The regional exception. *The Pacific Review, 5*(4), 390–401.

Porter, M. (1998). *On Competition.* Boston: Harvard Business School Press.

Poutziouris, P., Smyrnios, K., & Klein, S. (Eds.). (2008). *Handbook of research on family business.* Cheltenham: Edward Elgar Publishing.

Prahalad, C. K. (2005). *The fortune of the bottom of the pyramid.* Upper Saddle River: Wharton School Publishing.

Prahalad, C. K., & Lieberthal, K. (1998). The end of corporate imperialism. *Harvard Business Review, 76*(4), 68–79.

Prasad, S. B., & Ghauri, P. N. (Eds.). (2004). *Global firms and emerging markets in an age of anxiety.* Westport, Connecticut: Greenwood Publishing Group.

Puffer, M. S., Mccarthy, D. J., & Boisot, M. (2010). Entrepreneurship in Russia and China: The impact of formal institutional voids. *Entrepreneurship: Theory and Practice, 34*(3), 441–467.

Pukall, T. J., & Calabrò, A. (2014). The internationalization of family firms a critical review and integrative model. *Family Business Review, 27*(2), 103–125.

182 REFERENCES

Quinn, J. B., & Hilmer, F. G. (1994). Strategic outsourcing. *Sloan Management Review, 35*(4), 43.

Ramsden, J. J., & Kiss-Haypal, G. (2000). Company size distribution in different countries. *Physica A: Statistical Mechanics and Its Applications, 277*(1), 220–227.

Rasmussen, E., & Gulbrandsen, M. (2012). Government support programmes to promote academic entrepreneurship: A principal–agent perspective. *European Planning Studies, 20*(4), 527–546.

Reinhart, C. M., & Rogoff, K. S. (2010). Growth in a time of debt (digest summary). *American Economic Review, 100*(2), 573–578.

Ritchie, B. K. (2010). *Systemic vulnerability and sustainable economic growth: Skills and upgrading in Southeast Asia.* Cheltenham: Edward Elgar Publishing.

Roberts, J. G. (1973). *Mitsui, three centuries of Japanese business.* New York: Weatherhill.

Root, H. L. (2006). Opening the doors of invention: Institutions, technology and developing nations. *International Public Management Review, 7*(1), 14–29.

Ross, I. (1999). The Stern Stewart performance 1000. *Journal of Applied Corporate Finance, 11*(4), 122–126.

Roztocki, N., & Weistroffer, H. R. (2004). Evaluating information technology investments in developing economies using activity-based costing. *The Electronic Journal of Information Systems in Developing Countries, 19*(2), 1–6.

Roztocki, N., & Weistroffer, H. R. (2008). Information technology in transition economies. *Journal of Global Information Technology Management, 11*(4), 1–8.

Sacchetti, S., & Sugden, R. (2003). The governance of networks and economic power: The nature and impact of subcontracting relationships. *Journal of Economic Surveys, 17*(5), 669–692.

Sachs, J. D. (1992). Privatization in Russia: Some lessons from Eastern Europe. *American Economic Review, 80*(May), 43–48.

Sahin, K. (2011). An investigation into why Turkish business groups resist the adoption of M-form in post-liberalization. *African Journal of Business Management, 5*(34), 13330–13343.

Salamon, G. L., & Dhaliwal, D. S. (1980). Company size and financial disclosure requirements with evidence from the segmental reporting issue. *Journal of Business Finance & Accounting, 7*(4), 555–568.

Salvato, C. (2004). Predictors of entrepreneurship in family firms. *The Journal of Private Equity, 7*(3), 68–76.

Samoilenko, S., & Osei-Bryson, K. M. (2008). Determining strategies for telecoms to improve efficiency in the production of revenues: An empirical investigation in the context of transition economies. *Journal of Global Information Technology Management, 11*, 7, 56–75.

REFERENCES 183

Sarkar, M., & Cavusgil, S. T. (1996). The trends in international business thought and literature: A review of international market entry mode research: Integration and synthesis. *International Executive, 38*(6), 825–848.

Schermerhorn Jr., J. R. (2009). *Exploring management.* Hoboken, New Jersey: Wiley.

Schulze, W. S., Lubatkin, M. H., Dino, R. N., & Buchhiltz, A. K. (2001). Agency relationships in family firms: Theory and evidence. *Organization Science, 12*(2), 99–116.

Schulze, W. S., Lubatkin, M. H., & Dino, R. N. (2003). Toward a theory of agency and altruism in family firms. *Journal of Business Venturing, 18*(4), 473–490.

Schwab, K. (2010). *The global competitiveness report.* Geneva: World Economic Forum.

Sciascia, S., & Mazzola, P. (2008). Family involvement in ownership and management: Exploring nonlinear effects on performance. *Family Business Review, 21*(4), 331–345.

Scott, W. R. (1995). *Institutions and organizations.* Thousand Oaks: Sage.

Shah, J., Ramachandran, J., Vaidyanathan, R., Jha, M., & Samanth, D. (2001). Role of community dominance of trade channels in India: Exploratory study. *IIM Bangalore Research Paper*, 170.

Shien, E. H. (1983). The role of the founder in creating organizational culture. *Organizational Dynamics, 12*(1), 13–28.

Siegel, J. (2002). *Stocks for the long run : The definitive guide to financial market returns and long-term investment strategies.* New York: McGraw-Hill.

Silva, F., Majluf, N., & Paredes, R. D. (2006). Family ties, interlocking directors and performance of business groups in emerging countries: The case of Chile. *Journal of Business Research, 59*(3), 315–321.

Stajano, A. (2009). Competitiveness of the European economy. In *Research, quality, competitiveness* (pp. 35–125). New York: Springer US.

Steers, R. M., Shin, Y. K., & Ungson, G. R. (1989). *The chaebol: Korea's new industrial might.* New York: Harper & Row.

Steiner, G. A., & Steiner, J. F. (2006). *Business, government, and society. A managerial perspective, text and cases.* New York: McGraw Hill.

Stern, J. M., Shiely, J. S., & Ross, I. (2001). *The EVA challenge: Implementing value-added change in an organization.* New York: Wiley.

Suehiro, A., & Wailerdsak, N. (2004). Family business in Thailand: Its management, governance, and future challenges. *ASEAN Economic Bulletin, 21*(1), 81–93.

Svejnar, J. (2002). Transition economies: Performance and challenges. *Journal of Economic Perspectives, 16*(1), 3–26.

Takayasu, H., & Okuyama, K. (1998). Country dependence on company size distributions and a numerical model based on competition and cooperation. *Fractals, 6*(01), 67–79.

184 REFERENCES

Tàpies, J., & Fernández Moya, M. (2012). Values and longevity in family business: Evidence from a cross-cultural analysis. *Journal of Family Business Management, 2*(2), 130–146.

Terziovski, M., & Samson, D. (2000). The effect of company size on the relationship between TQM strategy and organisational performance. *The TQM Magazine, 12*(2), 144–149.

Thomas, J. (2002). Freeing the shackles of family business ownership. *Family Business Review, 15*(4), 321–336.

Thomsen, S., & Pedersen, T. (2000). Ownership structure and economic performance in the largest European companies. *Strategic Management Journal, 21*(6), 689–705.

Tricker, R. B. (2015). *Corporate governance: Principles, policies, and practices.* Oxford: Oxford University Press.

Tsui-Auch, L. S. (2006). Singaporean business groups: The role of the state and capital in Singapore Inc. In S. Chang (Ed.), *Business groups in East Asia: Financial crisis, restructuring, and new growth* (pp. 94–115). Oxford: Oxford University Press.

Vallejo, M. C. (2008). Is the culture of family firms really different? A value-based model for its survival through generations. *Journal of Business Ethics, 81*(2), 261–279.

Van Agtmael, A. W. (1984). *Emerging securities markets: Investment banking opportunities in the developing world.* London: Euromoney Publications.

Vecchi, A., Della Piana, B., & Cacia, C. (2014). Mapping family business groups from a cross-cultural perspective. In *Enacting globalization* (pp. 194–204). London, UK: Palgrave Macmillan UK.

Venter, W. P., & Kruger, S. (2004). The contribution of familiness' to the performance of family businesses. *Guidelines for Contributors to the Southern African Business Review 76, 8*(3), 1–20.

Venter, E., Boshoff, C., & Maas, G. (2005). The influence of successor-related factors on the succession process in small and medium-sized family businesses. *Family Business Review, 18*(4), 283–303.

Vilaseca, A. (2002). The shareholder role in the family business: Conflict of interests and objectives between nonemployed shareholders and top management team. *Family Business Review, 15*(4), 299–320.

Von Bertalanffy, L. (1972). The history and status of general systems theory. *Academy of Management Journal, 15*(4), 407–426.

Wade, R. (1990). *Governing the market: Economic theory and the role of government in East Asian industrialisation.* Princeton: Princeton University Press.

Walumbwa, F. O., & Lawler, J. J. (2003). Building effective organizations: Transformational leadership, collectivist orientation, work-related attitudes and withdrawal behaviours in three emerging economies. *International Journal of Human Resource Management, 14*(7), 1083–1101.

Ward, J. L. (1991). *Creating effective boards for private enterprises.* San Francisco: Jossey Bass.

Ward, J. L. (2011). *Keeping the family business healthy: How to plan for continuing growth, profitability, and family leadership.* New York: Palgrave Macmillan.

Watson, R., & Wilson, N. (2002). Small and medium size enterprise financing: A note on some of the empirical implications of a pecking order. *Journal of Business Finance and Accounting, 29*(3–4), 557–578.

Wenyi, C. (2009). The influence of family ownership on SME performance: Evidence from public in Taiwan. *Small Business Economics, 33*(3), 353–373.

Westhead, P. (1997). Ambitions, external environment and strategic factor differences between family and non-family companies. *Entrepreneurship & Regional Development, 9*(2), 127–157.

Westhead, P., & Cowling, M. (1997). Performance contrasts between family and non-family unquoted companies in the UK. *International Journal of Entrepreneurial Behavior & Research, 3*(1), 30–52.

Whitley, R. (Ed.). (1992). *European business systems: Firms and markets in their national contexts.* London/Newbury Park: Sage.

Williams, G. A. (2005). Some determinants of the socially responsible investment decision: A cross country study. *Journal of Behavioural Finance, 8*, 43–57.

Wilson, D., & Purushothaman, R. (2003). *Dreaming with BRICs: The path to 2050* (Vol. 99). New York: Goldman, Sachs & Company.

Wright, M., Filatotchev, I., Hoskisson, R. E., & Peng, M. W. (2005). Strategy research in emerging economies: Challenging the conventional wisdom*. *Journal of Management Studies, 42*(1), 1–33.

Yaprak, A., Karademir, B., & Osborn, R. N. (2006). How do business groups function and evolve in emerging markets? The case of Turkish business groups. *Advances in International Marketing, 17*, 275–294.

Yasser, Q. R., & Mamun, A. A. (2014). Implications of ownership identity and insider's supremacy on the economic performance of the listed companies. *Corporate Ownership & Control, 11*(4), 399–411.

Yasuda, T. (2005). Firm growth, size, age and behavior in Japanese manufacturing. *Small Business Economics, 24*(1), 1–15.

Yiu, D., Bruton, G. D., & Lu, Y. (2005). Understanding business group performance in an emerging economy: Acquiring resources and capabilities in order to prosper*. *Journal of Management Studies, 42*(1), 183–206.

Yiu, D. W., Lu, Y., Bruton, G. D., & Hoskisson, R. E. (2007). Business groups: An integrated model to focus future research. *Journal of Management Studies, 44*(8), 1551–1579.

186 REFERENCES

Young, M. N., Peng, M. W., Ahlstrom, D., Bruton, G. D., & Jiang, Y. (2008). Corporate governance in emerging economies: A review of the principal–principal perspective. *Journal of Management Studies, 45*(1), 196–220.

Zachary, R. K. (2011). The importance of the family system in family business. *Journal of Family Business Management, 1*(1), 26–36.

Zahra, S. A. (2003). International expansion of US manufacturing family businesses: The effect of ownership and involvement. *Journal of Business Venturing, 18*(4), 495–512.

Zahra, S. A. (2005). Entrepreneurial risk taking in family firms. *Family Business Review, 18*(1), 23–40.

Zahra, S. A., & Sharma, P. (2004). Family business research: A strategic reflection. *Family Business Review, 17*(4), 331–346.

Zahra, S. A., Neubaum, D. O., & Huse, M. (2000). Entrepreneurship in medium-size companies: Exploring the effects of ownership and governance systems. *Journal of Management, 26*(5), 947–976.

Zellweger, T. M., Eddleston, K. A., & Kellermanns, F. W. (2010). Exploring the concept of familiness: Introducing family firm identity. *Journal of Family Business Strategy, 1*(1), 54–63.

INDEX

A
adverse selection, 12
aggregation, 62–7, 69, 70, 73, 74, 77, 78, 125, 135, 139, 140, 156
altruism, 8–9, 13–14

B
balance sheets, 9–10, 44, 87
Board of Directors (BoD), 2, 13, 21, 22, 24, 25, 27, 29, 30, 34
BRIC countries, 19, 106
business houses, 139

C
capital market, 106, 108, 119–20, 126, 143, 149
capital stock, 7
chaebols, 139
Chief Executive Officer (CEO), 24–5, 137, 150

control structure, 5, 27, 40
corporate governance, 19, 21, 24–6, 28, 29, 31–3, 50, 56n1, 154
cousin consortium, 82

D
deferred or eluded succession, 35

E
economic growth, 10, 106, 107, 112, 114, 117, 118, 120, 121, 142
Economic Value Added (EVA), 97–8, 100n6
emerging economies, 47, 105, 106, 108–11, 113–17, 125, 133, 153, 155n4, 156n5
emerging markets, 105–26, 133–56
emotional value (EV), 54, 55
extra-familial transfer, 35

Note: Page numbers followed by "n" denote notes.

© The Author(s) 2017
M. Del Giudice, *Understanding Family-Owned Business Groups*,
DOI 10.1007/978-3-319-42243-5

187

188 INDEX

F

family business, 1–15, 19–56, 61–100, 123, 124, 136–8, 140–4, 146, 154, 155, 155n5
  extended family businesses, 2, 23
  household family businesses, 2
  open family businesses, 2
  traditional family businesses, 2, 23, 54
family capitalism, 5, 6, 15n1, 42
family capitalist investor, 50
family conglomerates, 137–53
family council (FC), 22, 30, 52
family groups, 72, 78–80, 88, 90–4, 136–9, 155n4
family holding, 37, 66, 70, 80–7, 89–90, 92–4, 99n4
family offices, 27, 141
family pacts, 23, 27, 30, 79, 82, 93, 139
financial capital, 8, 25, 121
financial value (FV), 55
flexibility, 9, 32, 42, 55, 83, 84, 86, 95
formal institutions, 116, 122–4, 154
founder, 2, 8, 11, 34, 36, 37, 66, 82, 93, 99n3, 138, 140–3, 146, 147, 152, 153

G

gender equality, 31
generational change, 11, 33–5, 37, 39, 54, 82, 86, 89–90
generational drift, 90–4
generational transfer, 11, 12, 37, 50
governance, 4, 8, 9, 19, 21–34, 37, 41, 50–2, 56n1, 67, 81, 83, 84, 87, 89, 115, 137, 153, 154, 156
governance structure, 8, 23, 26–8
Gross Domestic Product (GDP), 113, 114, 120
grupos, 139

Gulf Cooperation Council (GCC), 140, 141, 152

H

holding companies, 37, 66, 87–8, 139
human capital, 7, 51, 95, 113, 120

I

informal capital, 8
informal institutions, 116, 117, 122, 154
innovation, 10, 11, 38, 40, 47, 48, 52, 54, 79, 92, 152
institutional overlap, 3–4, 26, 52, 155n5
institutional vacuums, 117–19, 121–6, 154
intra-familial transfer or succession, 35

K

knowledge, 7, 11, 28, 35, 36, 38, 47–54, 63, 119, 141, 146, 151, 153

L

labor market, 11–12, 117, 118, 120–1

M

management committee, 22, 34, 75

N

nepotism, 11, 12, 146
Net Operating Profit After Tax (NOPAT), 98, 100
non-family businesses, 31, 154
non-family CEO, 24–5

O

ownership, 1–5, 7, 10, 11, 14, 19, 21, 23–31, 33, 34, 37–42, 53, 56, 64, 77, 78, 80, 82–9, 91, 93, 133–6, 141, 143, 151, 153, 154
ownership structure, 2, 19, 27, 30, 38, 53, 82

P

product market, 90, 117–21
pyramidal groups, 13, 50, 95, 135

R

risk aversion, 10–11, 54

S

serial entrepreneur, 49–54
serial family entrepreneur, 47–54
shareholder, 5, 7, 9, 12–14, 25–8, 30, 34, 46, 56n1, 67, 72, 78–80, 82–5, 94, 96, 98, 99n5, 119, 124, 137, 143, 152, 155n3, 155n5
shareholding, 5, 10, 21, 44, 45, 50, 65, 79, 91

share leverage, 69, 91–3
sibling partnership, 82
small and medium-sized enterprises (SMEs), 4, 5, 43
stakeholders (funders, workers, public administrators, etc.), 7, 20, 21, 25, 28, 34, 52, 53, 55, 78, 95, 96
succession, 3, 23, 33–8, 41, 46, 69, 79, 83, 89, 90, 92, 137, 138, 153
succession issues, 11–12
succession process, 30, 37–8
succession with abdication, 35
succession without abdication, 35

T

transaction costs, 116, 125, 154
Transition Economies of Central and Eastern Europe (TECEE), 111
transition economy, 105, 108, 111, 116, 123
transition process, 35, 37, 38

V

value creation, 7, 46, 89, 92, 94–8

Printed in the United States
By Bookmasters